The Confident Minds Curriculum

The Confident Minds Curriculum provides a simple and practical approach to culture change in schools, health care settings and organisations working with young people. Refraining from focusing solely on young people's growth, the curriculum provides logical and practical support to the people and systems in their environment to enable and maximise growth for positive and connected communities.

Crucial mindsets for healthy relationships, empathy, compassion, problem-solving, emotional intelligence and well-being are broken down into bite-size, teachable chunks. All blend together exquisitely to help people look at themselves and others with confidence, gratitude and compassion.

Easily applied to individuals, targeted groups and whole classes to meet the social emotional learning (SEL) or well-being curriculum, this book provides a guiding light for young people and their supporters to develop what is necessary for socially and emotionally intelligent environments.

Aimed primarily at the middle years (8–14), it is easily adaptable for younger and older students. Through role plays, discussions, journaling and practical activities each new mindset is divided into several lessons that teach individual learning components of new ways of thinking, feeling and behaving.

The Confident Minds Curriculum will appeal to teachers, educators and health professionals searching for a whole school or organisational approach to social emotional learning, well-being, compassion and personal growth. It is also an essential resource for homes where parents and carers can help further develop life skills that build character and optimism so their family can approach life with greater confidence.

Madhavi Nawana Parker is Managing Director of Positive Minds Australia, author, child and youth practitioner, and keynote and public speaker. The *Confident Minds Curriculum* is a culmination of over 20 years of dedicated work and care into the social emotional health of young people, families and educators in schools and health care settings around Australia. Find her at www.positivemindsaustralia.com.au.

The Confident Minds Curriculum

Creating a Culture of Personal Growth and Social Awareness

Madhavi Nawana Parker

LONDON AND NEW YORK

First published 2020
by Routledge
2 Park Square, Milton Park, Abingdon, Oxon OX14 4RN

and by Routledge
52 Vanderbilt Avenue, New York, NY 10017

Routledge is an imprint of the Taylor & Francis Group, an informa business

British Library Cataloguing-in-Publication Data
A catalogue record for this book is available from the British Library

Library of Congress Cataloging-in-Publication Data
A catalog record has been requested for this book

ISBN: 978-0-367-36131-0 (hbk)
ISBN: 978-0-367-36128-0 (pbk)
ISBN: 978-0-429-34404-6 (ebk)

Typeset in Bembo
by Cenveo® Publisher Services

This book is for all young people who try their best, despite the frustration of living with a brain and body that's still under rapid change and construction. Behind the impulses, errors in judgement and tide of emotions, your hearts are big, your minds are brilliant, your intentions are clear. May you continue learning what you need to, using your personal strengths to be the person you were always meant to be. May everyone who leads you seek out and uphold your essential goodness. The world is stronger because of each and every one of you.

Contents

Acknowledgments

This book happened thanks to my beautiful family, friends, colleagues and clients. My husband James, always forgiving of my terrible habit of talking through your favourite TV show—actually talking through pretty much everything—I love you. Your enthusiasm, encouragement and trust in everything I do propel so many moves I make. To our children, Soraya, Toby and Zach, whom I want to swallow whole every morning. Thank you for letting me greet you each day like we haven't seen each other for a decade. The three of you make my heart sing. You are quick to forgive my mummy rants about lost socks and stinky stuff and meet me each day with abundant love. You have my heart and I will do anything for you. You are nothing short of the nicest people I know. I love you.

To my parents, Mallika Nawana and the late Srinath Nawana (1939–1984), thank you for raising me and preparing me for life. Your genuine, hardworking, kind and generous natures were always something to strive towards. Namal Nawana, we have been through thick and thin from the day I arrived on your third birthday. I knocked on the bedroom walls to say good night to you for many years. I wrote you a code to decode what the knocks meant. Although you might have been secretly rolling your eyes, thank you for always knocking back. Srimal Nawana, for childhood adventures painting rocks from Silver Sands, blue opal nail polish and the hunt for clothes on the $5 rack. To my gorgeous nieces and nephews, who I adore—Dylan, Elea, Tylanni and Nael—you are such wonderful souls. I am blessed to be your aunty. You are loved and treasured every day. To my extended family from Sri Lanka, now scattered all around the world, I'm so grateful to have you in my life.

To my beautiful friends. I love you more than chocolate. You're all so kind-hearted, wise, hilarious and brilliant. What would I do without you? Thank you for your love, laughter, tears and adventure. You've embraced me wholeheartedly, warts and all through childhood, teenagehood, adulthood and whatever on earth you call where we're at right now. I couldn't possibly name you all here—you know who you are. Mark Le Messurier, my brilliant 'What's the Buzz?' coauthor and friend, we have created so much together over the years. The world is better because you're here. If only your brilliance could shine on every child.

You are one in a million. To the colleagues who inspire me with their dedication, I couldn't possibly name you all but a special mention to Virginia Evans, Natalie Natsias, Denise O'Loughlin and all the brilliant educators at Pulteney Grammar School; Kerry Kaesler, Ieva Hampson and the wonderful team at Scotch College. The Positive Minds Australia team, James Parker, Nikki Wadewitz, Nick Bennett, Katie O'Reilly and Leah Braun, thank you for your incredible contribution. Your work is changing the lives of young people and I am privileged to work with you. Everyone at Fullarton House, with special thanks to Rose Price (happily retired), John Hall (happily retired), Kay Bosworth (not allowed to retire), Bill Hansberry and Karen Hodson; I loved working with you and feel so grateful you're still part of my life. You continue to inspire me with your valuable work that is authentic and crucial to the lives of young people. Thank you to the spectacular folks at Freerange Future for your integrity and professionalism designing my website and ebooks. Thank you, Nicole Eglington, for reviewing my manuscript with such enthusiasm. To all the other stellar professionals who are changing lives every day to give young people the best chance of reaching their full potential, I hold you in the highest regard.

To the families and children with whom I work: You know how much you inspire me. It takes such courage to ask for help when life gets wobbly. You have gifted me with the enormous privilege of helping you navigate the curve balls in your lives. I take my work with you to heart and thank you.

To Dr James Kollias, Dr Tabitha Healey and Dr Joanna Price, this book wouldn't be here if I wasn't here. Thank you for your phenomenal kindness, humour, empathy and expertise. I hope I won't need you again, but if I do, I wouldn't want anyone else on my team. Thank you for saving my life. My family and I are forever grateful.

Thank you coffee. You are delicious.

Alison Foyle (Senior Publisher UK and rest of world), you might be in London, but it feels like you're just around the corner. Thank you for your warm enthusiasm throughout my writing career. I demand you come back to Australia soon so we can have another lovely long lunch together. Vilija Steven (Editor, Australia and New Zealand), your knowledge and expertise in your field is exemplary. I have loved our conversations over the last eighteen months. Thank you for helping shape many a move in this book and for being a sensational sounding board. To Matt Bickerton, Will Bateman, Apoorva Manuch and everyone else on Routledge's global team, you've been a pleasure, as always, to communicate and work with.

Thank you, James Parker, for the countless hours and dedication that went into reading the manuscript. You didn't complain once (not out loud anyway). Richard Mills for your excellent training and early morning conversations at the gym. Two awesome teenagers, Seamus O'Reilly and Tom Venus, thank you for your time, effort and design skills formatting my Social Emotional Learning wheel and pre- and post-curriculum surveys for the introduction. As you know, I am terrible at technology, but you're not. Thank you, Soraya Nawana Parker, Toby Nawana Parker, Zach Nawana Parker, Charlotte Bolton, Oscar Bolton, Georgie Bowering, Claude Bowering, Mia Bowering, Clyde Campbell, Boyd Campbell,

Kobe Campbell, Daisy O'Reilly, Rosie O'Reilly, Eamon O'Reilly, Emma Venus, Sam Venus, Anna Hardman, Jude Hardman, Zoe Hardman, Roszi Bentley, Maya Bentley, Ellie Bentley, Soraya Forbes and Olivia Beere for your beautiful stories and drawings. They made my heart sing.

If I forgot anyone in the acknowledgements, be assured I will feel guilty about it every day for the rest of my life.

With much love always, Madhavi

Preface

The Confident Minds Curriculum structure

Each chapter is divided into a number of lessons that break down the skills for the overall topic. It is recommended you incorporate the 'gradual model of release' guidelines, a teaching method using the following steps to teach a new skill:

1 Show students the skill first, by demonstrating it yourself. Share a relevant personal story, case study or show a clip where someone is demonstrating the skill.

2 Practise the skills together.

3 Step back, observe and avoid stepping in unnecessarily. Warmly encourage from the sidelines. As a school or organisation, you might set weekly goals to apply the new skills so everyone is on the same page.

4 Show your trust in their developing skills and abilities. Check in with gentle reminders and make sure there are plenty of structured and incidental opportunities to use and practise the skills.

Each chapter has several ways to encourage the new confident mindset concept. Each component is structured into an individual lesson. You can facilitate one clear lesson at a time or change the order within a chapter to suit your unique needs.

Each lesson covers the following components

New confident mindset concept

This part introduces a new way of thinking that's related to the underlying skills to improve the mindset. Take time to read this section on your own first, then explain it in your own words to your students.

Case studies

All case studies can be read or summarised to your students in a way that makes sense to them. Each case study reaches a point marked 'solution'. At this point, you might like to stop reading and allow your students to suggest ways the problem might be solved.

Brainstorms and mind maps

Brainstorms and mind maps help you find out what your students already know, supporting them to start thinking more deeply about a new concept without being led in any preplanned direction. Mind maps are as simple as putting the word or concept on the board and inviting your students to 'tell me something about this'. As they share their knowledge and beliefs, the mind map continues branching out into new areas that are related to the core concept. Continue extending each individual idea that has come out of the core idea into as much detail as possible. Mind maps are a great way to get student-led information flowing freely.

Brainstorms are another way of gathering information. Questions stir up thoughts and discussion, allowing a broad range of ideas to evolve together as a group.

Role plays

Role plays provide an opportunity to practise new thinking and skills without the pressure of really being in the situation. Students help each other see new ways of thinking and interacting. Role plays are often done in pairs with peers but can also be used as discussions and offered one on one between student and facilitator. Some of the role plays are best done as individuals. It's okay for the same role play to be attempted by several students. This approach opens up great opportunities for students to learn from many minds focused on the same problem.

Journaling

Journaling provides you and your students with an opportunity to freely and confidentially jot down your thoughts and feelings about a specific topic or event. It can also be used for gratitude practice and recording acts of kindness. Daily journaling is similar to having a regular debrief with a friend. It can be useful even without a specific format, encouraging students to use it however they like. Consider using journaling as part of your students' day.

In the Confident Minds Curriculum lesson plans, journaling is often used for reflection about the topic and answering questions that might better be considered privately.

Play and games

Every lesson ends with a short burst of play or games. While it might be tempting to skip these, remember most young people love and feel energised by play. While some will need encouragement to get out of their comfort zone, most will learn to relax and enjoy this less structured time. It's through play that young people can enjoy themselves for the fun of it—with no measurable outcomes placing pressure on them to achieve. Playtime allows for rest, resetting and creativity. If times permits, add one or two other games you already enjoy as a group to the one provided in the curriculum.

Introduction

Welcome to *The Confident Minds Curriculum*, where research is translated into practical activities. By working through the eight mindsets you and your students are heading in the right direction for greater confidence in yourself and others.

The program is specifically aimed at 8–14 year olds and can be adapted for young people on either side of this age group. The middle years are a crucial stage of social emotional development, and this book provides practical ways to help young people navigate them constructively. The early years are equally crucial to social emotional development, however, they should not be seen in isolation. In other words, it's insufficient to think that by training children well in the early years, they have everything they need to succeed after that. A similar approach is sometimes taken in terms of adolescence and early adulthood. These stages are more obviously challenging, where young people develop their sense of identity while juggling hormones, changing social networks and greater demands in the curriculum. The sometimes more challenging behaviour of an adolescent and young adult provides more clues about what is going on inside. The middle years can sometimes be the least obvious time to provide specific and targeted social emotional learning.

Becoming socially and emotionally skilled is a lifelong process. At different stages of development, new skills are needed to navigate the physical and emotional changes that occur. A recent study into the middle years found many changes happen inside the minds of this age group, and the well-being and social emotional curriculum can be helpful in supporting a smooth transition. The middle years are an important stage of development, with less obvious outward signs of what might be going on beneath the surface. Redmond et al. (2016)

The Confident Minds Curriculum offers a social-emotional learning framework for many skills, including healthy relationships, problem solving, decision making, optimism and emotional intelligence. Full of practical guidance, you will find simple methods for your students to build a confident and constructive outlook. Traditional definitions of success have suggested that to feel happy and connected, you need wealth, a certain career and high levels of achievement. These beliefs throw many people into a state of inadequacy and despair, convincing them more than their character, strengths and relationships with others is needed to be whole and worthy.

Meta-analysis studies around the world have demonstrated that social-emotional competencies can be taught in schools and other settings to make a positive difference in young people's lives. Students taught social-emotional learning skills like those offered explicitly in *The Confident Minds Curriculum* exhibit significant improvements in prosocial behaviour, self-confidence, empathy towards others, better emotional regulation and improved academic outcomes. Durlak et al. (2011)

The long-term effects of teaching social-emotional literacy in schools include better overall conduct from students, healthier relationships, lower emotional distress and better overall academic achievement. Schools are not the only place social-emotional literacy competencies can be offered to gain short- and long-term benefits for young people. Taylor et al. (2017) Programs like *The Confident Minds Curriculum* can be easily implemented outside of schools in clinical and community settings, gaining similar benefits to a whole school approach to social emotional learning. Durlak. Weissberg and Pachan (2010)

A confident mindset takes steady, conscious, commitment, effort and practice. It carries the potential to help you feel calmer, more optimistic and balanced in your thinking. Do remember, you may enter situations where you're so challenged or even feeling stubborn, the tenacity to use it won't come easily. Old ways have long histories and tend to creep back. Don't be disheartened; this is the same for everyone. There are no instant and permanent solutions to a confident mindset nor is there a one size fits all formula. Human behaviour has many complicated layers. Try and see each new skill as a step forward and congratulate yourself for your progress.

Different personalities, temperaments and environments will affect how soon you'll notice changes. Keep yourself and your students optimistic about your strength and capability to master it in good time.

It's also important to remember that progress won't reach its full potential in isolation. Mindsets can be developed and enhanced; however, these shifts best occur on a systemic level. That means everyone around the young people you're targeting works towards the same goals, doing what they can to encourage its place in the environment. Planning for a culture change where everyone works together and supports each other to think and behave with positive thinking, you're going to have greater progress than if only a handful of students and staff are focused on it.

Leadership and educators need adequate support, encouragement and training in successful implementation as well as a collaborative approach within a committed and connected group. The more supporters in the student environment aligned together, the better the outcomes will be. Greenberg et al. (2003) Silver bullets are absent in social-emotional learning programs, including *The Confident Minds Curriculum*.

If you're teaching a social-emotional learning curriculum on your own, don't lose heart. Every interaction with a young person has the potential to plant seeds of change. There's a lot that can be achieved by one person too. Young people thrive from interactions with positive and compassionate adults who care about them, support their capabilities and take the time to get to know them and guide them gently towards their potential.

By the end of *The Confident Minds Curriculum*, your students will have a foundation for a more capable way of thinking that lends itself to a more comfortable way of feeling. The degree to which that change will occur rises when there are more people around them using the same values and guidance. The process of improvement is a lifelong process. A confident mindset continues to evolve throughout your life, long after the skills are initially taught.

What can go wrong with mindsets?

The quality of your thoughts, will directly relate to the feeling that follows. Given most people are thinking all day, the challenge to try something new is worth the investment.

There are several layers to how people develop their mindsets—or thinking styles. Researchers tend to define thinking styles as mental frameworks people use to process information and solve problems in specific contexts.

How mindsets develop varies and often begins in early childhood. How you're spoken and responded to, what you're exposed to and what's happening around you interact with your personality, temperament and genetics. From here, you start developing your individualised thinking habits and frameworks. Saracho (1998); Zhang and Sternberg (2006)

Mindsets can easily become fixed and resistant to change in very little time. When you're consciously and unconsciously thinking all day long, the mental chatter often persists until you're fast asleep. The more you think a certain way, the stronger those connections become in your brain. Your thinking style or mindset can become a set pattern very quickly. Even a destructive thinking pattern that makes you feel uncomfortable gets heard and taken seriously by your subconscious mind unless you learn how to respond constructively. Thoughts are often automatic, powerful and relentless.

Even with the very best of intentions and training around using a confident mindset, you'll notice old, uncomfortable and unhelpful thoughts haunting and bothering you. Soon enough you'll learn how to accept them, answer back, ignore them and think about or do something else to balance your mindset.

What factors help or hinder the growth of a confident mindset?

A confident and balanced mindset can be hard to remember with the background noise of a rapidly changing world. Daily 'to do' lists, challenges at work and school, high levels of expectation and competition in learning and work environments all contribute to a heavy mental load.

An environment like this can be exhausting, throwing life out of perspective. It can also contribute to a, hopeless mindset that you're not enough unless you're 'as good as' the next person, pleasing everyone or have the latest status driven material possession. It can sometimes be hard to stay confident when you're looking for joy outside of yourself, your relationships and the quality of your character and mind.

Despite all of this, people are keeping their heads above water and overall doing rather well. The 24/7 newsreel will want you to believe that the world is falling apart despite strong evidence revealing less overall crime, better access to health care and improved education outcomes. Most people are living happier, healthier lives than ever before. Pinker (2018)

What has changed, then? It seems our excessive focus on achievement and happiness overriding kindness and care may have had an adverse effect on younger generations. This cultural shift means that young people who haven't learned significant social-emotional capabilities are more likely to behave in ways that are unkind or disrespectful towards others. Without character and values education, children can become excessively self-absorbed, undermining a more meaningful sense of community and connection. Weissbourd (2009)

Social-emotional guidance for young people, once handed down from generation to generation through hands-on learning, is harder to provide within busy families and fractured support networks. It's often the everyday incidental chats about life that sink into a young person's perspective and value system over time.

Another factor to consider is how children's minds can become overloaded in the information age. The amount of information might overload a laptop in a very short time! Social media, smartphones, Internet, and a never-ending stream of email are the most obvious sources. Although the human brain has infinite space for new information, it's the pace and number of times people are unnecessarily interrupted that can impact on emotional regulation and our ability to stay focused.

The World Health Organization (2018) has recorded increasing rates of anxiety and depression globally, with depression ranked second as a leading cause of disability worldwide. While bio-psycho-social predictors can't be ignored, low levels of social-emotional literacy that contribute to this challenge cannot be overlooked.

Dan Gilbert's happiness research at Harvard University, like many similar studies, found that what people think will make them happy doesn't last when it comes from outside of themselves. For example, winning the lottery will make you happy but not for as long as you might think. Just as becoming paraplegic will make you unhappy at first but not for as long as people think it will. Gilbert (2007)

Is there an optimum period to develop a confident mindset?

During early childhood, more than one million neural connections form every second. Harvard Center on the Developing Child (2009) While the best time to develop a confident mindset is when you're young and your brain is mostly plastic, it's never too late to challenge your thinking. This book is just as much for you as it is for the young people you are supporting. You will be thinking for the rest of your life, so you'll have plenty of opportunities to build this mindset no matter what developmental stage you are at.

Once a confident mindset is active, will that be the end of defeated thinking and unhappiness?

After learning these skills, defeated feelings will continue to appear. These feelings are part of everyone's lives, especially when things do not go as planned. You will naturally continue to experience a full range of both comfortable and uncomfortable thoughts and emotions.

What will change once you develop a more confident mindset is a newfound self-awareness and ability to respond to situations with improved clarity, making use of challenging conditions to leverage you to a better place. You will learn to cope with difficulties in a constructive way that doesn't weigh you down longer than is necessary.

Years of thinking patterns are about to be challenged. Many of these thoughts have become automated, so you don't even know they've happened. Be kind and patient with yourself as you navigate your way through these pages.

What is the most important underlying principle of a confident mindset?

There are many underlying principles, but a fundamental approach is to question potentially harmful beliefs in a proactive and purposeful way. Students learn that just because they have a thought, it doesn't mean that thought is correct. They learn that with practice, they can choose another thought.

Compassionate thinking: An integral part of a confident mindset

Compassion supports mental health, lowers anxiety, improves emotional regulation and is essential in building a confident mindset. Jazaieri et al. (2017) Being compassionate towards yourself and others has a significant impact on social-emotional literacy, optimism and an individual's ability to get along with others. Seppala et al. (2019)

Neuroscientist Jordan Grafman from the U.S. National Institute of Health conducted several studies in the 2000s showing fMRI brain images confirming the pleasure centres in the brain are equally active when giving as they are when receiving. Santi (2016) A similar study published in the Harvard Business School gave half the participants money to spend on themselves and the other half money to spend on others. Those who spent money on others left significantly happier than the group spending it on themselves. Dunn, Aknin and Norton (2008)

Focusing too much on yourself and your challenges doesn't allow much space for compassion and kindness towards others. Learning to see outside of yourself, contribute to others and do things without any expectations the gestures will be reciprocated will help you think and feel more hopeful. Fostering compassion through understanding rather than judgment, empathising where appropriate and doing what you can to relieve suffering around you proves to have many benefits. Doing good helps you feel good.

Using compassion as a first point of call when a student presents with difficult behaviour is another way to encourage your own and their confident mindset. All students want to get things right and behave well. When they don't, there's almost always something going on in the background. Privately asking questions like, 'You're really struggling to handle your feelings in the classroom—can you tell me why and how I might help?' is much more connecting and compassionate than, 'You need to behave better in the classroom, this isn't good enough.' The same applies for a student who is not handing work in. Asking, 'I've noticed you're not doing your homework. Is anything going on that's making it hard for you to get it done?' is more effective and connecting than, 'You need to hand in your homework or your grades will drop.' Responding with compassion opens the doors to communication to find out what's really going on behind the scenes, while contributing to healthy connections. Boundaries stay strong, expectations remain clear, firm and fair, but the delivery is compassionate to increase the likelihood they will keep listening and trying.

What new skills might be gained from reading *The Confident Minds Curriculum*?

The chapters that follow will remind you of many things you already know. Practical social skills, constructive problem solving, conflict resolution, gratitude, kindness and compassion are all considered. You will have the opportunity to strengthen your existing knowledge, as well as learn new skills to build and nourish a confident mindset.

The Confident Minds Curriculum might be a refresher course for students who already know what it takes to be autonomous and socially, emotionally skilled. For others, this is an excellent opportunity to learn simple tools to start thinking and feeling with confidence and optimism. The essential foundations for balanced thinking are offered here for you to continue building student's social-emotional competencies.

What skills do I need to teach a confident mindset?

Your personality, education, values, life experience and intuition can be brought to the table for this curriculum to reach its full potential. Without your unique perspective and existing skills, this would be a social skills cookbook listing off what you should and should not do. When you work with people, there's no such thing as a quick fix. There is never just one way to do things, and what works one day might not work the next. By bringing your prior knowledge and professional experience into the picture, you give programs like *The Confident Minds Curriculum* the best chance of success.

How to use *The Confident Minds Curriculum*

While the program is designed to follow the framework as closely as possible in the order suggested, modify the content to suit the young people in front of you. Adapt the language and don't be afraid to extend the chapters by teaching your prior knowledge on each of the topics. When you use *The Confident Minds Curriculum* in this way, it will be enhanced by your personal 'stamp'.

The social-emotional learning framework

The Confident Minds Curriculum is a structured social-emotional learning program that teaches all components in the social-emotional learning (SEL) wheel that follows. Young people will find it hard to reach full competency in all areas, as social-emotional learning is a lifelong process. The goal of programs like this one is that young people are able to feel they are competent enough to interact and proceed in prosocial ways. Don't feel defeated if a child shows slow improvement. Continue supporting them to develop these skills using your expertise and the lessons within this and other programs. At the core of change and optimism is a sense of belonging and capability. These do not develop overnight or immediately after engaging in a curriculum like this. Self-awareness and social-emotional development take time. Continue doing what you can to be a nonjudgmental, compassionate leader striving to build competency in young people. Your steady work matters even if the outcomes of your efforts aren't always clear.

Chapter structure

Each chapter is divided into a number of lessons that break down the skills for the overall chapter topic. It is recommended you incorporate the 'gradual model of release' guidelines, a teaching method using the following steps to teach a new skill:

1. Show students the skill first by demonstrating it yourself. Share a relevant personal story, case study or show a clip where someone is demonstrating the skill.
2. Practise the skills together.
3. Step back, observe and avoid stepping in unnecessarily. Warmly encourage from the sidelines. As a school or organisation, you might set weekly goals to apply the new skills so everyone is on the same page.
4. Show your trust in their developing skills and abilities. Check in with gentle reminders and make sure there are plenty of structured and incidental opportunities to use and practice the skills.

Each chapter has several ways to encourage the new confident mindset concept. Each component is structured into an individual lesson. You can facilitate one clear lesson at a time or change the order within a chapter to suit your unique needs.

The Confident Minds Curriculum social-emotional learning wheel

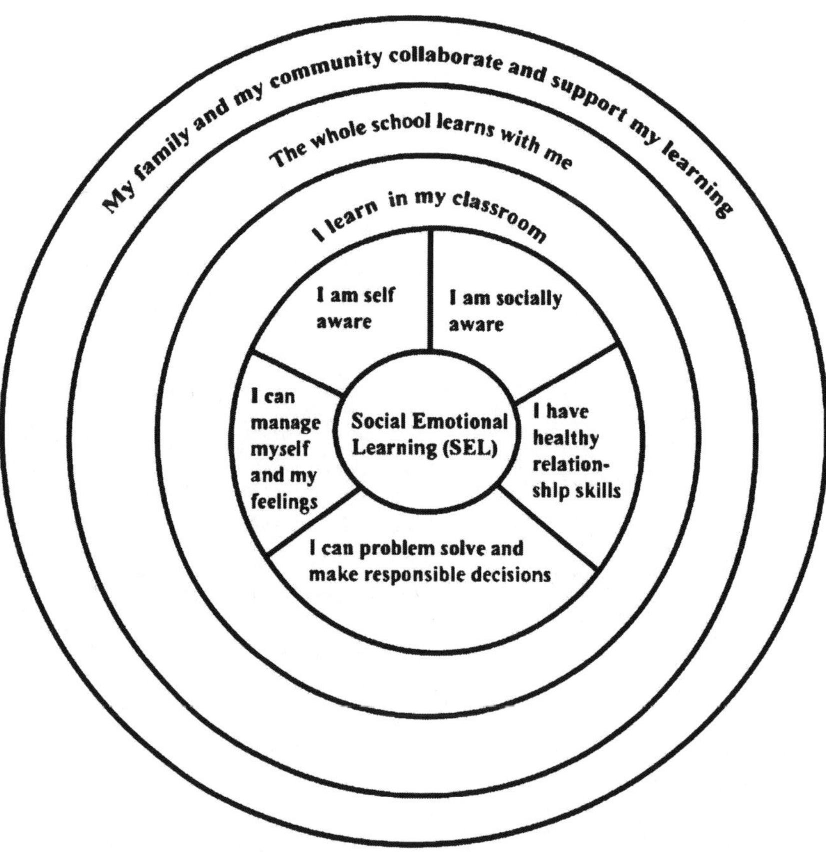

The Confident Minds Curriculum SEL wheel is based upon the CASEL 'Competencies Wheel.' (2017)

Lesson structure explanations

New confident mindset concept

This part introduces a new way of thinking that's related to the underlying skills to improve the mindset. Take time to read this section on your own first, then explain it in your own words to your students.

Case studies

Case studies are found throughout *The Confident Minds Curriculum*. Spanning across two decades of my professional practice, they provide you with insight on the broad range of challenges young people experience and how *The Confident Minds Curriculum* might assist. Names and recognisable details have been altered, but the core problem and solution are intact. You can use the case studies for personal interest or read them to your students, stopping before the point marked, 'solution' where they can think of their own ways to help the young person under the lens.

Brainstorms and mind maps

The Confident Minds Curriculum encourages you and your students to think for yourselves about what a confident mindset means to you. Mind mapping is an effective way to get information flowing freely, opening up layers that are under the surface while creating opportunities for knowledge to become denser and more useful. Mind mapping creates opportunities to discuss new ideas using open-ended inquiries, avoiding any leading questions from the facilitator that suggest what is 'right' or 'wrong'.

Mind mapping is student-led, allowing the facilitator to support broad discussions without excessive preparation. For example, if you were teaching your students how to handle anger, you could simply write 'anger' as your key prompt on the board. This strategy would then spark discussion around what anger might mean, when it happens, what people do when they feel it, the consequences of angry outbursts and much more. Brainstorming is also used throughout this book to help students get their ideas out quickly and to gain insight into how they see the confident mindset playing out.

Brainstorms and mind maps help you find out what your students already know, supporting them to start thinking more deeply about a new concept without being led in any preplanned direction. Mind maps are as simple as putting the word or concept on the board and inviting your students to 'tell me something about this.' As they share their knowledge and beliefs, the mind map continues branching out into new areas that are related to the core concept. Continue extending each individual idea that has come out of the core idea into as much detail as possible. Mind maps are a great way to get student-led information flowing freely.

Brainstorms questions stir up thoughts and discussion, allowing a broad range of ideas to evolve together as a group.

Role plays

Role plays provide an opportunity to practise new thinking and skills without the pressure of really being in the situation. Students help each other see new ways of thinking and interacting. Role plays are often done in pairs with peers but can also be used as discussions and offered one on one between student and facilitator. Some of the role plays are best done as individuals. It's okay for the same role play to be attempted by several students. This approach opens up great opportunities for students to learn from many minds focused on the same problem.

Journaling

Journaling is one way to get feelings out, recording both positive and negative experiences. Spending twenty minutes a day writing about your thoughts and feelings has been shown in many studies to lower depression and anxiety. Krpan et al. (2013)

Journaling has assisted many young people to clear their minds, improve their self-awareness and let go of negative thoughts. It is recommended students record their thoughts for many of the activities but also use their journal as a daily ritual for self-reflection and awareness.

Journaling provides you and your students with an opportunity to freely and confidentially jot down your thoughts and feelings about a specific topic or event. It can also be used for gratitude practice and recording acts of kindness. Daily journaling is similar to having a regular debrief with a friend. It can be useful even without a specific format, encouraging students to use it however they like. Consider using journaling as part of your students' day.

In *The Confident Minds Curriculum* lesson plans, journaling is often used for reflection about the topic and answering questions that might better be considered privately.

Play and games

Every lesson ends with a short burst of play or games. While it might be tempting to skip these, remember most young people love and feel energised by play. While some will need encouragement to get out of their comfort zone, most will learn to relax and enjoy this less structured time. It's through play that young people can enjoy themselves for the fun of it—with no measurable outcomes placing pressure on them to achieve. Playtime allows for rest, resetting and creativity. If time permits, add one or two other games you already enjoy as a group to the one provided in the curriculum.

***The Confident Minds Curriculum* is designed for both professional and student development**

The Confident Minds Curriculum might be your opportunity to shift from your comfort zone and practice some researched-based, practical ways to think about how you approach life. If you aren't already using a confident mindset, consider challenging yourself to master the thinking along with your students. Your students will appreciate your authenticity as you teach them what you are doing yourself.

Make sure you look after your own well-being as you enter a learning curve like this. It's not easy to add another layer to your already busy workload. Your well-being is crucial for the effective delivery of any program. Greenberg, Brown, and Abenavoli (2016)

A whole school approach, small targeted groups or individual counselling?

The Confident Mind Curriculum encourages a culture shift by being a whole school or organisation approach. Research demonstrates that behaviour change is speedier and more consistent when everyone in the community is approached similarly, while tailoring for individual needs as necessary. Greenberg et al. (2003)

A culture change approach helps build a cohesive sense of 'these are our values, beliefs and attitudes'. Together everyone develops a shared social-emotional language, whereby everyone is equipped with common strategies that become part of the overall culture.

Within health care settings, you might be using this curriculum with young people who have significant difficulties with their overall social-emotional literacy and well-being. You can teach these skills one on one as well as in small groups. Encourage parents to visit www.positivemindsaustralia.com.au to enhance their knowledge and skills and to enable follow-up at home. Role plays and discussions throughout the book can be provided to individual students as well as small groups.

Ultimately, you are the best judge of who needs *The Confident Minds Curriculum* in the environment you work as well as what the best delivery method will be for whom you target.

Survey results

Recently, 185 young people living in Australia aged between 8 and 14 undertook the online survey found below. You will find the survey results and their comments throughout this book to help keep you engaged with the minds of young people.

Students rated their answers on a scale of 1–5, with 1 being 'never' and 5 being 'always'.

1 I have enough friends.

2 I know how to be a good friend.

3 I have goals.

4 I know how to reach my goals.

5 I know people who can help me if a problem gets too big to handle alone.

6 I have enough adults who care about me.

7 I belong at my school.

8 I belong in my home.

9 I have talents and strengths.

Students answered the following questions:

1 What, if anything, do you worry about?

2 How do you calm down when you're upset?

3 What do you need most from your parents?

4 What do you need most from your teachers?

5 What do you need most from your friends?

While the survey was not used as a diagnostic tool, it provides insight into how young people see themselves, others and their experiences.

Encouragement

It is important to encourage yourself and your students throughout this process and beyond. No one achieves anything in isolation, and any new skill takes time and practice to master. Encouragement is different from praise. When you use nonspecific praise, you might say 'You're smart' or 'You're good.' This approach focuses only on the outcomes of their efforts. Encouragement, on the other hand, is commenting on their efforts and the process of learning.

Ways to encourage your students to build a confident mindset include:

'I can see you're working hard to think this through.'
'I've noticed you have put a positive spin on some really tough times.'
'I'm really enjoying watching you take on the challenge to be kind to yourself.'
'You're making such an effort to understand other people's differences and accept them for who they are. It's not easy, but you're doing it so well.'
'Your hard work is really paying off.'
'You have been getting along with some really tricky personalities lately, and you've stayed out of trouble. Keep it up. You're doing great.'
'Thank you for the effort you put into being compassionate. It's making a difference to our school.'
'I can see how much confidence you've built since you started ignoring your inner critic. Impressive.'
'You work hard.'
'I imagine it's really hard, but you make it look easy!'

Pre- and post-curriculum surveys

At the end of this introduction you will find two surveys. One is to be filled out by the adult teaching or counselling the young person. The other is designed to be taken by the students themselves for self- awareness and reflection. Questions in the survey are directly related to the skills taught in *The Confident Minds Curriculum*. By responding to the survey both at the start and the end of the curriculum, you will be able to ascertain where a student has improved and where they continue needing assistance. An online version is also available at www.positivemindsaustralia.com.au.

Collaboration with families

Where possible, copies of *The Confident Minds Curriculum* should made available for borrowing or purchasing wherever the program is offered. When families and carers follow the program at home, this not only enhances the young person's confidence in the program but strengthens their skills. Where family support is unlikely or not possible, continue your excellent work. Every seed you plant will count, even if it takes longer or is less apparent in some of your students.

Supporting materials and activities

You will find plenty of free resources and downloadable tools to complement the book at www.positivemindsaustralia.com.au.

Take your time

While the idea of thinking more confidently can be exciting, try not to rush your way through this curriculum. Take your time. Remember, human thought and behaviour take years to shape. It will take time for a new mindset to develop, and there will be backward steps along the way. With time, understanding and compassion for your students, you'll see good results coming your way.

If a child or group of young people is taking a while to understand the content, split one lesson into two or three smaller lessons. A short, five-minute burst with minimal material can be more useful for some students than spending half an hour to an hour covering a lot more content.

How long will the curriculum take?

Again, this is up to you and your circumstances. Each chapter has around five to ten lessons full of activities and discussions. In total, the book offers approximately 50 lessons and several hundred activities. In most schools, the program is delivered at a healthy pace over six months to one year. Lessons can be as short as five or ten minutes at a time, once or twice a week, or as long as 45 minutes per week, every week for a school semester or year. The curriculum can go for longer if you add your own components to deepen student skills and understanding.

What support is available?

Online training will be available from 2020 at www.positivemindsaustralia.com.au. Group training will be available across Australia and in some parts of the world from 2020 on an invitation basis. Free online resources at www.positivemindsaustralia.com.au will further your knowledge and skills as well as courses and ebooks.

A final word before beginning

What matters most of all is that you enter this process with self-confidence based on your personal strengths and professional expertise. You're about to teach a curriculum your students can use long after your role in their learning has come to an end. Follow your instinct, take what is useful at the time and adapt or remove what isn't. Maybe those parts are for later, perhaps they're not for you. Trust your intuition, professional judgment and expertise.

I wish you all the very best and thank you for the opportunity to bring my work into your workplace.

Madhavi Nawana Parker
www.postivemindsaustralia.com.au

Pre- and post-curriculum survey for The Confident Minds Curriculum

Parents/carer/ facilitator survey

Before commencing *The Confident Minds Curriculum*, please take this short survey. This will help gather data before the program. You will be reminded to take it again at the end of the program to measure improvements and changes.

Thank you.

For each question, please highlight or write down one answer in degrees of modality.

1 (always), 2 (sometimes) or 3 (never)

Child's Name .... *Date*................................ *DOB* ..../......./.......

Name of person filling form ....

If you wish to add any additional comments, please use the other side of the page.

Does the child:

1. Show mutual respect and open communication in friendships?	**1**	**2**	**3**
2. Show concern for other people's challenges and differences?	**1**	**2**	**3**
3. See themselves in a positive and supportive way?	**1**	**2**	**3**
4. Handle disagreements and differences with fairness, respect and healthy communication?	**1**	**2**	**3**
5. Know to look for positive and helpful things in difficult situations?	**1**	**2**	**3**
6. Use a balanced and solution-focused method to solve problems?	**1**	**2**	**3**
7. Manage challenging feelings like anger, disappointment and frustration calmly and constructively?	**1**	**2**	**3**
8. Know what they need to be physically and mentally healthy, energized and comfortable?	**1**	**2**	**3**

9. What are the child's strengths?

Pre- and post-curriculum survey for The Confident Minds Curriculum

Student survey

Before commencing *The Confident Minds Curriculum*, please take this short survey. This will help gather data before the program. You will be reminded to take it again at the end of the program to measure improvements and changes.

Thank you.

For each question, please highlight or write down one answer in degrees of modality.

1 (always), 2 (sometimes) or 3 (never)

Your Name .... *Date*............................... *DOB* ..../ ..../ ....

If you wish to add any additional comments, please use the other side of the page.

I know how to...

1. Show other people respect and communicate in a friendly way.	**1**	**2**	**3**
2. Show people I care about them when they are having a tough time.	**1**	**2**	**3**
3. Encourage myself in a positive way.	**1**	**2**	**3**
4. Be fair and respectful when I have a disagreement with another person.	**1**	**2**	**3**
5. Look out for positive and helpful points in difficult situations.	**1**	**2**	**3**
6. Solve problems by staying calm and focusing on solutions.	**1**	**2**	**3**
7. Handle challenging feelings like anger, disappointment and frustration in calm and constructive ways.	**1**	**2**	**3**
8. Take care of myself physically and mentally.	**1**	**2**	**3**

9. My strengths are:

References

Collaborative for Academic, Social and Emotional Learning. 2017. 'Core SEL Competencies', *CASEL*. Available at https://casel.org/core-competencies/

Dunn, E. W., L. B. Aknin, and M. I. Norton. 2008. 'Spending Money on Others Promotes Happiness.' *Science* 319, no. 5870: 1687–1688.

Durlak, J. A., R. P. Weissberg, A. B. Dymnicki, R. D. Taylor, and K. Schellinger. 2011. 'The Impact of Enhancing Students' Social Emotional Learning: A Meta-Analysis of School-Based Universal Interventions.' *Child Development* 82: 405–432.

Durlak, J. A., R. P. Weissberg, and M. Pachan. 2010. 'A Meta-Analysis of After-School Programs That Seek to Promote Personal and Social Skills in Children and Adolescents.' *American Journal of Community Psychology* 45: 294–309.

Gilbert, D., 2007. *Stumbling on Happiness*. New York: Random House.

Greenberg, M. T., J. L. Brown, and R. M. Abenavoli. 2016. *Teacher Stress and Health: Effects on Teachers, Students and Schools*. Edna Bennett Pierce Prevention Research Center, Pennsylvania State University, and Robert Wood Johnson Foundation.

Greenberg, M. T., R. P. Weissberg, M. U. O'Brien, J. E. Zins, L. Fredericks, H. Resnik, and M. Elias. 2003. 'Enhancing School-Based Prevention and Youth Development through Coordinated Social, Emotional and Academic Learning.' *American Psychologist* 58, nos. 6-7: 466–474.

Harvard Center on the Developing Child. 2009. 'Five Numbers to Remember about Early Childhood Development.'

Jazaieri, H., L. McGonigal, I. A. Lee, T. Jinpa, J. R. Doty, J. J. Gross, and P. R. Goldin. 2017. 'Altering the Trajectory of Affect and Affect Regulation: The Impact of Compassion Training.' *Mindfulness* 9, no. 3: 283–293. doi:10.1007/s12671-017-0773-3.

Krpan, K. M., E. Kross, M. G. Berman, P. J. Deldin, M. K. Askren, and J. Jonides. 2013. 'An Everyday Activity as a Treatment for Depression: The Benefits of Expressive Writing for People Diagnosed with Major Depressive Disorder.' *Journal of Affective Disorders* 150, no. 3: 1148–1151.

O'Reilly, S., and T. Venus. 2019. SEL wheel artwork and pre- and post-curriculum surveys in collaboration with Madhavi Nawana Parker.

Pinker, S. 2018. *Enlightenment Now: The Case for Reason, Science, Humanism, and Progress*. New York: Penguin.

Redmond, G., et al. 2016. *Are the Kids Alright? Young Australians in Their Middle Years: Final Report of the Australian Child Wellbeing Project*. Flinders University, University of New South Wales and Australian Council for Educational Research.

Santi, J., 2016. *The giving way to happiness*. New York: Penguin Putnam.

Saracho, O. N. 1989. 'Cognitive Style in the Play of Young Children.' *Early Child Development and Care* 51: 65–76.

———. 1998. 'What Is Stylish about Play?' In *Multiple Perspectives on Play in Early Childhood Education*, edited by O. N. Saracho and B. Spodek, 240–254. Albany: State University of New York Press.

Saracho, O. N., and B. Spodek. 1981. 'Teachers' Cognitive Styles: Educational Implications.' *Educational Forum* 45: 153–159.

Seppala, E. M., E. Simon-Thomas, S. L. Brown, M. C. Worline, C. D. Cameron, and J. R. Doty, eds. 2019. *The Oxford Handbook of Compassion Science*. New York: Oxford University Press.

Taylor, R. D., E. Oberle, J. A. Durlak, and R. P. Weissberg. 2017. 'Promoting Positive Youth Development through School-Based Social and Emotional Learning Interventions: A Meta-Analysis of Follow-Up Effects.' *Child Development* 88: 1156–1171.

Weissbourd, R. 2009. *The Parents We Mean to Be: How Well-Intentioned Adults Undermine Children's Moral and Emotional Development*. New York: Houghton Mifflin.

World Health Organization. 2018. 'Monitoring Health for the SDGs: Sustainable Development Goals.'

Zhang, L., and R. J. Sternberg. 2006. *The Nature of Intellectual Styles*. London: Routledge.

CHAPTER 1

Healthy relationships

Introduction

A broad range of personalities co-exist in homes, schools and workplaces every day. Without balanced thinking skills for understanding and accepting different values, personalities and temperaments, things can easily fall apart. As social connection is a primary indicator of happiness, teaching young people how to have healthy relationships with others is crucial. Harvard Study of Adult Development (1937–present)

Social-emotional learning programs like the Confident Minds Curriculum teach young people helpful ways to see themselves and others, so they learn to get along respectfully, even when they don't see eye to eye. Even the most reserved person is wired deeply for connection and belonging. How much they need to be with others is undoubtedly on a spectrum, but no one flourishes well without belonging to a social group.

Maintaining healthy relationships throughout your life rates highest on global happiness, well-being, overall health and resilience indicators. Children and adults deeply connected to a broad range of people are more likely to be self-confident, happy, emotionally balanced and well behaved. People who don't enjoy the sense of belonging that healthy relationships bring are at higher risk of addiction, unhappiness and poor physical and mental health. Harvard Study of Adult Development (1937–present)

Your thinking style or mindset is an integral part of how your relationships with others will play out. Behind everything you feel, say and do, there is a leading thought process. Being trained to use hopeful thoughts about yourself and others helps build self-confidence and confidence in others, leaving you with a better chance at healthy relationships. A hopeless mindset produces unrealistic expectations and is more likely to end up in conflict and isolation. Research has proven that people can be trained to be happier and more optimistic, so they can focus on healthy relationships instead of attaching happiness to success or belongings, which doesn't provide long-lasting optimism. Achor (2018)

Young people with healthy, rational optimism are less fixated on judging differences and more focused on seeing another person's strengths and finding ways to connect with them. A person with a negative or hopeless mindset, on the other hand, might see a newcomer as a threat to their position in a group, or because of a natural tendency to find fault in others, struggle to build friendships unless the other person is entirely agreeable with their values, beliefs and attitudes.

Viewing others with an open mind, creates opportunities to make friends with a broad group of people. Optimistic people are more socially accepted and more willing to allow others into their social networks. Brissette, Scheier and Carver (2002) This is not blind optimism, it is about understanding and accepting personal differences as a normal variation between people. Someone willing to look for the best in others becomes very good at replacing fault finding with strengths seeking. They are still able to differentiate between unhealthy relationships and healthy relationships, but do not see differences as a threat or reason to cut off a friendship.

This chapter looks at simple ways to teach students a healthy relationship mindset. It explores how to find the best in others and ideas to interact that are friendly and balanced. Practical ways to accept, embrace and grow from personal differences are taught explicitly, along with the underpinnings of friendship.

Lesson 1.1

Character and intention

New confident mindset concept: Healthy friendships focus on character and intention instead of wealth, status and popularity

Focusing on *who* people are rather than *what* they are opens up more significant opportunities for authentic and reciprocal friendships. In early childhood, forming a self-identity is an integral part of becoming who you are. Most young people go through this during their teens and early adulthood. Finding yourself and your place in the world is a natural part of maturing. By focusing on character and intention, you're less likely to value yourself and others based on outward achievements and status. A more open, understanding and authentic self-concept and view of others naturally follow. Connecting through character and intention builds a positive and healthy foundation for robust relationships, contributing to overall optimism and resilience.

Mind map and brainstorm to explore character and intention

Begin with a brainstorm, asking your students the following questions:

- What do you most like in a person's character?
- What do you like people to notice about your character? Do you show appreciation for people with these character strengths?
- What do you find most frustrating about other people (habits, comments they tend to make, personality styles, behaviours and attitudes)?
- Is there anything about you other people might not understand and find frustrating?
- Is there anything you personally do that you find frustrating in others?

Some students, especially those who are less self-confident, might struggle with the openness and self-awareness this activity calls upon. For others, this will be a new concept altogether, and they may need time to process it before they are ready to contribute. Just go with the flow, without pressure, and see what comes of it. If you're willing, hold yourself accountable too and share anything relevant to the discussion.

Once the brainstorm is complete, you can start the mind map. For the first mind map, write 'Character' in the centre of the page. See what your students understand about what character means and its role in friendships. If time permits, start a second mind map with 'Intentions' written in the centre of the page and see if your students can differentiate between clumsy social behaviour resulting from impulsivity or limited social skills sabotaging good intentions or related to unhealthy plans and intentional cruelty.

Case study: Helping Alessi understand and appreciate others for their character and intention

Alessi was one of the kindest students I had ever met. In all the years I'd seen him, he never had hurtful intentions towards others. Alessi would do anything to help friends and family at the drop of a hat. The only problem with Alessi was he had a massive superiority complex. You might be thinking this probably means he had an inferiority complex—after all, many who show this kind of arrogance are deeply insecure underneath all the fanfare.

Not Alessi. Alessi found anyone with a different point of view or a different level of understanding to him infuriating. He struggled to talk to people he didn't consider intelligent or as capable as himself.

Alessi had always struggled to see things from other people's perspectives. His empathy was low. Not in a cruel way—just in the way that other people's thoughts and feelings didn't exist in his trajectory. When other children spoke to him, he'd either ignore them completely, roll his eyes, grunt, sigh, yawn, or on one of his less relaxed days he'd tell them how ridiculous their thinking was.

Needless to say, Alessi had no friends, despite his kind heart, gentle soul and strong desire to be a good friend. He was often lonely. He had no idea what his strengths were other than 'I'm smarter than most people my age,' and 'I know more about things than most people.' He didn't know how to calm down or to be kind to himself when he was struggling or had made a mistake. He wasn't very active and ate very little.

Alessi begged me to help him make friends but had no insight about how his behaviour might have an impact on his chance at doing this.

Solution

With permission, we filmed him at playtime. Alessi, not convinced he ever spoke or behaved out of turn, sat spellbound watching himself in the yard. Even Alessi could see the atmosphere of intolerance that radiated from his every pore. Interaction after interaction seemed to start peacefully yet end abruptly with Alessi throwing his arms up in the air, rolling his eyes or just walking off midsentence.

Viewing himself objectively was the first step towards helping Alessi develop an understanding of how his words and actions might affect others. He also saw himself as a heavy presence for the first time, wandering from person to person carrying unintentional judgment and objection. This approach was not an exercise in shaming. I made it clear to Alessi that everyone is learning and that he is not the only child who struggles to handle their feelings calmly when frustrated by other people's views. I emphasised the importance of forgiving himself for his mistakes and being kind and considerate towards himself during this challenge.

From here, I was able to help Alessi see we're all connected not only through our similarities but also through our differences. I taught him that underneath our differences we share the same needs. Everyone wants to feel safe, supported, liked and loved. Many people see their way of thinking as the best way of thinking, and most people have the best of intentions. We role played positive interactions (which at first he thought were ridiculous, given they had never actually happened), and we brainstormed ways he could use his strengths to connect with others.

Alessi agreed to engage in a kindness and compassion challenge where he would set out to understand, accept and be kind to others, even if they drove him mad with their 'inferior' thinking. He would listen without putting what they said into a 'right' or 'wrong' category, and he'd remind himself to keep his lips closed while they spoke. Slow, deep breathing was essential to keep him focused on his goal and calm enough to achieve it.

At first progress was slow, but after a few weeks the challenge became second nature. The positive attention Alessi was enjoying for the first time in his life made all the effort to accept differences much more comfortable.

While Alessi remains alone in his thoughts and perspectives more often than not, he is no longer alone. He has a small group of friends he can rely on at school and on the weekends. His parents and teachers are relieved, and he's now considered at much lower risk for anxiety and depression in his teenage years.

Character and intention role plays

- Amara struggled with jealousy. She couldn't stand it when other people got more attention than she. Other people's happiness bothered her too. Show what this looks like as Amara is greeted by a peer who tells her he has just made the state basketball team and is off to travel interstate.
- Ella loved her best friend, Ana, who kindly understood Ella's social clumsiness, bad timing and poor taste in social comments. Show an interaction between the two of them, where Ella has just told her new teacher she looks pregnant. Ella is missing the point as the teacher tries to explain that she is not pregnant, but Ella is just not listening. Show how Ana responds respectfully and sorts things out without making a big deal.
- Asha pretty much owned everything. She had an expensive laptop, the latest phone, a new puppy, a swimming pool and designer clothes. Asha seemed

to have the most friends too. Show an interaction where Jemma wants to be friends with Asha, but Asha is making it clear that she has certain 'standards' before she 'lets' someone be her friend.

- Erin came into school every morning smelling pretty bad. She was new to the neighbourhood and was struggling to make friends. She struggled to know what to say and do around her peers, and no one knew what to make of her. Show an interaction where someone takes the time to get to know Erin and what makes her tick.
- Josh didn't want anyone to know how much his family was struggling financially, so he found ways to sound wealthy. He went to a prestigious college which he would never have gone to unless his grandparents had paid the fees. Josh is struggling with this 'lie' he carries. He can no longer keep up with the possessions and overseas holidays the other kids have, and the pressure to try is overwhelming. Show a discussion between him and his teacher as he plans to 'come out' and share who he really is. His greatest fear is being judged and losing his friends.
- Amal got angry so quickly and misunderstood what seemed like the smallest of things. Show an argument between her and another student where Amal accuses her of being unkind and uncaring because she forgot Amal's birthday. Show Amal's reaction as she starts to calm down. How might Amal clear things up?
- Zara set up arguments between friends that made her look good and others look terrible. Zara was intentionally mean because she had grown up in a family where her experiences had been painful and damaging. She found meaning in conflict. Show what this might look like and one way Zara could be encouraged to turn things around.

Play and games

Character and intention game

Stand the group in a social circle. Every time you call out something they think is intentionally unkind or inappropriate, they tap their head while rubbing their tummy. When you call out something they believe is a result of an impulse or socially clumsy with good intentions, they stand with one leg up, the foot resting on the opposite knee. (This is the start of the yoga tree pose.) You can choose your poses or let the students nominate them.

Game scenarios

- James, feeling embarrassed, asks Rasheed if his new sports uniform fits okay, knowing it is way too big. Rasheed answers, 'Mate, you look like a clown!'
- On the soccer field, Sameera laughs when Jillian misses the goal. She rolls her eyes and says, 'Good shot, Jillian.'

- Elsa has broken her sister's favourite pencil sharpener. She throws it in the bin to hide the evidence. When her sister asks Elsa if she knows anything about it, Elsa replies, 'No, but I'll buy you a new one with my pocket money.'
- Suran is feeling anxious about walking to school on his own. His dad offers to walk him halfway. Suran is relieved at first, but when they get close to school, he sees some friends and realises he is the only grade 6 student with a parent joining them. Suran growls at his dad and says, 'Get lost, you're embarrassing me.'
- Benjamin doesn't make the basketball team. He's so upset. He starts telling everyone who did make the team that he didn't want to get selected because he's going to do club basketball instead (which is way better).

Lesson 1.2

The inner critic vs. the inner champion

New confident minds concept: Getting to know your inner critic

Most people have an inner critic, a hopeless and helpless voice playing in your mind that criticises you and others for all your perceived faults. When things don't go according to plan, the inner critic is the voice of blame. According to the inner critic, whatever went wrong is yours or someone else's fault. The inner critic is a natural fault finder. Taming it is essential for healthy, harmonious relationships.

You will learn in detail about the inner critic in chapter 3. For now, the aspect of the inner critic that needs attention is its judgment of potential friends. Those who aren't considered popular, fashionable, traditionally successful or helpful for your social status aren't regarded highly. The inner critic resists differences and imperfections, pushes others away unless they fit into the image it wants to uphold about you and your social network.

Blindly paying attention to your inner critic puts you at risk of not getting to know people who could become great friends. When you question thoughts coming from your inner critic, you'll find that your initial ideas do not necessarily reflect reality. On the flip side, you can teach yourself to use an 'inner champion' mindset that is encouraging and optimistic about yourself and others. It understands others and allows the reality that no one is perfect or the same as you, and differences offer a richness and depth to a relationships that similarities alone cannot.

Mind map and brainstorm: Exploring the inner critic and inner champion

In the centre of the board, write 'Inner Critic'. Support your students to explore what it is, what it sounds like and how it feels. After this, write 'Inner Champion' on another board and support your students to explore what this concept means to them.

Journalling: Identifying the inner critic and inner champion

Allow some time for students to write about their own inner critic. When do they hear it most? What does it say? Is there any truth to it's beliefs? Once they have identified their inner critic, they can write a new script by their inner champion. To inspire the dialogue, remind them the inner champion speaks kindly and with encouragement, like they would speak to their best friend. Respond to each inner critic statement in their journal with an inner champion statement. Remind them it will take practice to get used to this kind of self-talk and over time, it will feel more natural.

Case study: Alice builds an inner champion

Alice had so much going for her. A great family, fantastic friends and a caring school. Her outside looked much better than her inside. Anyone who knew her thought she was happy and confident. On the inside, she had an out of control inner critic. All day long it said things like 'You're going to mess this up,' 'No one likes you,' 'You're boring,' 'You don't belong here,' 'Your friends aren't good enough' and much more.

Alice listened intently to her inner critic. She believed her thoughts and never questioned them. Because of this, Alice struggled to concentrate at school and entered into conflicts with her friends whom she saw as imperfect. It started to affect her sleep. She'd been told to think about other things until the thoughts went away, but nothing was working, and she was unhappier by the day.

Solution

Alice was not especially enthusiastic when she came to see me. Her opening line was, 'Nothing works!' I empathised with her frustration and let her know I had one new thing to try, hoping she wouldn't reject it or say she'd already tried it.

I let Alice know about the inner critic and how it's entirely automatic and hard to control. I explained that the voice of the inner critic is just made up of thoughts that she has unintentionally created. I asked her to try one thing for a week, to question her beliefs. Each time she was listening to the criticism, instead of churning it over (which makes the thinking stronger) I asked Alice to think to herself, 'Is this true?' While sometimes she found it hard to disagree with the thoughts, at least half the time the question helped her see things from a more productive perspective.

Once she was in the habit of doing this, I was able to teach her how to build her inner champion and how to divert her thoughts into more positive and constructive directions. Another focus was on helping Alice remain positive about her friends and be a champion to them by accepting them for who they were and remembering they can't be perfect or agreeable all the time.

Ask your students to record what they hear their inner critic saying. For every critical statement, ask them to draw three branches and write down alternative inner champion statements. Replacing negative beliefs with positive ones can become a daily habit. When children put themselves down, they can think of three compliments from the voice of their inner champion. This kind of self-exploration and development of self-awareness is an essential part of a healthy, lifelong relationship with themselves and others.

Role plays

Some of the following role plays are best done as individuals. It's okay for the same role play to be attempted by several students. This approach opens up great opportunities for students to learn from many minds focused on the same problem.

- Alessandro wants to join a new club at school. Show him telling a friend whatever his inner critic is telling him. In the end, Alessandro backs out and doesn't attend the tryouts.
- Paulo never stops thinking. Show him lying in bed trying to fall asleep while telling his dog all about the worries of his day as well as his concerns about the next day that hasn't even happened yet.
- Desi has always wanted to go to university to be a vet. She fails a science test for the first time. Show how her inner critic tells her that she'll never be a vet.
- Jemima has always been shy. She looks up to Reilly in her class and wants to be his friend. Show how Jemima's inner critic tells her she's not good enough to be Reilly's friend.
- Gill hasn't had the best of days. Everything seems to be going wrong. It feels unfair. Show how Gill's inner critic says this day should not be going the way he deserves.
- Tammy loses her laptop on the bus. She phones the bus company, but it's no good, it's gone. Show her inner critic criticising her for her mistake and how her mind goes into catastrophe mode as she realises she's going to have to tell her parents.
- Tobias was excited about playing the drums at school. A letter came home just before he started and he finds out the drums are no longer being offered. Tobias doesn't want to play any other instrument. Show his inner critic saying this is somehow his fault and that he'll never learn to play the drums.
- Amal is struggling to learn to read. He's in the upper primary. He's tried hard every day of his life. He feels embarrassed and worries he will never learn to read correctly. Show what his inner critic says to make him feel even worse than he's already feeling.
- Anise is afraid of flying in a plane. Last time she flew there was turbulence. She had a mild panic attack and was embarrassed afterwards. Her dad has just told her they are going to Disneyland for Christmas. Her brothers and sisters are pumped with excitement. Show Anise's inner critic telling her a disaster is on the way.
- Jasmine wants to make friends with Alannah. They both find the same things funny, and they have lots of similar interests. Show Jasmine's inner critic talking about Alannah negatively as it tries to convince her that Alannah isn't good enough to be her friend.

Play and games

Inner critic/inner champion playoff

Divide the group in two. If the session only involves you and your student, you can each take on the role of one side or the other. The first side is the inner critic and the second is the inner champion. Line up both sides so they are facing each other. Cut out inner critic statements for students to call out. The person in front of them responds by coming up with an inner champion statement to cancel it out. This is excellent practice for developing positive and constructive self-talk.

Inner critic statements

'I'm hopeless!'

'No one likes me.'

'I'm boring.'

'I'll never get into university.'

'My friends aren't good enough for me.'

'I'm not good enough for my friends.'

'I'll never pass maths.'

'I can't be friends with someone so unpopular.'

'My school is hopeless.'

'I'll never have enough friends.'

'I'm weird.'

'My life is horrible.'

'My parents are embarrassing.'

Lesson 1.3

Understanding and acceptance in your friendships

New confident mindset concept: Understanding and acceptance

Friendships thrive through common ground, open-mindedness, mutual respect and empathy. Bonds are strengthened further by understanding that differences are a natural part of human diversity and can be a positive aspect of friendship. Friendships can become complicated when a person can't see past differences. People are undoubtedly different, but at the heart of it, share more in common than not.

People naturally want to be feel, seen, heard and valued for who they are. The more time you spend with another person, the more differences you may notice. When you're accepting in friendships, you focus on each other's strengths and grow to appreciate each other for who you are. You value and understand the other person unconditionally, without expecting them to change on account of you interests and beliefs. You give them the freedom to be themselves, creating a healthy foundation to get along.

Mind map: Accepting others

In the centre of the board, write 'Understanding and accepting others in friendship'. Support your students to explore this concept in more detail.

Goal: Being understanding, accepting and nonjudgmental

For one week, set the goal for everyone to try and ignore other people's looks, popularity and possessions. Instead, endeavour to see interactions for what they are: people uniting for connection and belonging, seeking to be heard, valued and understood. Help your students remember the goal by writing a prompt in a clearly visible place, such as 'We understand and accept each other,' or 'We see others for who they are. We see more in people than their faces, money, popularity and achievements.'

Help them remember with prompts like matching friendship bracelets or by carrying a pebble or card as an additional reminder.

Provide the following instructions to stay focused on the goal: When your mind wanders away from a person's character, gently bring your attention back to the moment. Tell yourself, 'Think about their insides, ignore their outsides. I am understanding and accepting of all people.'

Aristotelian interviews

One of Aristotle's most relevant writings that fits in with the Confident Minds Curriculum relates to his theory about three foundations that underlie a friendship.

The first foundation Aristotle identified is that of 'utility', where the person is useful or helpful to you. The second is 'pleasure'. Together you experience and share pleasure. This might be through sport, games, play, conversation or hobbies. The third, most powerful and enduring foundation is the friendship based on mutual appreciation of each other's 'goodness and character'. Pangle (2003)

Aristotle emphasised how connecting through goodness and shared values relied on time, trust and a mutual desire to lift each other. He acknowledged the place for all three foundations, while highlighting that friendships of goodness and character have the best chance of becoming lifelong, reciprocal and mutually fulfilling relationships.

Young people can explore Aristotle's friendship philosophy in the context of themselves and what they offer their relationships, as well as in terms of how they connect with others. The ultimate goal from this activity is for young people to find something good in each person they meet and to keep building these three foundations in all their relationships.

Once you have explained Aristotle's philosophy of friendship, help students understand the foundations in themselves and others. Divide students into pairs. Be prepared to demonstrate an Aristotelian interview first, so students can learn by observing you. In pairs, students take turns to give their partner feedback based on the three foundations.

Aristotelian feedback statements:

You are useful and helpful because...

You bring other people pleasure and fun by...

You have good character because...

Allow time for a short debrief after this activity. Ask your students whether these three foundations could become a base for their relationships with others. If they are keen, why not place a banner or poster in your room as an additional prompt?

Aristotelian journaling

Allow five to ten minutes for students to reflect on and build self-awareness based on how their partner perceives they fit in with the Aristotelian foundations. Students can answer the following questions in their journal, sharing responses afterwards if there's time.

Self-reflection Aristotelian statements:

I am useful and helpful in friendships because I...

I bring pleasure and happiness in my friendships when I...

I bring goodness to my friendships because I...

Both Aristotelian activities increase self-awareness as well as awareness of other people's strengths and value. This can be a helpful exercise in connecting students on a deeper level. Perhaps extend it further by creating compliment circles where students give each other feedback based on Aristotle's framework.

Play and games

First impressions game

(Thanks to the Office of Human Resources, U.S.A. for this game.)

Participants take a seat in a social circle. Each person writes one fact about their background, interests or history that most people don't know. Students then fold up the cards and put them in the middle of the circle.

The facilitator opens the cards and reads them out one at a time. Participants write down which person in the circle they think the card is talking about. Each person then states their guess, followed by the writers revealing themselves to the group. After the game, ask your students how they decided what traits described who and why.

Lesson 1.4

Breaking down divisions

New confident minds concept: Seeing yourself in others by breaking down divisions

Viewing yourself as 'same as', 'different from', or 'better/worse than' others creates divisions that indicate there is a 'right way' to be versus a 'wrong way' to be.

Your value system is what makes sense to you at the time, whether it fits in with social norms or not. It's unlikely you will meet someone who has identical values, skills and interests as you. Despite your differences, you can still be friends. Neither of you is better or worse when the division of right and wrong cease to exist.

When you find it difficult to relate to another, one way to break down divisions is by seeing yourselves in each other. How are you similar? By putting others, irrespective of gender, skin colour, size, wealth, education, introversion, extroversion etc. into the category of 'human', it's much easier to see beyond your differences. Placing your attention on differences can inhibit empathy, compassion and healthy relationships.

While it's easy to stay in your comfort zone, mixing with people who go to the same school, live in the same neighbourhood and like to do the same things, this limits opportunities for building rich and diverse friendships. There are many different kinds of people with their own kind of charisma. There are the thinkers, the quiet achievers, the talkers, the jokers, the doers, the observers and so on. Finding ways to value and celebrate differences rather than viewing them as right or wrong will be infinitely more helpful to the quality and number of your relationships. There is so much from to learn through differences.

Breaking down divisions doesn't mean you go out of your way to meet people who make no sense to you or have values or character that are unkind or unclear. It's about getting out there, engaging openly and being willing to talk to people you meet without judgment or unnecessary categorisation into 'my kind of friend' or 'not my kind of friend'.

Mind map: Breaking down divisions

In the centre of the board, write 'Dividing people', and follow this with a mind map, 'Connecting people'. Remember, there are no right or wrong answers. Young people will learn best when they think for themselves with your gentle guidance.

Visualisation: Finding me in you

Students close their eyes. Offer a moment to think of someone they have a hard time getting along with. Ask your students to imagine they are that person. Imagine what they are thinking and feeling. Imagine what it's like to be them. After the visualisation, ask your students to journal as many things as possible they have in common with the other person. Students are often surprised at finding examples of common ground. This exercise can build stronger empathy, understanding and opportunities for a friendship that might not have otherwise existed.

Finding me in you interview

One way to empathise with and get to know another person is by putting yourself in their shoes. Divide your group into pairs and encourage them to ask each other the following question:

What's it like to be you?

This question might not sound extraordinary, but it is an opening to understanding another person. With the right timing, this can even be a good question to ask students in conflict who have engaged in a restorative conference. It helps each person get outside their own mind and see the world through the eyes of someone you don't see eye to eye with.

Journaling

Ask your students to record three people they have avoided getting to know because they seem too different. Challenge them to consider talking to one each day over the next week without judging them.

Getting to know each other interviews

Mock interviews can help students find out more about each other safely and predictably. In pairs, students take turns to ask and answer the same set of questions. Remind your students to listen without judging the person's answers as right or wrong. Before asking them to do the interviews, show courage and let one of your students interview you in front of the class.

If you could pick anyone to come over for dinner, whom would you choose?
What's your idea of a perfect day?
When did you last sing to yourself or to someone else?
What is the greatest thing you've ever done?
What was the most embarrassing moment of your life?
What is your favourite memory?

Play and games

We have more in common than difference game

Provide your students with an A4 paper or card they can divide into six portions. Allow a few minutes for students to write down six things they are interested in or care about. Without writing any names, all six portions from each student goes into a container. Start by reading out your own answers. One by one, have students pick out a piece of paper from the shared container. Students run to one side of the room each time they hear an interest they relate to. If the interest doesn't fit, they run to the opposite side. A variation is getting each student to call out their own answers, however some children find it difficult to put their personal interests up for open discussion.

End with a reminder that people have more in common than difference. It's part of the human negative bias that hones in on difference and draws attention to it. You don't have to listen to or accept it. Try and focus on your common ground without seeing your differences as a threat.

Lesson 1.5

Being responsible for the feeling you bring into a space

New confident mindset concept: Be responsible with your facial expression and feelings

Magnetic resonance imaging (MRI) scans of the human brain can identify a unique set of neurons called mirror neurons that fire away when you're looking at another person or even watching them on film. Mirror neurons act like an emotional mirror. This means if you see someone get hurt, you will feel that hurt as if it's happening to you. While you won't get the physical pain, you will get a pang of 'pain' as your mirror neurons reflect what you see. Jacobin and Mazziotta (2007)

You have probably watched television shows where people get hurt (not seriously hurt but the funny kind of hurt), and you find yourself cringing—even calling out in horror. Humans have a unique connection to each other where seeing another person suffer is enough for us to feel that suffering. Mirror neurons in many ways create an emotional interconnectedness.

Understanding mirror neurons allows students to be more aware of how facial expressions, body language and overall emotional energy affect others (whether you want them to or not).

A word of caution: some people naturally struggle (because of neurological or personality differences) to manage their facial expressions and body language. We need to be understanding about this and do what we can to support them to develop these skills in their own time. They should never be made to feel guilty about this.

Mind maps: Body language and facial expressions

In the centre of the board, write 'Body language and facial expressions'. See what your students understand about how these factors link to friendships and feelings. Once you've completed this mind map, write 'Emotions are contagious' on the board. Hopefully, students will be able to relate to this and understand the value of being self-aware and respectful of the impact their actions and feelings have on those around them.

Mirror, mirror on the wall

Divide students into pairs and ask them to share a story that involves a dramatic punch line. If your students are struggling to think of one, perhaps tell a story of your own or recount one you already know. Here's mine:

When I was about five, my brother was enthusiastically trying to teach me to play softball. One day, as the story goes, I was holding the softball bat tightly in my hands. He stood behind me showing me how to swing. Before he had a chance to step back, I swung the bat so hard it smashed right into his face. Crunch! I'll never forget that sound!

Usually, when you tell a story like this where someone gets hurt or strong feelings like embarrassment or fear come up, your listener will react strongly as if the story is happening right there in front of them. When students respond this way, remind them they are experiencing a mirror neuron response. Whatever you say and do will create a feeling or reaction in whoever is watching and listening. Humans are deeply connected in many ways, and the mirror neutron network is one of them.

Goal setting: Smiling

You've had the experience of meeting someone who doesn't smile. Something feels uncomfortable about it. Drawing attention to this valuable social skill can encourage students who have a flat or negative facial expression to fake a smile until it comes more naturally to them. It's no surprise you're less likely to want to get to know a person who doesn't smile than a person who does.

Smiling is vital for healthy relationships. Mirror neurons respond to a smile in ways that light up the brain's pleasure centres, passing the positive feeling of joy from one person to the next. Not smiling, on the other hand, spreads feelings of doubt and discomfort that can get in the way of a good interaction. Emotions are contagious. People catch them from the attitude that comes from your face as well as your nonverbal cues. Achor (2015)

A word of caution: many people find looking at people's faces (let alone smiling) tough. Many people on the autism spectrum, for example, may struggle to maintain eye contact and smile at the same time. Some say if they look someone in the eye, they can't listen at the same time. It's important to be respectful about the diverse ways people come across and focus primarily on their character and intention.

Set a goal with students to smile when they make eye contact with, get closer to or are approached by someone friendly. Allow those who struggle to develop the skill to work on smiling at their own pace, with your gentle encouragement. Every so often, check in with your students to see if they have been smiling more, and if they've noticed this changes how they feel and how others feel.

Case study: When smiling doesn't come naturally

Malanna struggled looking into people's eyes. If she looked in their eyes, she couldn't concentrate on what they said. People often got a bad impression about Malanna and considered her rude and snobby. Malanna's character and intention didn't reflect her facial expressions and she was desperate for help.

Solution

Malanna began working towards her goal by learning the trick of looking at people's foreheads, instead of their eyes. She practiced this with as many people as possible. She also spent time imagining herself looking at people's faces and smiling when she had moments on her own at home. Just picturing this in her mind helped build pathways for eye contact and smiling in her brain as if she were really doing it.

Malanna also practiced smiling and eye contact in the mirror. Once she was good at doing this, her goal became smiling at three children in her class before settling down for the day. While smiling is still a work in progress for Malanna, this is no longer obvious to others. She smiles more often, feels less tense and is enjoying lots of smiles in return.

Play and games

Don't you smile at me!

Allow your students to walk around the room freely. They have a straightforward goal in this game. Make eye contact with everyone; smile at no one! A place full of laughter and connection soon follows.

Lesson 1.6

Be kind

New confident mindset concept: Be kind

Be kind. Too obvious?

How often are children taught this explicitly and encouraged to practice it diligently? This basic social skill and fundamental social value can easily become a guiding principle and part of mission statements and values in schools and workplaces. It is reasonable to say most people appreciate receiving kindness from others and that kindness connects people. If another person is difficult to get along with for now, and kindness is a struggle, students can aim for being neutral (not kind and not mean).

To help define kindness further, you might direct your students to look at dictionary meanings behind kindness. A personal favourite to display in classrooms is:

> *Kindness is loaning someone your strength instead of reminding them of their weaknesses. (Original source unknown)*

Case study: Building Jamima's kindness muscles

Jamima seemed polite and sweet-natured, but behind the scenes she caused heartache and pain towards anyone she felt threatened by. Jamima was easily intimidated—especially by happy and confident peers. Jamima had a problematic past and challenging relationships with her family. She had social skills well beyond her years when interacting with people she didn't feel threatened by, but underneath it all, she was sad, confused and lonely. Jamima's only joy was making others feel unhappy and insecure about their friendships. She would artfully set up arguments, steal belongings and ask people questions or make comments that were designed to hurt. Jamima would often say things like 'Did you know you're the only person not invited to Jemma's party—oh, sorry, I can't believe I just said that!'

Jamima's relational aggression was dividing the school community. A team was brought together to support the students she was hurting, as well as Jamima herself, to find out why she was hurting others.

Solution

When Jamima came to see me, her first comment (accompanied with a substantial eye roll) was 'I hate my life. Don't suppose you fix that?'

I knew Jamima was the sort of child you had to have entirely on your side before there was any chance of helping. I could have asked her to be more respectful and that her eye rolls and sarcasm wouldn't be tolerated. Instead, I showed her the empathy that was understandably difficult for others who lived and learned with her day every day. I said, 'I'm sorry you're hurting. You're a great person. You won't always feel this bad. What's going on?'

Jamima replied, 'Everyone hates me. I have no friends.' I waited. She blurted out, 'I do mean stuff, and I don't care.'

As the conversation unfolded, I could tell her heart was aching as I watched her pick away at the already frayed edges of the rug we sat on together.

I asked, 'How do you feel when you're being mean?' 'How do you feel after you've been mean?' 'Are you ever kind?' 'How do you feel when you're kind?' 'How do you feel after you've been kind?'

Jamima's answers showed that while she enjoyed being mean because other people's pain distracted her from her own, she felt terrible afterward. As much as she struggled to be kind to others (because in her life, few people that mattered to her had been nice), she always felt good once she got in the swing of things. I reminded her how kind her heart was and that she had only lost her way a little. I let her know this happens to all of us when we are hurting, and that one of the best ways to hurt less was by being kind—causing no harm and maybe even bringing a little joy. Jamima agreed to a three-day challenge where she would record every caring thing she had done for the day. If she harmed others, she owed it to herself to engage in two kind acts to balance things out.

Jamima did it. Her peers were surprised, having never experienced her kindness, but they welcomed her back in. Whenever Jamima resisted the impulse to hurt because of jealousy or frustration, it became easier for her to reconsider and do something nice—or nothing at all.

While Jamima's problems were far from solved, they were undoubtedly heading in the right direction. The more kind she was to others, the weight gradually lifted from her shoulders. Occasionally she would help others without any prompting, and her tense interactions became few and far between. On most days she could be found happily settled into a friendship group—not gathering information to cause conflict but just for the fun of it.

Brainstorm: Be kind

Ask the following questions:

'What does it mean to be kind?'
'How do you feel when you're kind?'
'How do you feel when you've been mean?'
'How does it feel being kind compared to being mean?'

The idea of this brainstorm is to get young people linking their feelings to their actions. Don't expect admissions of guilt from children who are being mean on purpose; this is a broad activity to develop their emotional self-awareness.

Role plays

- Jason is sitting alone, but you're blissfully happy having one-on-one time with your best friend. How could you be kind to Jason as you walk past?
- You're late for school, and your little brother trips and falls. The contents of his unzipped bag go everywhere. How can you be kind?
- Everyone in your class is picking on a student in your school. You're not feeling brave enough yet to stand up for them. You're naturally shy and worry they'll choose you as the next target if you get involved. How can you be kind?
- Your stepbrother has no friends. You love him, but you also find him tiring to be around and you understand why he struggles to make friends. His heart is genuine, and you have friends coming over—something he rarely gets to do. How can you be kind without making the experience awful for yourself?
- Your best friend's mum is seriously ill. You find talking about it hard as it reminds you of a family member who is also very unwell. You feel guilty you're not able to help them or hear them out. How can you be kind without it affecting your feelings beyond what you can handle at the moment?
- Your friend is socially awkward and often says things that unintentionally offend others. He is starting to realise that other people feel uncomfortable around him. Your friend comes to you asking, 'Am I weird? Why does everyone roll their eyes when I say anything? Why are you my only friend? Is there something wrong with me?' How can you be friendly and helpful at the same time?
- Your mum needs your help to go to the shop for her while she feeds the baby. You're exhausted, and you get nervous about going into the shop alone. You can see your mum is feeling desperate and you want to help, but you are drowning in uncomfortable feelings. How will you be kind?
- Your sister has very few friends. You're less than a year apart, so you share a lot of the same friends. When she has someone over, they always end up wanting to play with you because your social skills are naturally stronger. One of your sister's friends whispers to you at school, 'I only come to your sister's playdates because you're there. Don't you think she's kind of weird?' How will you be kind?

When kind is hard, be wise

Sometimes there are situations and relationships that challenge your ability to be kind. To enable the best chance of a balanced response, try asking yourself, 'what's the wisest thing I can do right now?' Tuning in to your inner wisdom can help move you away from reactivity and emotion. As this is not by any means easy, especially in the heat of emotions, consider a poster in the room, along with encouragement and reminders to support developing this skill further.

Play and games

Secret buddy game

To practice being kind, take the names of your group and pop them in a pot. Each day or week, depending on your judgment, ask students to draw a name from the pot. For the agreed period, students must be kind to the student whose name they draw. They must not let on they are the secret buddy. All they need to do is be kind to that person. At the end of the period, students guess who their secret buddy was. Rotate the names and support the students with class rewards for being extra kind.

Lesson 1.7

Being a great listener

New confident mindset concept: Listening well

Listening is an essential skill for healthy relationships. Feeling heard and understood builds trust between people. What sometimes gets in the way of active listening is thinking about what you'll say next or letting your mental chatter distract you from the here and now.

People often seek to talk and express what's important to them. While what they say won't always resonate with you, showing you're listening is one of the most respectful things you can do in a conversation. Healthy friendships thrive when people listen as much as they speak.

Mind map: Listening

Write 'Listening' on the board to get your students thinking about the why and how of being a good listener. Allow time for self-reflection and discussion afterwards.

Building the steps for great listening

The following steps can be written on the board or made into a poster. You can come up with your own strategies based on the mind map activity and add them to this framework.

Step 1. Make face and eye contact (without staring). Look at the person, not around the room or at other people. Smile or reflect an expression that matches what they are telling you.

Step 2. Listen deeply to the person (not what's racing around in your head). Try to switch off your opinions and thoughts. Be right there with them, right now.

Step 3. When there's a break in the conversation, this is a chance to show empathy and understanding, proof that you've been listening. You can say things like 'I get it,' 'I understand,' 'That's tough,' 'That's awesome' and so on. Reflecting back the meaning of what they've said is also good in short bursts.

Step 4. Don't offer advice unless they ask for it. If you're not sure your opinion is wanted, it's safer to ask 'Would you like my advice?'

Step 5. Show you listened by checking in with them next time you meet. For example, if the person told you about a holiday they were planning, next time ask how it was.

Role plays

Divide your students into pairs to practice listening to a topic they are likely to find boring. Allow students to choose from the items below or come up with their own. Students work hard to listen attentively for two minutes while the other person talks in laborious detail about their subject. Then swap over, so each person has a turn at listening and speaking. Often, you'll find them laughing as they struggle to make conversation on topics that are entirely mind-numbing for them.

Role play listening topics

Painting a wall. Using a CD player. The pattern on your school uniform. Filling your school diary with the week's homework. Emptying a bin. Mowing a lawn. Sweeping the floor. Hanging up a painting. The canned fruit and vegetable aisle in the supermarket. Watching paint dry. Emptying the dishwasher. How to hang up and bring in a load of laundry. The importance of hygiene.

Listening to, 'no' and 'stop'

A great friend and listener tunes into their conversation partner. When people have had enough of a situation or do not want to do something, they are likely to use words like, 'no' and 'stop'. Many young people can get in the habit of trying to coerce their friend to change their mind. Even in minor differences of opinion, learning to respect a 'no' or 'stop' without expecting the other person to come up with an explanation, is crucial in healthy relationships. Open a discussion with your group by asking what they think of the following statement:

> **'No' and 'stop' are complete sentences.**

Allow some time to talk about what this means and how important it is to respect these words and the person who said them, seriously.

Play and games

I went to the market and bought a...

Most people know this old favourite. You can come up with your own variations too. The game is straightforward. Everyone sits in a circle and the first person starts with 'I went to the market and bought a...' (they choose something they bought). The next person offers the same beginning, recalls what the person before them bought and then adds their own. The game continues until everyone has added an item and the list is long!

Lesson 1.8

Finding the good in others

It never hurts to see the good in someone. They often act better because of it.

Anonymous

New confident mindset concept: Looking for goodness and strengths in others.

Young people are often, by nature egocentric. They tend to struggle more than adults to cope when there are differing opinions or qualities in others they don't like. Knowing you can always choose to search for good in others, even when you think and feel differently, not only builds compassion but deepens the connection between people. Most people, feel better about themselves when they know others notice their essential goodness. This is also important for parents and teachers who are often worn down by the sometimes challenging behaviours and emotions of young people. By focusing on their goodness as much as possible, it is easier to maintain a bond, despite the difficulties that arise.

Mind map: Looking for the good in others

In the centre of your board, write 'Looking for the good in others'.

Watch your students explore this gently directed topic and enjoy observing their understanding evolve.

Case study: The goodness in Jai

When Jai started school, his family and teachers were overwhelmed by his high levels of energy and low impulse control. Jai hardly ever did the right thing and had worn out the other students. His home life was challenging, and he lacked a deep connection with others.

On a typical day, Jai would call out in class, roll his eyes, question the teacher, ignore the teacher, disrupt learning and get into a brawl at playtime. The principal's office was very familiar to Jai. Once Jai got into the principal's office, it was like the weight of the world had lifted from his shoulders. The principal was a kindhearted person who knew Jai was missing more social-emotional literacy skills than she could poke a stick at. She'd made it her goal to find the good in Jai. Identifying positives in someone who presented all day with negatives was not easy.

Solution

Together they would sit, and the principal would ask philosophical questions that got Jai thinking about what he believed in and what mattered to him. Once she'd found a handful of positives, she found Jai's opportunities to lead others using the skills he had and connected him with mentors (both students and teachers) who had similar values and interests.

While it took time, it was entirely worth the effort. Jai started to be understood on a deeper level. Students and teachers were finally able to see beyond the impulses and were much more forgiving when he had a momentary loss of self-control. Jai always had to make things better, but he was never shamed and felt proud of himself as he identified himself as a 'good guy'.

Jai is now in grade 6 and thriving. Like all people, he has bad days but is quick to pull himself back into line and do everything he can to make things better.

Role plays

Students can work in pairs to solve the next set of role plays. Ideally, each scenario gets resolved by at least two pairs to enable a variety of creative solutions. To encourage this, only four role plays are presented.

- Rosie loved school. She was blessed with great friends and could see the good in everyone, except in Sameera. For some reason, Sameera made Rosie feel uncomfortable, and it didn't help that Sameera was often dishonest and got Rosie into trouble for things Sameera had done. Show how Rosie could see beyond Sameera's dishonesty and find some good in her.
- Alice didn't like her French teacher. Her French teacher didn't particularly like Alice either. They had a personality clash, and it was affecting how Alice was doing in French class. One day, to both their surprise, they found each other at a wedding. The seating had been planned earlier. Alice and her teacher were seated next to each other. Show how they could communicate so they can find the good in each other.
- Selinia's brother's best friend, Ali, was often mean to her. He spent a lot of time at their house and did everything he could to keep Selinia quiet and out of the way. Selinia was not the kind of person to fight back, but she knew what Ali was doing was mean. She was also very unimpressed by her brother not sticking up for her. Selinia's parents weren't helpful either and told her to be polite to their visitor and toughen up. Show a solution that is fair and involves Selinia, Ali and her brother talking respectfully.

- Jasmine was a kindhearted soul who was often picked on by others. While she never did anything to upset anyone, she didn't fit in. Her parents had met with her teachers to ask what could be done to help Jasmine fit in. With her parents' permission, student leaders met to discuss what they thought Jasmine had in common with others and to identify her strengths and values. Show how this looks and how it might turn out.

Interviews: Finding the best in each other

Divide the group into pairs. Offer five to fifteen minutes to ask each other the following questions designed to find the best in each other:

- What's one thing people could learn from you?
- What problem in the world are you best equipped to solve?
- How do you contribute to the love in your family?
- What's better in the world because of you?

If there's time afterwards, you might like to allow some time for students to journal and reflect on what they learned about themselves and others through the interviews.

Play and games

The good hot and cold game

Ask each of your students to write down one good thing about their class or group. (In one-on-one sessions, children can share one good thing about their life with you.) In group or class work, take everyone outside. When it's each person's turn, the group looks away while the positive note from the first player is hidden. Once the note is out of sight, the group must find it together. The person calls out 'hotter' as everyone gets closer to the hiding spot and 'colder' as the group moves further away. When the note is found, the student reads it out aloud for everyone to enjoy.

You probably won't get through all group members, but you can save the notes and the game for another day when everyone needs a mental circuit breaker and change of pace.

Lesson 1.9

Forgiveness

New confident mindset concept: Forgiving yourself and others for your mistakes

Relationships tend not to run smoothly all the time, especially in young people. Conflict or differences in opinion can often be forgiven when both parties are able to let go of the need to be right. Everyday squabbles experienced by young people should rarely cause the end of a friendship as social clumsiness and mistakes are common throughout childhood. Even with the best of intentions, people say and do the wrong thing. Punishing someone by ignoring or withdrawing from them is not a solution. Usually, these moments of social-emotional clumsiness are an unintended hiccup. Holding on to a grudge is not useful to anyone.

Forgiveness doesn't mean you have to be best friends. In some cases where the friendship is unhealthy, forgiveness can show that you are 'done' with it. You no longer carry that anger around with you like a chip on your shoulder. You accept that some people are not yet able to behave respectfully, and you free yourself from the burden of expecting more by forgiving and moving on.

Staying angry because someone has hurt your feelings or disappointed you makes emotional pain worse on all accounts. Most of the time, people act the way they do because they think it's right. If it's not the right thing for you, then it can help to see them as misinformed. Everyone behaves better when they know better.

Forgiveness is not easy. Making a conscious decision to be forgiving or at least understanding of your own and other people's mistakes is a healthy step towards improving not only your relationships but your well-being.

Mind map: Forgiveness

In the centre of the board, write 'Forgiveness'. Gently guide your students to explore what this means, why it might be hard, when it might be more comfortable and why it's usually helpful.

Make it better statements

Begin a discussion about how other people's words and actions can make things better, making forgiveness easier. Here are some ideas to get you started:

- Say, 'I'm sorry.'
- Ask, 'How can I make it better?'

- Ask, 'How can I make things up to you?'
- Ask, 'What do you need to forgive me?'
- Offer a hug.
- Do their chores for them.
- Make them a card.
- Write them a poem.
- Make a list of 10 reasons why you're sorry.
- Tell them how bad you feel about what happened.

Consider making a poster for students to use as a reference point for repairing harmed relationships.

Case study: Learning to forgive yourself

Albert had an uncanny knack of saying things he later regretted. Albert didn't have a bad bone in his body, but his impulsivity and social-emotional immaturity meant he'd say whatever came to mind. He often said things like 'I can see why you didn't make A grade soccer—you're pretty uncoordinated.' Even when he tried to compliment others, it would come out wrong. The morning I saw Albert, he'd just told a friend, 'You're so good at art, which is a good thing because you're really bad at maths.'

Albert never got far in his friendships. While others had become understanding thanks to the compassionate nature of the school looking beyond the behaviour to his underlying intentions, it was Albert who wouldn't forgive himself.

Managing his frustration towards himself for the things he said and did was becoming more difficult for Albert. He had started banging his fist into his head after he realised what he'd done. This habit was not only becoming painful but also compulsive.

Solution

Firstly, Albert was reminded of the school's value system. The children had been taught that whenever another person acted up, they should ask themselves, 'Is this person being mean on purpose?' I asked Albert, 'What are your intentions? Do you want to hurt other people?' Of course, the answer was a firm 'No way!'

Next, I talked to Albert about focusing on his intention. Did he think he was trying hard every day to be better at thinking before speaking than he was the day before and the day before that? Of course, the answer was a resounding 'Yes!' I reminded him all we can do is focus on improvement. We all have things we could do better. If at the end of each day we know we have tried our best to improve, then we are doing well!

Finally, I asked Albert to treat himself with the same kindness and forgiveness he gives others. I asked him to apologise to himself when he engaged in negative self-talk and to apologise also when he hit himself on the head after an impulsive statement. I also taught Albert to talk to himself kindly after making a mistake by saying something like 'My heart is good; my words are fast; I'm getting better every day.'

Albert wrote a list of ways he could slow down when he saw a person and think before speaking. He decided to count to three in his head before he said anything. He also agreed to try not to judge others. For example, if he thought someone was bad at something, that was a judgment and best not said.

Albert continues to work hard on managing his impulses and getting along with others. While every few days he will take a step backwards and say something he regrets, he knows how to forgive himself and apologise to himself and the person he unintentionally harmed. He gets better every day at staying on track, with the goal of improving his efforts from one day to the next!

Discussion: Forgiveness

Share an appropriate time you said or did something you later regretted. How did you feel? What did you need to feel better? Did someone help? How did it feel to be understood or forgiven? How did it feel to be misunderstood and held angrily in someone else's heart and mind?

Allow some time for students to journal or talk in pairs or small groups to share an experience where forgiveness was necessary. Ask them to try the following positive self-talk: 'I am a kind and forgiving person. I will see the best in myself and others.' To reinforce the point, you can display this or a similar statement where your students can see it.

A forgiveness goal

Suggest for the next week, every time someone does something that annoys, if it's harmless, you forgive them for not knowing any better, even if that person is doing it on purpose. Have a brief discussion at the end of the day or week to ask what it felt like to be forgiving rather than staying annoyed or angry. Students will need to tune into their instincts about what can and can't be forgiven. Some behaviours may need to be followed up on and require help and support from an adult.

Play and games

Forgive no one

Here's a chance to have some fun with carrying anger and judgment without any consequences. It's also a chance to feel what it's like not to receive forgiveness. To play, one person stands up in the front (you show them first as usual) and says something of their choosing (or from the list) and then asks the group to forgive them. Let them have some fun going up to a few students and asking one of the 'make it better' statements from earlier. The answer always needs to be negative, refusing forgiveness.

- 'I broke your phone.'
- 'I left the five dollars that I owe you at home.'
- 'I lost the house key, and we are locked out until night time.'
- 'I yelled at you, and I regret it.'
- 'I let your cat out when I was feeding it, and it ran away.'
- 'I forgot about your birthday.'
- 'I kicked the soccer ball in your face by accident.'
- 'I knocked over your milkshake, and I don't have any money left to buy you another one.'
- 'I lost your wallet when I promised I'd take care of it.'
- 'I said I could help you with your homework tonight, but now I can't.'
- 'I told someone about your own news.'
- 'I said something bad about you behind your back, and I regret it.'

Make sure you and your students add your own ideas to the list to make it relevant for you.

References

Achor, Shawn. 2015. 'The Science of a Smile.' *Success* magazine, November 2.

______. 2018. *The Happiness Advantage: How a Positive Brain Fuels Success in Work and Life*. New York: Currency, 2018.

Brissette, I., M. F. Scheier, and C. S. Carver. 2002. 'The Role of Optimism in Social Network Development: Coping and Psychological Adjustment During a Life Transition.' *Journal of Social Psychology* 82 (1): 102–111.

Iacoboni, M., and J. C. Mazziotta. 2007. 'Mirror Neuron System: Basic Findings and Clinical Applications.' National Institute of Child Health and Human Development, *Journal of Neurological Progress*.

Pangle, Lorraine Smith. 2003. *Aristotle and the Philosophy of Friendship*. Cambridge: Cambridge University Press.

Lesson 2.1

How to focus on similarities, accepting (even embracing) differences

New confident mindset concept: Finding connection with others using an open mindset

When meeting someone new, thoughts and beliefs connected to that person may run through your mind. Often they involve a grouping system of categories like right vs. wrong, different vs. same, good vs. bad.

When someone lands in an opposing category to what you identify with, that division is enough to knock over compassion, empathy and openness to a new friendship in its tracks. Many people have missed opportunities to build friendships with people they might otherwise have bonded well with, merely because of their reflexive observations and judgments.

We can all find connection with others. Openness to connection doesn't mean you blindly build friendships with anyone; it means you look beyond people's exterior and search for something special in everyone. You learn to recognise that humankind connects through a shared desire to be appreciated and loved, respected and connected. A compassionate mindset assumes that everyone is doing their best based on the environment, knowledge and skills they have at the time. A compassionate person finds it more comfortable to like other people, without holding excessive or unrealistic expectations about them. This makes it easier for them to like themselves too.

When you're not using a compassionate mindset and you're stuck in your comfort zone, it's easy to become attached to what you believe in—after all, you came up with it, so it feels right. Egocentric thinking can fool you into thinking the other person has to be wrong in order for you to be right. A closed mindset won't allow a respectful and empathic halfway point, where you both have equally valid views and ways of doing things.

An open mindset, on the other hand, focuses on finding similarities and embracing or at least accepting differences. It understands you can strongly believe in one thing while another believes in the opposite. It affirms that you can both still have valid points of view and indeed you're both entitled to that.

Case study: Learning to appreciate and value others

Anoka was proud of who she was becoming. It was her first year in high school and she felt she was figuring out what mattered to her. Life was good. She had a great group of friends with similar values and interests, she liked her teachers, and her home life was the most peaceful it had been in years. Studying politics and gender was her passion, and she knew right from the moment she began studying these, she wanted to make a difference in the world, and that meant everything to her.

All was well until Anoka started to see herself as different from the girls and boys outside her friendship circle. She often looked down on them through her perceived belief she knew better than them. Anoka felt they were all caught up in useless pursuits—failing to see life for what it was. She often commented to her friends how 'those girls' and 'those boys' are 'shallow' and 'clueless'.

For the first few months, her friends listened and to some degree agreed. Anoka had always felt like a bit of a leader to them. When she spoke, she spoke with conviction.

As Anoka grew in confidence, she took it upon herself to spread the word about everything she believed to be true. The way she did this was by paying people out for their beliefs or lack of ideas. Anoka showed no compassion or understanding towards anyone who saw the world differently from her, yet she felt sure she was helping them by proving them all wrong and teaching them a 'better' way. She spoke out often and wondered why no one was listening.

One day Anoka was called to the principal's office. She came in shaking and couldn't imagine why the meeting was called. The principal, a kind man with a playful moustache, smiled with a warmth that said, 'It's okay.' He got straight to the point and let Anoka know there had been complaints made against her from parents and students.

Anoka burst into tears. What could she possibly have done to deserve complaints?

Her principal explained parents were concerned their sons and daughters were feeling bullied and many had come home feeling upset. Even girls in her friendship group had heard enough negativity and wanted the old Anoka back who let everyone be themselves and get on with things their way. They were already finding it hard enough to figure out who they were and what they cared about without Anoka passing judgment on them all.

Anoka and the principal chatted for a while, and Anoka agreed she could do with some help.

Solution

The first point of call was to show Anoka empathy for what she was going through. She was only 13 years old and it's only natural she'd make mistakes. She needed to know it was okay she'd lost her way a little and that everything would work out just fine.

I asked Anoka if she'd thought about seeing things from other people's perspective. Sure, her beliefs were valuable and noteworthy—but what did other students believe in? What made her beliefs correct and theirs incorrect? How would she feel if they said her thoughts were clueless? Would she like that? Was it essential for her friendships to survive that everyone believed in the same things?

Together, we came up with compassionate ways of maintaining her beliefs but respecting other people's points of view. I reminded her of the Golden Rule: treat others how you would like to be treated.

We talked about how Anoka could make a difference, focusing on what she cared about while letting other people make a difference in ways that were meaningful to them.

I asked Anoka to write a list of what she had in common with the people she had distanced herself from based on their beliefs. It was clear she had more in common with them than not.

Finally, we created a plan to repair the damage she'd unintentionally created. Anoka one by one made eye contact with everyone she had hurt and gently whispered, 'I'm sorry I made you feel small.' To her closest group of friends who had hung in there so long listening to her insults, she thanked them for putting up with her and asked, 'How can I make this better?'

Once Anoka left the need to be right and to push differences out, life got better again for her. She felt lighter and happier. Anoka hadn't realised how painful it was to carry around the belief she was better and knew better than others.

I can't wait to see what the future has in store for this brilliant young person.

Brainstorm: Finding similarities and embracing differences

Ask the following questions:

Can two people believe opposite things and both be right? Give an example.

Do your beliefs have to be 'right' for you to believe in them? Explain.

What might happen if you mainly focus on differences between you and others?

Have you ever made an unlikely friend? (Someone you seem very different from on the outside but on the inside you have a lot in common.)

Conversations like these open your students' hearts and minds to human connection, focusing on similarities rather than differences. The more connected, understanding and compassionate everyone is despite differing values, the more harmonious interactions become.

Mind map

Write, 'My way vs. your way.' Allow your students time to process what this means. Remember there are no right or wrong answers.

Lesson 2.1

Role plays

- Al's public speaking and creative thinking skills were exceptional. He was excited when he was invited to join the debating club and couldn't wait to get involved. Al had strong ideas about what was right and wrong, and to everyone else's frustration, he took any ideas different from his own as a personal attack. Debates quickly turned into arguments, where Al took offence and started to put other people down. Show a way that might help Al take a more balanced approach when he doesn't agree with someone else's point of view.
- Jamal wanted to text his friends now that he was in high school. He thought texting was important for staying in touch. His parents believed texting wasn't important and refused to let him do it. Jamal saw his mum and dad as mean and old-fashioned. Show a way they can all understand each other.
- Billie loved watching cricket with his family; it was his favourite sport. His older brother found watching cricket long and boring; he preferred tennis. When cricket and tennis were both on TV at the same time, Billie would shout at everyone saying cricket was much better than tennis. He demanded they only watch the cricket. Find a way to help Billie compromise.
- Amy was vegetarian and was upset with her parents for not following her request that they, too, stop purchasing and cooking meat. She felt that eating meat was wrong and took time to express this daily. Show a conversation between Amy and a parent as they find a way to meet somewhere in the middle.
- Anushka and Jemima made friends on the very first day of preschool. Now in high school, they noticed they no longer believed in the same things. Jemima was okay with it and loved her friend for who she was. When Anushka scoffed at people who liked things she didn't like, Jemima didn't take too much notice and focused on what she knew made Anushka awesome. Anushka, on the other hand, had zero tolerance for Jemima (or anyone else) when she said or did things that conflicted with her own point of view. Show how this looks and sounds. Help Anushka find similarities and accept differences in others.
- Serena loved studying feminism with her mum and dad and was proud she had a strong understanding of gender equality from a young age. As the years went by and Serena reached middle school, this translated into her disliking boys and seeing them as the enemy. Show how this starts to look in her friendships at school and her relationship with the males in her family. Offer a way for Serena to uphold her values and beliefs without driving a wedge between the genders.

- Sol was asked to sit with Ella, the new girl in his class. Sol took an instant dislike to her. Sol was quiet, Ella was loud. Sol liked to think things through, Ella acted on impulse. Sol was respectful towards his teachers, Ella pushed the boundaries. Support Sol in finding similarities and an understanding for Ella so he can help her adjust to her new school.

Journaling

Allow five minutes for students to journal about a person they struggle to see eye to eye with. Their goal is to find three things they have in common with them and find an empathic interpretation of the person's behaviour they struggle with most.

Play and games

I believe eye to eye

Divide students into pairs. The idea is for one person to call out five to ten statements they believe in. There are ideas below for you to role model first, so your students see how the game works. The person they state their belief with, whether they agree or not, has to look them right in the eye and say, 'That's just not true because…' The opposer can come up with any reason they like (the more absurd, the more fun they will have) to prove the person wrong. Make sure that each person has a turn to both share beliefs and oppose beliefs. It's crucial that eye contact is maintained throughout the game. Here are some beliefs to get you get you started:

I believe where I live is the best country in the world.
I believe everyone should play sport.
I believe that summer is better than winter.
I believe that playing is a waste of time.
I believe healthy eating is overrated.
I believe everyone needs to believe in something.
I believe I'm better than everyone else.
I believe bullies should go to a school just for bullies.
I believe learning to swim is essential if you own a swimming pool.
I believe schools should have longer play breaks.
I believe bullies should be banned from the playground.

Lesson 2.2

The trouble with, 'me, me, me': Learning to see beyond your own lens

New confident mindset concept: It's not all about you

Thinking compassionately doesn't mean ignoring challenges or dismissing them. It's about seeing beyond them. Problems are part of the ebb and flow of life. Everyone struggles sometimes, not just you. When you are able to think compassionately, you can see other people have their own challenges and you are not alone. You don't focus all your attention on self-pity and seeing yourself as a victim.

While it's easy to get caught up in what's going wrong in your own life (after all, you have to live through it), to maintain a healthy outlook, you need to keep things in perspective. The earlier you can teach your students they're not the only ones experiencing a problem at any given time, the closer they will get to broadening their understanding of the human experience. Few people's lives go precisely to plan. Most days involve several unexpected bumps and turns.

When you allow too much time to focus on what's going wrong for you, self-pity will usually follow. Thoughts like 'Why me?' 'Everything always goes wrong in my life!' and 'Nothing ever goes to plan!' switch compassion and optimism off, shifting our attention towards egocentricity and a sense of hopelessness.

By encouraging students to see their own challenges and hardships as part of the overall human experience, you are bringing the world right into the room with you, developing a sense of global compassion and connection. Self-pity, which serves no constructive purpose, can't survive these conditions. When you focus beyond your own experience and extend your care and compassion to others, you are better placed to thrive. In the words of Dr. Jamil Zaki, professor of psychology at Stanford University, 'Humans are the champions of kindness.' Zaki's MRI data shows that being kind to others registers in the brain as a pleasurable experience. Humankind finds it more valuable to do what's in the interest of the group than to do what's most profitable to the individual. Zaki (2017)

Case study: From victim to capable

Liana was often sullen, angry and jealous. It was hard to know how long she had been like this, but it seemed to be a mix of natural temperament and a lack of people challenging her to see the world differently. Liana held a strong victim mentality. She was so caught up in her own experiences that she spent most of her time complaining, sighing and focusing on all the negative things life had 'dealt her'. She was continually blaming others for her difficulties.

The first thing she said was, 'You'll have to book me in every day for a year to hear everything I've been through.'

It wasn't that Liana hadn't been through her share of difficulties; she had. Liana's parents had recently separated after years of conflict, her best and only friend was moving schools and her grandmother was gravely ill. She experienced all of this as an only child, so she didn't have anyone close to her own age at home to share the journey with her.

Liana's challenge was that she genuinely felt like she was the only person on earth experiencing these difficulties. Her restricted global view was unhelpful. Liana's hardship dominated her thinking, day and night. She was utterly convinced that everyone else was having a much happier and more relaxed time with life.

Solution

Before problem solving and developing a more balanced mindset, it was essential to hear Liana out. She needed to describe her own thoughts and feelings without fear of judgment. I gave Liana plenty of empathy and understanding—after all, this was a young girl in distress, unhappy with her life and losing friendships by the day.

Once we'd connected through her hardships and my understanding and appreciation of what she was experiencing had grown, it was time to help her gain some perspective.

I asked Liana, 'I wonder how many other children in the world have watched their parents go through divorce?' Liana looked at me as if I'd brought up something that had never occurred to her. It's funny how sometimes a problem feels like its only yours because the pain is so great. I joked that I bet Google had the answer, which it did.

Liana's Google search found that around the world 50 to 71 percent of marriages end in divorce. It took Liana several moments to gather her thoughts after the surprising results. I asked, 'I wonder if every child feels it differently—if the country matters … if how old you are when it happens matters … if being an only child makes it better or worse?' I asked the questions casually and said we'd probably never know the answers for sure, but it's a curious thing worth considering.

Over the weeks, we did this with everything that upset her. First, she'd debrief and the weight would lift from her shoulders. The thoughts and feelings were no longer just hers. I was carrying them with her.

Next, we'd ponder how many other children her age were going through what she was. Each time, she found it less surprising and more heartening. I would remind her, 'You're not alone, Liana.'

Finally, I asked Liana, 'How do you think you could turn your pain into someone else's joy by sharing your strengths and personality?' I was encouraging her to extend herself outside of her own experiences.

While it took some time, everyone around her noticed that the look on her face had softened. She became less reactive. She smiled more, helped more and listened more. Her mindset was healthier and no longer only about her. Liana finally began enjoying life.

When I asked her if we still needed 365 appointments to get through everything, she laughed out loud.

Mind map and brainstorm

In the centre of the board, write 'Problems'. Allow plenty of time to see what direction this takes your students.

Following the mind mapping exercise, it's time to brainstorm. Ask the following questions:

- Do you think that somewhere in the world, there is another person who has experienced similar challenges to you? How would you know?
- What makes a comfortable life?
- Do people with plenty of money have it easier than people with less money? Explain.
- Is anyone the only person to go through specific problems? Explain.
- Why do you think some people never tell anyone else how they're struggling?

Group discussion: What does it mean to be a 'victim'?

Ask your students what they think the word 'victim' means.

The Cambridge Dictionary identifies a victim as 'someone who has been hurt, damaged, or killed or has suffered, either because of the actions of someone or something else, or because of illness or chance'.

Students should be able to offer interpretations of the Cambridge quote around the age of 10. Remind them, there are no right or wrong answers.

Note: It's crucial this activity doesn't demean the struggles of people who've experienced hardship. Painful experiences naturally cause hurt and discomfort and need acknowledgment and understanding. This activity is about empowering children to see that they don't have to be defined by their hardship and that hardship is a shared human experience.

Journaling

Have students draw a line vertically through the centre of the page. One side can be titled, 'My toughest times'. The other side can be titled 'Other people's toughest times'. If appropriate, demonstrate your experiences on the board first.

The idea is to record the many tough times you have faced. Beside each example of a challenging experience, consider whether or not someone else has been through something similar. Sometimes it feels like you're the only person on earth going through something, but usually others are facing it too. If your tough time is likely being experienced by others, place a tick in the 'other people's toughest times' column.

You can finish by encouraging students to close their eyes and send collective good wishes to everyone around the world going through similar struggles.

Role plays

- Si was often alone on the playground. Sometimes he liked it that way, while at other times he struggled with it. He was new to the country and the school, and felt uncomfortable about how different the culture and environment was. He missed home and felt angry that his parents had made him move. Show how the school counsellor might help Si feel more hopeful about his situation by opening his eyes to what's going on around him.
- Aliah was always positive and friendly to others. She was well known for being kind and compassionate towards others and would be the first to put up her hand to help someone in need. Aliah was supporting a struggling student with her homework in her own time. While it was tough making the time for it, the student was doing much better because of her help. One afternoon, Aliah overheard the student saying, 'Aliah thinks she's so much better than everyone just because she understands the school work. I think she's the most annoying person I've ever met.' Show how Aliah finds a way to use compassion and thinking outside of her hurt to deal with this constructively and peacefully.
- Andrew was struggling to fit in. He was on a scholarship at a school where everyone there generally had a lot of money. Afraid to make new friends, he didn't want anyone to come to his house and see how little money they had. Andrew's teacher had noticed he was keeping to himself and asked him why. Show how his teacher might help Andrew see things differently so he can open himself up to making new friends and invite them over without feeling embarrassed.
- Melissa's parents had just separated. She found it hard to be around friends whose parents were still together. Show Melissa explaining to her friends how her jealousy is affecting her behaviour. Consider how her friends might empathise with Melissa while suggesting that this is just one part of her life, not all of it.
- It was two weeks before the school ski trip when Lucy slipped on a wet floor and broke her leg. Lucy was devastated she couldn't go anymore and dumped those feelings on everyone around her. Most of all, she got fixated on blaming her dad for mopping the floor and not warning her. She fell into a deep sense of unhappiness and jealousy, especially during the week everyone

went off on the trip. Show how Lucy can get out of her own head and focus her energy on something constructive. How can she increase compassion for others and acknowledge that while what's happened is tough, blaming others and feeling jealous is only hurting her and the people she loves?

- Biella was tired of working after school in her family restaurant. She felt she had no life and just wanted to go home and play like her friends. Show a conversation between her and her parents where both sides develop compassion and understanding for each other.
- Jonnie's parents didn't let him have friends over. They were shy people and didn't like the noise. Jonnie had learned to be quiet at home, and because he didn't have any brothers or sisters, this usually wasn't a big challenge. The problem was that Jonnie liked people—and noise—and he was sad he didn't have friends visit on the weekends. Now he'd started high school, he wanted friends over more than ever. Show how Jonnie and his parents might come to an understanding by showing each other compassion and working towards a compromise.
- Lovita didn't want to share a room with her sister anymore. There was no other option and they would be sharing a room until her older sister moved out of home. Show how Lovita can remain kind to her younger sister (who loves sharing a room with Lovita) and reach a compromise that is compassionate while also finding a way to think about sharing that helps her remain positive.

Play and games

Top this! My life is worse than yours

This game is played in pairs. Taking turns, both players try to top each other's problem. The idea is to get silly, have a laugh and see how far you can go to be the more prominent victim. Here is an example to try out.

My life is worse than your life, top this...

I share a room with a cockatoo and a little brother...

I can top that! My life is way worse, I share a room with a galah, a little brother and his mouse that never sleeps...

My life is way worse, my parents never bought a cage for the cockatoo and it flies all around my bedroom all night long...

I can top that, my brother's mouse that doesn't sleep escapes because my brother never closes the cage door and I have nightmares because of that...

While the idea is to be absurd and have some fun, this is an excellent opportunity for the group to connect and explore the common thread of hardship.

Lesson 2.3

Building self-compassion

Anyone who has boarded a plane has heard the attendant remind passengers to put on their own oxygen mask *before* helping others in an emergency. This analogy is often used to remind us to care for ourselves so we are better placed to care for others. Self-compassion in reality is easier said than done.

Most people aren't in the habit of investing in themselves first—especially when caught up in the demands of school, work and family life. Younger children tend to be better at this than older ones who may have drifted away from being able to live in the moment. The sweet spot between compassion for self and compassion for others can take time to find.

The difference between self-compassion and self-esteem

Self-compassion (relating to yourself with kindness, care and understanding—even when you've made a mistake or 'failed' at something) is a confident mindset practice that differs from self-esteem. It's a stable state of mind that, when maintained, won't fluctuate based on your success and achievement.

Self-esteem lends itself to evaluating yourself positively and is often linked to a sense of achievement and comparisons with peers. It can fluctuate, depending on what's happening in your life. When you're feeling successful, your self-esteem rises, when you're feeling less successful, your self-esteem can drop.

By role modelling and teaching a self-compassion mindset, you're helping young people understand that being kind to yourself without conditions is not selfish but reasonable and healthy. People who care for themselves will be infinitely better at managing their feelings, contributing to their various roles and, where appropriate, caring for others.

Self-compassion is about treating yourself like you would treat a good friend. Encouraging, expecting the best and taking care of them when times are tough. A self-compassionate person understands that mistakes are part of the human experience rather than a personal failing. Being self-compassionate gives you the best chance of a healthy relationship with yourself and others.

It's not uncommon for people to find self-compassion challenging. Some may even feel afraid to try it. Researchers found an interesting link between compassion and self-compassion. After nine weeks of compassion training, people came out of the study less fearful and more prepared to practice the art of self-compassion. The data from this study also demonstrated that compassion could be cultivated through training. Jazaieri et al. (2012)

The practices in this lesson are especially important for facilitators, as young people may be more self-centred due to their age and developmental stage and therefore more self-compassionate than adults.

Case study: Duncan teaches his teacher

Duncan, who had always struggled to behave well, loved his teacher. He knew he was hard work by the exhausted look on her face that she tried so carefully to hide. Duncan's teacher, Jasmin, showed him compassion because she knew Duncan always tried his best. When Duncan made a mistake or acted up, she was the first to forgive and the last to punish. She would show him the understanding he'd always yearned for, looking beyond his outward actions to see what was going on behind the scenes.

While Jasmin was well versed in showing Duncan and her other students compassion, when it came to herself, she was often exhausted and would often fall ill from an exhausted immune system.

One day, Duncan took her by surprise and came into her classroom after sports practice. It was almost six o'clock, and as usual, Jasmin was preparing for the next day. While Duncan knew this was how most teachers and educators rolled, he felt she was doing way more than most—and at the sacrifice of her health and well-being. Duncan boldly told Jasmin, 'I think you need a holiday to learn how to be as nice to yourself as you are to me. I think you're kind of mean to yourself. You tell us we don't need to be perfect and that we need to look after our well-being, but—well, I don't see you doing what you tell us to do.'

Jasmin was proud of Duncan. She'd known him since preschool and had taught him on and off over the years. He was now in his final year of primary school and she was often amazed at the deep thinker he'd become.

Duncan didn't mean to rush her, but he knew his dad was waiting outside, so he asked, 'When are you going to be as nice to yourself as you are to me?' Jasmine, her voice choking up, knew the boy was right. 'Now, Duncan. Right now.' She could hardly speak and mouthed the words, 'Thank you.'

Solution

I'd been mentoring Jasmin over the last few months and when she shared the story, I asked her to write down a list of things she loved doing that weren't outcome focused. In other words, while she loved teaching and helping her students, there was an outcome attached to everything she did. Jasmine rarely did anything just for the fun of it.

She agreed to choose one activity from her list each day.

It wasn't easy making time to enjoy herself, but once she got the hang of it, she was a convert. Jasmine loved this so much she taught her whole class to do the same and explained the value of doing one fun or relaxing thing every day without the pressure of a predetermined outcome. Students were encouraged to teach this trick to their parents to continue to the ripple effect of self-compassion. Fun for the sake of fun became a common goal within the school community.

Mind map: Self-compassion

In the centre of the board write, 'Caring for myself'. (If your students understand the words 'Self-compassion' then write that instead.) Allow some time for them to explore what it means and how they are going to make it happen for themselves.

Role plays

- Rose was exhausted. As year level student leader she had a lot more on her plate than other students—mainly because she took her role so seriously. Rose also had dyslexia, which meant she had to work harder than most to understand and hand in her work on time. Her grandmother had moved into the family home and was seriously ill. Often it was Rose's job to care for her. Rose was not sleeping well, worrying night after night about how on earth she would keep up with the workload and maintain her role as student leader while caring for her sick grandmother. Most nights she fell asleep crying. Rose finally brings this up with her best friend, who helps her find space for self-compassion.
- Liesl loved walking. She rarely took a walk for no reason because she was always doing things that had a purpose or to meet other people's needs. Show a discussion between Rose and her dad where they talk about how to include walking just for her own enjoyment, without feeling guilty.
- Jamie could always make the students in his class laugh. The way he did this was by putting himself down. Jamie made jokes about the colour of his skin, his family's cultural background, his grandparents and how he struggled with learning. Show a conversation where a student in the class approaches him and challenges him to find a new form of humour that doesn't involve him being mean to himself.
- Adam felt guilty every time he put his feet up to watch a movie. His family worked on a farm and they never stopped. He helped during the week every night after school but on the weekends, he was exhausted—especially now he was also doing the town's newspaper route. What made things worse was when Adam brought this up with his family, they believed he shouldn't be putting his feet up—hard work was important in their community. Show a compassionate conversation between Adam and his parents where they both try to express their thoughts and feelings to reach a compromise, allowing self-compassion for both parties.

- Sofie, the eldest of six children, loved her baby sister, who was ten years younger than her. When she got home from school, she loved those cuddles and all the gorgeous gurgling sounds she made. However, Sofie was starting to resent her little sister. Sofie's parents expected a lot from her and more often than not, Sofie was left to care for her sister while her parents did other things. One day at a friend's party, Sofie's parents asked if she could take her little sister into the swimming pool. Sofie didn't feel comfortable with this much responsibility—she was looking forward to relaxing in the pool with her friends. Show how Sofie might share her worries with her parents and express how much she needs to be self-compassionate right now.
- Jack was struggling to keep up with his school work. If he took a break, he risked falling behind. If he sped up, he would get little sleep and feel extremely stressed. Show how Jack could communicate this with his teacher and how they might find a healthy work-life balance.
- Ness was kind to everyone but herself. She worked in a soup kitchen on the weekend and helped a lot around the house. When Ness broke her leg, she believed she was a burden on her family. Ness felt guilty about how much help she needed. Show a way Ness can be self-compassionate and feel good about it.

New confident mindset concept: Compassionate self-talk

When you're stressed and overwhelmed, your self-talk is often constant, negative and self-defeating, always expecting the worst is about to happen. An overwhelmed mind tends to skip back to the past, race through the present and leap into the future. Those thoughts are rarely self-compassionate, helpful or positive. 'I haven't got time for X,' and 'I can't believe that happened,' and 'I'm sick of Y being so difficult!' are the kinds of thoughts you might hear. Some thoughts go by so quickly, you can hardly catch their meaning. This kind of destructive self-talk gets absorbed both consciously and unconsciously, often leading to painful feelings and belief systems that are out of balance.

To build self-compassion, self-talk that's hopeless or helpless must be reset. Self-talk that's kind and encouraging—like what you would say to a friend going through a tough time—is precisely the kind of self-talk that builds self-compassion.

You might suggest to students who are unkind to themselves, 'Be nice to yourself!' or 'Don't be mean to yourself!' Remind them they deserve kindness and care and don't have to wait to get it from someone else. They can give positive feedback to themselves every single day.

Self-talk awareness activity

Now that you've explained compassionate self-talk, gather your students somewhere quiet for a moment so they can notice what's going on in their minds. Set a timer for five minutes.

When the silent time is over, ask your students if they'd like to share what went on in their minds. Were they surprised by the number and nature of their thoughts?

Journaling: Compassionate self-talk

Take journals out to write down all the kind, understanding and caring things they tend to say to others. Now ask them to write what they tell themselves when they have made a mistake or are feeling down.

Finally, ask students to draw a picture of themselves (older students may prefer to write their name on the paper and write words only) and surround their picture with at least ten encouraging, self-compassionate self-talk statements they can tell themselves. If they are struggling to come up with some, remind them they could get inspiration from the list of kind things they say to others.

Most people will not remember to talk to themselves nicely, no matter how much sense this might make to them. You will need to remind them (and yourself) to do this.

Goal setting: Compassionate self-talk

To help get things more automatic and concrete, your students will need practice. Goal setting is a great way to keep everyone focused. You can set a goal for your class or entire school, that for every negative comment they make to themselves, they need to come up with one positive self-talk statement. The more focused attention on this new skill, the easier it will be developed. You can write a prompt on the board, remind them verbally and ask them how they think they went each day with being compassionate in how they spoke to themselves.

Role plays

For each of the scenarios below, ask students to practice compassionate self-talk:

- You were given something precious to take care of, but you lose it and now you're mad at yourself.
- You failed your driving test. You didn't study that hard, but things have been really busy.
- You found yourself gossiping about someone you don't like at school. It's not usually how you do things, but you caught yourself off guard and now feel bad.

- You drop a beautiful birthday cake everyone is waiting for at the dining table.
- You cook a meal that tastes nothing short of awful.
- Your puppy is difficult. You shout at him and he starts to whimper. You're cross with yourself for losing your cool.

Adults modelling compassion and self-compassion

To improve your students' chances of being more compassionate to themselves and others, you need to take the lead as much as possible. Begin by using compassionate language with young people who are hard on themselves.

Compassionate statements to offer young people

'Be kind to yourself.'

'Be fair to yourself.'

'You're more than your feelings.'

'Forgive yourself—you're not the first person to make this mistake.'

'You look like you could do with some TLC.'

'You deserve some time to take care of yourself.'

Compassionate self-talk statements to display

I will be kind to myself.

I will be fair to myself.

I am more than my feelings.

I forgive myself. I'm not the first person to make this mistake.

I could do with some TLC

I deserve time to take care of myself.

Make sure you treat yourself with the same kindness and compassion you treat others. Children are often watching and tuning in to how we respond to challenges. If you blame yourself or find faults in yourself, you're not only hurting yourself, you're role modelling that you're not okay with your mistakes and challenges.

Lesson 2.4

Seeing the best in yourself and others

New confident minds concept: Seeing the best in yourself and others

Giving and receiving compassion reduces opportunities for loneliness, conflict and social disconnect. Studies have consistently shown how the brain reacts most positively when you're kind and compassionate. One study asked people to play an economics game using two opposing mindsets, a 'savings' mindset and a 'donating' mindset. The rules according to the two mindsets were explained by telling one group their losses during the game were donations, while informing the other group their gains were savings. The donations group reacted calmly and generously when they lost, while the group given the savings mindset reacted more aggressively, playing the game more selfishly. The explanation for the mindset was the only difference; the rules themselves were exactly the same. People played nicer when they felt their loss was another person's gain. Cooper et al. (2010)

Compassion is about putting yourself in another person's shoes, seeing life from their perspective and doing right by them through empathy, kindness and care. Compassion is also a shift to finding the best in others. When there are personal differences, an individual with a compassionate mindset is less likely to express negative judgments or anger. Instead, they seek to find the best in the other person. If a compassionate person finds it hard to connect with or understand others, they will at the very least remain neutral, accepting that the other person has their reasons for behaving the way they do.

Mind map: Compassion

In the centre of the board, write 'Compassion'. If your students are still developing their understanding about what compassion means, you might like to write 'Being kind and caring'. Allow plenty of time for discussion.

Case study: Turning compassion fatigue around

Elijah's daily interruptions had driven his classmates to compassion fatigue. Despite the robust nature of the school's value system, which endeavoured to give every student a sense of hope and belonging, Elijah's behaviour was relentless. Day in and day out, he called out words, sounds, song titles and occasional swear words. Elijah's challenges stemmed primarily from his neurological differences, and his family and teachers understood that new skills were going to take time for him to develop. Previous behavioural intervention had helped to some degree, but progress was slow.

As the school year went on, students were beginning to talk about Elijah behind his back and even make fun of him. As the school had a zero-tolerance bullying policy, the staff wanted my support to nip the negative talk in the bud.

Elijah was a kind-hearted boy who loved people. He was developmentally delayed and painfully embarrassed about his identity as the class clown. He had been like this for as long as he could remember.

Solution

Elijah began structured lessons on relaxation and social-emotional learning. Elijah also debriefed about feeling different from everyone.

As well as seeing Elijah, I got together with Elijah's class while he saw the school education officer for literacy. The class loved the chance to respectfully debrief about the challenges they had offering a compassionate response when Elijah experienced difficulties managing his behaviour.

Showing compassion towards someone you're frustrated with is hard enough for adults, let alone young people in early high school dealing with their own challenges. The class needed support just as much as Elijah. We talked about how everyone makes mistakes and poor judgments, and how easy it is to do that when you're struggling. While there would be no tolerance of bullying, attention was turned towards teaching the class better ways of responding to Elijah's challenging behaviours.

One of the first things we did was talk openly about their experiences of Elijah's disruptive behaviour. We talked about how negative thoughts about people often ended in unresolved feelings like guilt and regret. Holding those feelings inside made things worse. The class embraced the opportunity for debriefing and problem solving.

Next, I asked the class to step into Elijah's shoes to see things from Elijah's perspective. How might Elijah feel after an impulsive round of comments? Is it possible he lies awake at night thinking about it? Does Elijah want to be liked? Does he need to belong?

Everyone closed their eyes and imagined they were Elijah. As I narrated, I described his daily experiences prompting the group to think about the associated feelings.

At the end of the exercise, we problem solved ways to maintain compassion towards him. Finally, we came up with a 'hopeful and compassionate' leadership role. Sustaining sympathy had proven to be difficult, and the students liked the idea of taking turns to lead for the week and be most responsive to Elijah.

When Elijah triggered frustration and impatience, they came up with a range of strategies to help them be compassionate. These included seeing themselves in him, shifting focus onto his strengths, taking a break and asking for help from a 'compassion leader', complimenting Elijah, and telling him, 'It's all good, mate—we know you don't mean to say that stuff.'

The compassionate community built around Elijah was exemplary. The incredible, silent work going on around him by teachers, students and health professionals meant his negative self-view and frustrated energy never became intentionally hurtful. Elijah knew he belonged and that everyone around him believed in him for who he was. While Elijah has a long way to go, each school term we celebrate the ongoing improvements in his behaviour and learning.

Role plays

- Jesse finds a stray kitten meowing outside his house. Jesse loves animals and takes it inside to give it somewhere warm to sleep for the night. His parents get furious at him and tell him it's not allowed inside. How might Jesse stay compassionate but follow his parents' rules?
- No one has taken a liking to the new girl in the class. She has come from another school and is like no one you've met before. You know it's wrong that she is alone every lunchtime, but you are unsure if you have anything in common with her—at all. How could you activate compassion when no one around you wants to help out?
- Your teacher has been grumpy lately. She's not unkind or unfair, but the lessons are uninspiring, and a month into her moody phase, the class is starting to talk behind her back. You know she's a great teacher and you are upset everyone is saying awful things about her. How will you steer your class towards compassion and kindness without them thinking you're clueless?
- Your parents buy you anything you like. It's school sports day, and you have every colour-matching accessory possible. You're entirely dressed up for the day and love every last piece of your outfit. You walk in the sports day parade with pride. As you walk past a group of students, you see one of them dressed in her team colours with no accessories and a look in her eyes that says, 'I feel left out.' How will you show compassion without talking down to her or making her feel small?
- Your favourite TV show is on. You have been waiting all day to watch it. Just as you settle in with a hot cup of cocoa, your little brother comes in crying. Your parents separated a few months ago and he's missing Dad and doesn't want Mum to know. How will you be compassionate without missing your show?
- You're not a big spender and don't care about material things, so your savings are healthy. Your older brother is an impulse buyer with

no savings, and he begs you for a loan of $50 to buy a secondhand skateboard in top condition. He wants it right now, but you know he will lose interest in it after a few days. How could you respond with kindness and compassion?

- You've received two party invitations for the same day. You already said yes to the first invitation, but you don't get along well with the person having the party. Your good friend then invites you to his party, but it's on at the same time as the first one. How will you handle this respectfully and with compassion?
- There's a boy in your class you've known since you were four. Your personalities are direct opposites. You often feel annoyed in his presence. He asks if he can come to your house on the weekend as he's never had a playdate at someone's home from school. How will you respond compassionately?

The loving-kindness meditation

Ten minutes of a daily loving-kindness meditation showed an increase in people's ability to turn outward and show care and compassion for others, as well as a reduction in selfishness. Seppala et al. (2014)

The following loving-kindness meditation is the one used in the study. You can reduce how much of it you do if your time is limited.

> Close your eyes. Sit comfortably with your feet flat on the floor and your spine straight. Relax your whole body. Keep your eyes closed throughout the whole visualization and bring your awareness inward. Without straining or concentrating, just relax and gently follow the instructions.
>
> Take a deep breath in. And breathe out.

Receiving loving-kindness

Keeping your eyes closed, think of a person close to you who loves you very much. It could be someone from the past or the present, someone still in life or who has passed; it could be a spiritual teacher or guide. Imagine that person standing on your right side, sending you their love. That person is sending you wishes for your safety, for your well-being and happiness. Feel the warm wishes and love coming from that person towards you.

Now bring to mind the same person or another person who cherishes you deeply. Imagine that person standing on your left side, sending you wishes for your wellness, for your health and happiness. Feel the kindness and warmth coming to you from that person.

Now imagine that you are surrounded on all sides by all the people who love you and have loved you. Picture all of your friends and loved ones surrounding you. They are standing nearby, sending you wishes for your happiness, well-being and health. Bask in the warm wishes and love coming from all sides. You are filled and overflowing with warmth and love.

Sending loving-kindness to loved ones

Now bring your awareness back to the person standing on your right side. Begin to send the love that you feel back to that person. You and this person are similar. Just like you, this person wishes to be happy. Send all your love and warm wishes to that person.

Repeat the following phrases, silently:

May you live with ease, may you be happy, may you be free from pain.

May you live with ease, may you be happy, may you be free from pain.

May you live with ease, may you be happy, may you be free from pain.

Now focus your awareness on the person standing on your left side. Begin to direct the love within you to that person. Send all your love and warmth to that person. That person and you are alike. Just like you, that person wishes to have a good life.

Repeat the following phrases, silently:

Just as I wish to, may you be safe, may you be healthy, may you live with ease and happiness.

Just as I wish to, may you be safe, may you be healthy, may you live with ease and happiness.

Just as I wish to, may you be safe, may you be healthy, may you live with ease and happiness.

Now picture another person that you love, perhaps a relative or a friend. This person, like you, wishes to have a happy life. Send warm wishes to that person.

Repeat the following phrases, silently:

May your life be filled with happiness, health and well-being.

May your life be filled with happiness, health and well-being.

May your life be filled with happiness, health and well-being.

Sending loving-kindness to neutral people

Now think of an acquaintance, someone you don't know very well and toward whom you do not have any particular feeling. You and this person are alike in your wish to have a good life.

Send all your wishes for well-being to that person, repeating the following phrases, silently:

Just as I wish to, may you also live with ease and happiness.
Just as I wish to, may you also live with ease and happiness.
Just as I wish to, may you also live with ease and happiness.

Now bring to mind another acquaintance toward whom you feel neutral. It could be a neighbour, or a colleague, or someone else that you see around but do not know very well. Like you, this person wishes to experience joy and well-being in his or her life.

Send all your good wishes to that person, repeating the following phrases, silently:

May you be happy, may you be healthy, may you be free from all pain.
May you be happy, may you be healthy, may you be free from all pain.
May you be happy, may you be healthy, may you be free from all pain.

Sending loving-kindness to all living beings

Now expand your awareness and picture the whole globe in front of you as a little ball.

Send warm wishes to all living beings on the globe, who, like you, want to be happy:

Just as I wish to, may you live with ease, happiness and good health.
Just as I wish to, may you live with ease, happiness and good health.
Just as I wish to, may you live with ease, happiness and good health.

Take a deep breath in. And breathe out. And another deep breath in and let it go. Notice the state of your mind and how you feel after this meditation.

When you're ready, you may open your eyes.

Research on the benefits of practicing the loving-kindness meditation continue to grow.

Let your students know it's okay if compassion doesn't come naturally to them

Being compassionate is often harder than being judgmental and negative. Compassionate thinking takes practice. Most people are in the habit of noticing what's wrong with everyone else—because it makes you feel better about who you are when you know you're better than someone else. Instead of denying human nature, understand it and do your best to see the best in others, to lift them up, to sit with and share their struggles and to wish the best for them.

Play and games

Lift me up

Write the statement 'Lift me up' on the whiteboard. Briefly explain how compassion is one way of lifting yourself and others. Ask the group to work out together how they can spell the words on the floor by using their bodies to make the statement.

I still think you're awesome

This game is played in pairs and requires plenty of trust within the group. Each person is asked to think of something about themselves they wish to be different. The idea is to tell this to their partner. The partner responds with 'I still think you're awesome because…' The objective is for students to come up with compliments showing what they value and admire about each other.

Lesson 2.5

Creating opportunities for empathy

New confident mindset concept: Empathy

Empathy is being able to see things from someone else's perspective, even if it's different from your own. Insight or empathy is an essential foundation skill in the process of compassion. Noticing and understanding other people's perspective and feelings strengthen the human bond. To go beyond that and see differences without passing judgment or expressing superiority over others heads you towards a higher level of compassion. The final step is empathic concern, where you focus on doing what you can to relieve another person's suffering. An empathetic mindset can be deeply satisfying, freeing you from concentrating on your perspective alone. When people show each other empathy, relationships flourish.

Research by Jamil Zaki (2019) shows empathy is not a fixed trait where you're born with it or not. It's a skill everyone can strengthen through practice.

Mind map: Empathy

On the board write 'Empathy: Understanding how other people think or feel.' Allow plenty of time for students to explore empathy and how they feel when they give it and receive it.

Brainstorm: Empathetic statements

Ask your students what they like to hear from others when they are going through a tough time or when they feel misunderstood. Offer what is meaningful to you at a time like this too.

If your students need help to get started, offer the empathetic statements below and make sure you use them regularly. The more empathy a child receives, the stronger it becomes within them.

> 'I can see this is tough for you.'
>
> 'I understand.'
>
> 'You're having a hard time, I know that.'
>
> 'Anyone would find this difficult—you're doing a great job, hang in there.'
>
> 'You're not alone to feel this way.'

Statements like these not only soothe feelings, they deepen the connection between you and your students as well as their understanding of other people's opinions and experiences.

Adding hope to empathy

Young people need hope. While the optimism chapter later in this book explains in detail about instilling hope in young people, I've included it here, as empathy is delivered warmly when it also offers hope.

Ask your students what they could say to offer hope to someone feeling hopeless. Statements like 'I know it's hard right now, but it won't always be this hard' show you understand the struggle and feel hopeful it will not last forever.

Remind your students after the brainstorm to try to lift others with empathetic and hopeful statements whenever possible. They won't always remember as this may not come naturally to developing young minds. With your role modelling, their practice and some visual reminders around the room, it will feel more natural in good time.

Role plays

- You are struggling with your little brother following you around everywhere. You love him a lot and enjoy his company, but you need your space now that you're older. Show how you can resolve this by showing your brother empathy and helping him build empathy for your own feelings.
- Your best friend's mum is sick in hospital and it's hard to know if she is going to get better or not. What could you say and do for your friend that shows empathy and hope?
- Your friend is an excellent person, and her personality is rare and exciting to you. You understand she says and does things most people think are immature for her age, but you see past that and know her strengths. She doesn't get invited to parties, but you do. Your friends let her join the social group during school hours because they get along so well with you. No one has taken her on more than that. One day, she comes to you and asks why she doesn't get invited to parties. How will you handle it with compassion and hope?
- You walk home after school every day. A student from your class whom you find a little challenging starts walking with you as she lives just around the corner. You don't want to hurt her feelings, but you prefer to walk alone. It's your time for peace before you get home and she likes to talk a lot. After thinking about what to do, you've decided the kind thing is to let her walk with you. What kind of thoughts can you use to bring out compassion and kindness so the walk has the best chance of being something you can manage and learn to enjoy?
- A student in your class cries whenever she doesn't get her way. You find your mind buzzing with negative attitudes towards her. What empathetic thoughts could you choose instead?

- Your teacher returns to work after her close friend has died unexpectedly. No one wants to talk about it even though your teacher emailed the class to explain her absence. What could you bravely say to show empathy and offer hope?
- Your parents do not want any more pets in the house. Show an empathetic two-way conversation where you all show each other empathy and care without changing what you want.
- Someone at a party is behaving in a way that's annoying the guests. What might be going on? How can you respond compassionately?
- Your friend is grumpy with everyone and hasn't talked to anyone since yesterday. What might be going on for him?
- Your sister loses it at everyone. Being around her can be tough, especially since she started high school. What kind of thoughts can you find to be compassionate and hopeful towards your sister?
- Your little brother won't leave you alone. You need your own space and he won't give it to you. What might be going on for him?
- Your teacher has yelled at the class more times in one day than he has all year. Everyone is confused. What might be going on for him?

Empathy challenge

If there is anything you do empathically for your community, now is your chance to share the story with your students. More than the details around what you do, share mostly about how it makes you feel and how it affects other people's lives.

Ask your students if there are any kindness pursuits they find interesting. Homeless shelters, taking their dog to meet elders in a residential home, raising money for a disadvantaged group, cooking a meal for someone in need, helping out at an animal shelter are all examples of activities that build awareness and empathy about what others experience. The more exposure students get to a variety of experiences and people, the stronger their insight becomes.

Read books about different cultures, places and experiences too. Books can broaden a person's understanding of people and build empathy.

Empathy building activity

Think of a person who seems different from you in every way you can imagine. They might have different interests, values or cultural beliefs. They may even be someone you're in conflict with. Try thinking of all the things you share in common. Perhaps you go to the same school; maybe you both have siblings or are only-children. Don't forget this one either—you both belong to the human species, so believe it or not, you share 99.9 percent of your DNA.

Suggest to your students that every time they meet someone who makes them feel uncomfortable or judgemental because of their differences, to look deeper to find a common thread.

Homework project: The human face of hardship

Allow students a week or so to look deeper into an area of human hardship. Help them collate images into a collage that tells a story without words about what the person or group of people are going through. Putting a face to the experiences often read or heard about in the media will deepen students' understanding of what people go through in difficult times. If appropriate, display the images in your classroom.

Discussion: It's not all about you

One way to help students strengthen their compassion is by gently exploring the question 'Is life only about you?'

It's important to make sure this doesn't come out sarcastically or judgementally, as the question is often used in a moment of frustration towards an entitled or ego-centric child: 'It's not all about you!'

When offered sensitively, especially in a warm and supportive group, it can be a great perspective builder to understand that no one is at the centre of the world. Answering this question in the right context can be quite humbling.

Our common threads display

Ask your students to bring along a photo of themselves (or use self-portraits). Pin their faces around the edges of the board, titled 'Our common threads'. Begin a brainstorm about the group's likes and dislikes, making sure someone is taking notes. Next, go through the answers, asking students to raise their hand when they relate to a like or dislike. Ask a student to help collect the responses. Finally, support students to work together with some pins and lots of string. Connect each child to all their likes and dislikes until your board is delightfully busy and full of common threads.

Well-wishing

When success gets measured by traditional standards of achievement like wealth, performance and status, it can be hard to practice compassion—because it's you against the next person.

Wishing others well rather than competing against them deepens compassion and connection between everyone. Start with simple forms of well-wishing. When you hear an emergency services siren, stop what you're doing and invite the group to wish those helping and the receivers of assistance a positive outcome. As your students get better at thinking this way, you can engage in well-wishing others before a test, audition or race. At the highest level of well-wishing, you and your students can make wishes for people you don't know well, whether it's for good luck, a happy day, winning the lottery or having a spectacular life!

Well-wishing keeps you connected to others and takes you outside of your own needs and experiences. It's high-octane fuel for compassion.

Play and games

Pick the worst thing

Students take it in turns to sit at the front of the group and offer two statements outlining an embarrassing or difficult time they've had. The rest of the group listens and has to decide which of the two experiences were the worst for the storyteller. Remind them to put themselves in the other person's shoes for a moment to see if they can genuinely work out which would be the worse experience for that particular person.

References

Cooper, J. C., T. A. Kreps, T. Wiebe, T. Pirkl, and B. Knutson. 2010. 'When Giving Is Good: Ventromedial Prefrontal Cortex Activation for Others' Intentions.' *Neuron* 67, no. 3: 511–521. doi:10.1016/j.neuron.2010.06030.

Jazaieri, H., L. McGonigal, I. A. Lee, T. Jinpa, J. R. Doty, J. J. Gross, and P. R. Goldin. 2017. 'Altering the Trajectory of Affect and Affect Regulation: The Impact of Compassion Training.' *Mindfulness* 9, no. 3: 283–293. doi:10.1007/s12671-017-0773-3.

Killingsworth, Matt. 2013. 'Does Mind-Wandering Make You Unhappy?' *Greater Good* magazine, July.

Scarlet, J., N. Altmeyer, S. Knier, and R. E. Harpin. 2017. 'The Effects of Compassion Cultivation Training on Health-care Workers.' *Clinical Psychologist* 21: 116–124. doi:10.111/cp.12130.

Seppala, E. 2017. *The Happiness Track; How to Apply the Science of Happiness to Accelerate Your Success*. New York: HarperCollins.

Seppala, E. M., C. A. Hutcherson, Nguyen, J. R. Doty, and J. J. Gross. 2014. 'Loving-Kindness Meditation: A Tool to Improve Healthcare Provider Compassion, Resilience, and Patient Care.' *Journal of Compassionate Health Care*. doi:10.1186/s40639-014-0005-9.

Weng, H. Y., R. C. Lapate, D. E. Stodala, M. Rogers, and J. Davidson. 2018. 'Visual Attention to Suffering after Compassion Training Is Associated with Decreased Amygdala Responses.' *Frontiers in Psychology*, May 22.

Zaki, Jamil. 2017. 'Building Empathy: How to Hack Empathy and Get Others to Care More.' TEDx Marin. Available at https://www.youtube.com/watch?v=-DspKSYxYDM

______. 2019. *The War for Kindness: Building Empathy in a Fractured World*. New York: Crown.

Lesson 2.5

CHAPTER 3

Taming your inner critic

Introduction

Your thinking style is a result of many factors, including genetic makeup and personal experiences, as well as individual values, attitudes and beliefs. While these factors have joined together to affect how you've thought until now, try not to see yourself as captive to them. What many people might not know is you can adjust your automatic thinking style by consciously learning to choose more supportive thoughts. Your genes, experiences and personality don't have to dictate how you want to think for the rest of your life.

World-renowned neuroscientist Dr Richard Davidson's research confirms you can rewire and build a healthier thinking style at any stage in your life. Through self-awareness and connection to others, no matter what your genetics, personality or environment push you towards; you can build a new, more optimistic thinking pattern. Davidson (2018)

When you pause long enough and tune into your thoughts, you might notice ongoing chatter, or 'self-talk'. Positive or negative thoughts churn away in your mind about yourself, other people, the past, present and future. To tame them, you need to notice and acknowledge them, check in if they might be useful and know when they are destructive so you can learn how to attune to healthy, realistic optimism.

Among the unhealthiest thoughts people carry are those of self-doubt and self-depreciation. The inner critic almost always needs taming. Humans have the unique ability to use rich and complex language to contemplate and communicate. When you're calm, rational and present, confidence can flourish. When thinking is restricted to past problems, future concerns and negative assumptions about yourself and others, the dialogue can become defeating. Blindly following the background noise of negative, unhealthy self-talk can lend itself to negative, hopeless and uncomfortable emotions.

When coached to talk to yourself in confident, realistic and motivational ways, your self-talk can improve your sense of capability and performance. When a defeating mindset full of self-doubt hopelessness and fault finding dominates, your thoughts and performance will not reach their full potential. Tod, Hardy and Oliver (2011)

Cognitive behavioural therapy (CBT) research over the last few decades confirms that following an event, you generate a thought associated with it. Depending on the kind of thought, you will have a particular type of feeling. Being trained to change your thinking for the better can improve your mood and how you feel, no matter what you are going through. Bernard, Ellis and Terjesen (2006) to build a confident mindset and gain feelings of capability, you need to check in with the quality of your thoughts. Developing self-awareness about your thoughts each day means you can develop more control over your thoughts. After all, you created them.

From where did these thoughts come? Sometimes the voice in your head is the voice you heard in your childhood. Parents, caregivers and other significant adults spoke to you in a particular style. Sometimes their communication was encouraging and constructive, helping you develop positive self-talk. Inevitably, at different times, their comments might not have been as supportive or hopeful as you would have liked. You can't change your early dialogues; they have come and gone. Try and remember that most adults did their best for the young people in their care, with the skills and knowledge they had at the time. If the experience was less than helpful to the dialogue in your mind, there's no need to despair. You don't have to listen to it anymore, and you're not a slave to it. You are going to learn how to create a new dialogue that's much more pleasant.

Lesson 3.1

The inner hero vs. the inner critic

New confident minds concept: Inner hero thinking

The inner hero style of self-talk is balanced, appreciative and encouraging. For the record, it doesn't blindly view you through rose-coloured glasses; it's realistically optimistic, fair and confident. When it focuses on what you can improve on or do differently, it does so with kindness, wisdom and clarity. The inner critic, on the other hand, critiques randomly and ruthlessly, where everything is defined and interpreted with pessimism and negativity.

To develop an inner hero mindset, you need to recognise what thinking habits your mind has already established. Most people who struggle to think confidently are too critical of themselves and practise what psychologists call negative self-talk. Another way to look at this is by seeing unhelpful and irrational thoughts as inner critics. To stamp out an inner critic, you need to create and practise the opposite—an inner hero. It takes a lot of time and practise to develop—and the inner critic will try to push it out. Hang in there; it won't be holding you captive much longer.

Case study: Finding the inner hero when your inner critic is a bully

Everyone who knew Sara adored her. She did well in class, stayed out of trouble and never had a bad thing to say about anyone. Despite her calm exterior, Sara was full of self-doubt. No matter how good things looked on the outside, Sara's inner critic was her living nightmare. If she did well on a test, it told her, 'It was just a fluke.' When she came first in a race, it said, 'The others let you win.' When she made a new friend, it scoffed, 'They'll figure out how boring you are soon enough and you won't be friends for long!' Sara helplessly played close attention to what her inner critic said. It got worse the more she listened to it and eventually, she began listening to it like an instruction manual. When it told her 'Don't bother' or 'You're too dumb to try that,' Sara found herself listening.

Sara's parents started noticing her eyes had lost their sparkle and her expression was no longer bubbly and joyful. Most things that came out of her mouth were sarcastic and rude. She quit the netball team and her grades dropped. It seemed all of this happened in the blink of an eye. No one saw it coming.

Sara was behaving out of character, so her parents asked me to work with her at school. While her inner critic had always been there, she managed to ignore it most of the time—or at least hide its effect and get on with life. In the months leading up to seeing me, her inner critic had taken over and was all she could listen to.

In our first meeting, we sat down and I asked her to close her eyes. I did too. I asked Sara to pay attention to what was running through her mind. We did this for just over five minutes. When she opened her eyes, I asked, 'What just went through your head?' She smirked and said, 'I don't think you want to know!' I asked, 'Why not?' She laughed, 'I don't want to hurt your feelings—please don't make me tell you!' I assured her I'm a big girl and could handle it. We had a giggle and then she shared her thinking with me.

While it began as critical towards me, it ended by being critical of herself. Sara's thoughts went something like this:

- 'I can't believe I have to do this!'
- 'I don't want to be here.'
- 'What would she know anyway?'
- 'Get me out of here!'
- 'This is boring.'
- 'I hate my life.'
- 'I'm going to fail my maths test tomorrow because of this.'
- 'Oh man, it's my turn to wash the dishes tonight.'
- 'Worst day ever.'
- 'I hope I don't have to come here again; it's such a waste of time.'
- 'I bet Mum forgot to buy my pimple cream today—she never remembers anything.'
- 'I can't believe it's only week three and I have to come to school for eight more weeks.'
- 'This is taking forever.'
- 'What am I going to wear to Jackie's party? All my clothes are so embarrassing.'
- 'I hate how Mum and Dad don't buy me new clothes until my birthday.'
- 'My family is weird.'
- 'My brother is a pain and I bet he's going to make me walk the dog tonight even though it's his job.'

I'll stop here, but you get the point. In such a short amount of time, Sara's self-talk was negative, doubtful and unforgiving of herself and everyone in her life. She hadn't had one confident thought. I even asked her, 'Did you think of anything good in that time?' She didn't have to tell me the answer. We both had a laugh.

Solution

Sara was given a journal and asked to write down five nice things she could say to herself. Sara found this hard, but after a while, she completed the task. They included, 'I'm funny,' 'I care about my friends,' 'I care about my family,' 'I love art' and 'I'm a great swimmer.'

I asked her to pick one, write it on a card and to stick the card by her bedside or on her bathroom mirror. I asked that she say that statement to herself every time she passed the card, with a minimum of telling it to herself twice a day. She rolled her eyes, but agreed. I encouraged her to do this every day for a week until our next session. I also asked her to pay attention to the kinds of things her inner critic said to her each day and to respond with a clear message that told it to go away! We also named her inner critic Fred, and I taught her to see Fred as separate from who she was.

Over the next few weeks, she learned the strategies outlined throughout this chapter. The initial change was almost immediate, although she slipped back into her old ways regularly. I let her know this would take a while and that she was doing great and needed to remind herself of that too.

I also met with her parents, who wanted the very best for their daughter. Both of them had experienced difficult childhoods and didn't want to see Sara fail at school. They'd unintentionally placed a lot of pressure on her to constantly perform. They fluctuated between excessive praise, only giving attention and affection when she was performing well, to extreme criticism when she struggled, accusing her of being lazy and not trying hard enough. They also modelled a lot of negative self-talk. When things went wrong, they would quickly blame others or themselves and they rarely expected things to go well. Sara hardly ever heard them sounding cheerful or excited about anything. Together we set goals focusing more on Sara's effort than her outcomes, showing her consistent love and attention no matter how well she was performing.

Her teachers became the cheerleaders to help kick Sara's inner hero into action. They were already supportive and attuned to cheering her on, encouraging her efforts and involvement at school with warmth and enthusiasm. There was a lot of work ahead, but we were on the right track. Her parents were grateful too, and they were finally learning to tame their inner critic while helping their daughter navigate her way through a tough time.

Mind map: The inner critic vs. the inner hero

To get your students understanding their inner critic and inner hero, explain the concept verbally, then begin a mind map.

On one side of the board, write 'Inner critic' and on the other side write 'Inner hero.' Allow plenty of time to build a diverse collection of ideas within the group.

Once enough ideas have been generated, ask your students to consider, map and compare the feelings they experience when exposed to their inner critic vs. their inner hero. This will deepen their self-awareness of the impact their thinking styles have on them.

Brainstorm: Inner critic

- When something goes wrong in your life, what do you say to yourself? How do you feel afterward?
- When something goes wrong in your friend's life, what might you say to them? How do you feel afterward?

Role plays

During the following role plays (best done in pairs), students are encouraged to demonstrate an outcome from listening to their inner critic, and an outcome from listening to their inner hero.

- Jensen found a stray cat and secretly starts feeding it. He wants to keep it, but his parents have made it very clear they're a no-pet family. When his mum finds out, she demands he take it immediately to the animal shelter down the road. She has no interest in hearing his thoughts. She's furious!
- Ella and Brandon are what their teacher calls 'frenemies'. When they get along, things are brilliant. They are friendly and support each other. They laugh and don't take things too seriously. When things go wrong between the two, things get ugly fast. Today, Ella found Brandon paying her out about her new sneakers in front of a group of other students. They both make eye contact and the tension is intense. Show both Ella and Brandon's inner critic and inner hero at work as they both prepare to talk this through together.
- Ray listened to everyone talk about the party on the weekend. He didn't get an invitation and this wasn't the first time he was the only one left off the class invite list.
- Sophie's mum worked hard to keep the family afloat. Sophie's dad had died the previous year and everyone missed him. Sophie had a soccer presentation on Saturday morning and her brother, who had just started school, had one too. Sophie's mum explained that she couldn't make it to Sophie's as she needed to be at her little brother's.
- Sports Day was often tough for Jack. He loved sport but wasn't particularly fast or coordinated. His team needed four more points to win the day, and it came down to the relay. During the race, when Jack was handed the baton, he dropped it and took a long time to pick it up again. Once he did,

he tripped and hurt his leg. It was safe to say that Jack's performance was the reason his team lost and all the points went to the other sides.

- Hamish took his little brother out for a walk to the neighbourhood playground. He'd never done this before without his parents. Hamish was having such a great time on the equipment after bumping into his friends that he forgot to keep a close eye on his brother. When Hamish got home, his mum asked where his brother was. Hamish's jaw dropped when he realised he'd left him behind. Hamish bolted back to the playground and found his little brother crying his eyes out. His mother was furious.
- Jess borrowed her sister's iPod without asking her and lost it the very same day. It had all her sister's photos on it, and she never backed anything up. Show Jess's inner critic as well as her inner hero as she decides what to do next.
- Bella wanted a part-time job at the café and had finally reached the last interview stage. She felt hopeful and excited, even though there was no guarantee of winning the position. That night, Bella's best friend Leila called. She was full of beans and told Bella she'd just got a job at the café. Bella hadn't told Leila she had applied for the same position. She quickly congratulated her friend and said she couldn't talk. As she hung up the phone, she froze and her thoughts raced away from her.
- Luke just broke a window at his family's new home. It was an accident with a cricket ball. No one has seen it yet, but his parents will be home soon.
- Jonah's sister Mayla just won four tickets to a concert to see Jonah's favourite band. Mayla doesn't like the band one bit but knows how badly her brother wants the tickets. She says she's taking three friends. Show what might be going through Jonah's head right now.

Journaling: Thought exchange

Allow your students 5 to 10 minutes to write down the kinds of things their inner critic says. Their task is to write down three counter thoughts from their inner hero. Remind them the inner critic can only be silenced by ignoring it or by answering back with inner hero thinking.

Safely handling your inner critic

Following on from the earlier mind map about the inner critic and its associated feelings, remind your students how negative thoughts from the inner critic create feelings that match. Whatever you think will generate a feeling. The inner critic usually creates uncomfortable feelings, while the inner hero is more likely to make energising ones.

Allow time for students to journal at least five things they can do with the feelings that arise from the inner critic. Ask them how they will remember to use these tools to make sure their inner critic doesn't lead to an emotional meltdown. This step is important as young people will struggle to bring out their inner hero thoughts if they aren't feeling calm enough.

Play and games

Inner critic vs. inner hero

Divide the group in half, one group playing the inner critic and the other representing the inner hero. If you're doing this activity with only one student, let them have a go at both sides. You or a student can stand in the centre of both groups and read the problems out. The two groups stand on opposite sides and have to think what the inner critic and inner hero might say. After the activity, make sure you take time to debrief and talk about how the two experiences felt.

- My brother needs me to help with his homework, but I'm so behind with my own.
- I lost my teacher's set of keys to the sports shed.
- I didn't win student leader—this is the third year I've tried.
- I have no one to hang out with in my new school.
- I was looking after my best friend's cat and it ran away and hasn't been back in two nights.
- I'm finding maths hard.
- I don't seem to get invited to many people's houses on the weekend.
- I am the only person in the class who can't finish the cross-country challenge.
- I have lost my school locker key three times and we are only six weeks into school term.

Lesson 3.2

Understanding the inner critic and cognitive distortion

New confident minds concept: Volcanic thinking vs. waterfall thinking

Cognitive distortion comes from an unrealistic interpretation of an event. A child-friendly term for cognitive distortion is 'volcanic thinking'. When too much faith is placed upon the inner critic, volcanic thinking forms part of the negative attribution bias students and teachers are likely to experience when they are feeling stressed, anxious or overwhelmed.

Imagine you saw your two closest friends having a milkshake together without you. A cognitive distortion or volcanic thought might be 'They hate me being around' or 'I bet they're talking about me and don't want to be my friend anymore.' However, there are many reasons they might have a milkshake without you. They might have had a chance meeting and both had money for a milkshake, perhaps they might be discussing how to help a mutual friend you don't know, or maybe they want to catch up alone and it's nothing personal. There are many reasons they might not include you.

Other volcanic thoughts damaging your self-confidence is your inner critic labelling you as a loser, dumb, boring or not good enough. These inaccurate characterisations are not who you are—they are thoughts made up by your inner critic and you can choose to ignore them. Your inner critic is the voice creating those volcanic thoughts. Just like you wouldn't call someone else names, don't let your inner critic call you names either.

Comparing yourself with others is perhaps one of the more challenging consequences of an inner critic's thinking. Rating your self-worth against others doing the same work or activity rarely ends well. There will always be someone else who is better at doing something than you are. When you perceive someone else as doing better than you, a volcanic thought might sound like 'I'm not as good as they are, so I may as well quit.' Comparisons like these create divisions of better than and less than, leaving you vulnerable to feelings of inadequacy and competition. As we learned in chapter 1, this restricts the development of healthy relationships with ourselves and others.

As the creator of your thoughts; with time and practise you can create new beliefs to replace the old ones. The unique views from your inner hero are realistically optimistic about what the future can hold. These optimistic interpretations are referred to in this lesson as 'waterfall thoughts'. They are the calm, balanced and positive understandings that the inner critic gets in the way of you hearing.

Mind map: Volcanic vs. waterfall thinking

Once you have explained the concept of cognitive distortions or volcanic thinking, it's time for a mind map to see what it means to your students.

In the centre of the board, write 'Volcanic thoughts', to express wobbly, explosive and negative interpretations of events. Next, write 'Waterfall thoughts' to explore calm, balanced and positive interpretations of situations and events in more depth.

Replacing volcanic thoughts with waterfall thoughts

Creating confident thoughts takes a great deal of focused attention, self-awareness and authentic practise. Although it's a great start, it's usually not enough to just ignore your destructive thoughts—they need to be actively replaced with more balanced and capable ones. Explain to your students that whatever you choose to think about creates a neural pathway in your brain. The more often you experience these thoughts, the stronger that pathway becomes. The only way to make destructive, pessimistic or unhelpful thoughts disappear is by filling your mind with constructive, balanced and confident ones. A child-friendly term for confident beliefs is 'waterfall thoughts'.

Confident thoughts may be hard to create and maintain at first, so if you're struggling to find them and your inner critic says 'You're not good enough,' tell it to go and bug someone else. Be kind to yourself—volcanic thoughts don't have to get in the way. After all, you can always choose another thought, always. In good time, you'll be a master of waterfall thoughts, expanding your own territory of confidence, even when life gets hard.

Journaling: Volcanic and waterfall thoughts

Ask each student to write down their volcanic thoughts. Once everyone has a list, it's time to come up with a more balanced waterfall thought to replace each volcanic one.

For example:

- Instead of 'I hate my life,' try 'Some things in my life I really enjoy.'
- Instead of 'Everything is always hard for me,' try 'Things get hard sometimes, but I usually get through it.'
- Instead of 'This is boring!' try 'I'll try hard to find something interesting here.'
- Instead of 'My school is the worst,' try 'My school isn't perfect, but it has its strengths.'
- Instead of 'No one will like me at this party,' try 'I will smile and be friendly to everyone and see what happens.'

Note: Let your students know they don't have to believe the waterfall thoughts yet. The subconscious mind believes whatever you tell it, so the more waterfall thoughts you create and repeat, the more you will accept them.

Finally, be kind and patient with yourself as you master waterfall thinking. Negative, volcanic thoughts come easily; confident ones are much harder work.

Role plays

Offer the following scenarios and ask your students to come up with at least two outcomes. One will be a result of a distorted volcanic thought, and the other a result of a balanced waterfall thought. This kind of discussion helps students see there are multiple ways of looking at other people's behaviour. Depending on how you perceive a situation you will uncover a variety of different thoughts and feelings.

- Your best friend had asked you to come over on the weekend to celebrate her birthday, but at the last minute she decides to cancel the party.
- Your friend promises to bring you back something from his family holiday, but when he gets back, he has nothing for you. You notice a couple of other students in the class have a gift from him.
- You play soccer for your school and club. You're captain this year and it's been your best season ever. The coach comes over at the end of a game and introduces you to Samal, who's just arrived from interstate. He's two years younger than you and is going to play in your team. Your coach says, 'Mate, wait until you see this kid on the field. He reminds me of you—in fact, he's the next you!' You shake hands with Samal, who invites you to kick the ball around. He's good and this bothers you.
- You arrive at school one morning, and when you say hello to your best friend, he looks at you but doesn't reply.
- You get home from school, and your mum yells at you for not feeding the dog two nights in a row. When you ask her for a hug, she says, 'Not now'. She's grumpier than you've ever seen her, but you don't know why.
- You can't find your friends today at lunchtime. When the bell goes at the end of lunch, you see them all coming out of the school hall laughing and looking really happy together.
- Your family has a new pool. It's a sweltering day, so you call your friend over for a swim. She tells you straight out she can't come because she's going to a pool party at one of your other friends' houses that you've heard nothing about.

- You want to be a student leader. You know you have a lot to offer and have proven yourself in the role before. You have a lot of friends in your class you're sure will vote for you. When the student leader gets announced, you are surprised and upset your friends ended up voting for someone else.

While this is only a small handful of discussion points, make sure you remind your students about the differences between volcanic thinking and waterfall thinking whenever appropriate. For example, if there's a conflict between friends, help your students think creatively about all the other reasons things might be as they are. Instead of getting caught up in inflexible black and white distortions that presume the worst, let them know it's okay to have feelings of sadness and frustration, but it's essential to move forward and do something constructive with the situation.

Play and games

Waterfall thought meditation

Find a spot for everyone to get comfortable and read the following meditation:

> Close your eyes and get comfortable. Notice your breath. Is it fast, slow or steady? Breathe nice and slow, in and out. *(Allow a minute or so of focused breathing.)* Imagine walking out of this room and finding yourself in a rainforest with a beautiful waterfall in front of you. The sun is high above your head, spreading its warmth across your shoulders. The waterfall is embracing the sun too. The water is sparkling and alive. You love this waterfall and you never tire of looking at it.
>
> As a big blue butterfly dances around the base of the waterfall, you notice the rush of the water and the intriguing sound it makes as it crashes on the rocks and sprays across the bank. Loud, yet peaceful, stable and consistent, you find the sound energising and uplifting. You feel happy. Every now and again you sense a gentle spray on your face. It makes you smile. Your mind begins to turn inward. Think about your strengths and talents. Think of all the things that are better because of you.
>
> Take your time and enjoy. Let these positive thoughts run freely down the waterfall. Bring forth all the memories and happy thoughts, letting them fall in front of you. Quietly enjoy this for a little while longer ... and when you're ready, bring your attention back to your breath. Return your mind to where you are. Tell yourself something kind and encouraging. Pause and enjoy the compliment. In a moment, open your eyes and smile at the people around you. Welcome back from your waterfall.

Lesson 3.3

Naming your inner critic and talking back to it

New confident minds concept: Naming and depersonalising the inner critic

By giving your inner critic a name (make it a good one), you can begin to separate it from yourself. That means next time your inner critic is telling you, 'You're no good, so don't bother,' you can remember this is not you, it's your distorted volcanic thinking trying to take control. Now that you've named it, you can talk back to it (like positive self-talk in your head) with something like 'Hey, Bob, that's enough out of you—I'm not listening. I know who I am.'

Many students have made brilliant names up for their inner critic, so allow plenty of time to get creative. Younger students often enjoy drawing their inner critic and inner hero too. Your inner hero doesn't need a new name—because that's you!

Comic strip between the inner critic's volcanic thoughts and the inner hero's waterfall thoughts

Extend understanding by creating a series of comics showing two characters with the opposing thinking styles in a disagreement. Creating a characterised version of your inner critic and practicing different ways of talking back to it will help students develop greater self-awareness.

Role plays

Now that everyone has given a name to their inner critic, it's time to practise talking back to it. Divide the group into pairs and ask each person to share the name they've chosen. One person plays the inner hero and the other plays the inner critic. The inner critic states the distorted volcanic thought and the inner hero answers back using the chosen name with a waterfall thought to defeat it.

Ideally, students create personal, relevant role plays, but here are some examples to get you started.

- 'You will never get into A grade soccer. You've been trying for years and it hasn't got you anywhere.'
- 'You aren't going to make friends in such a big school; you don't have the personality for it.'

- 'I wouldn't bother trying out for the play; you won't get the part.'
- 'Your parents will never get you a dog; they don't care enough about you.'
- 'You'll never pass maths; your teacher hates you.'
- 'You'll never get good grades; you're not smart enough.'
- 'There's no point going in the triathlon; you'll be last over the finishing line.'
- 'You're hopeless at training your dog.'
- 'You're no good at anything; just stop trying.'
- 'You don't have what it takes to be successful at anything.'

Activity: Inner hero card to yourself

Provide your students with construction paper they can fold into a card. Allow them some time to do a self-portrait or drawing of their inner hero. Ask them to write five compliments to themselves just like they'd say to a friend they like. Once they have written their praises, they can pass it to the people on either side of them who add a compliment to show what they have noticed as their strengths. These cards can be kept handy to read over at their leisure or posted up at home as a reminder they have many authentic strengths and qualities.

Lesson 3.4

Not allowing your inner critic to exaggerate or minimise your experiences

New confident minds concept: The magnifying glass and minimising glass

Your inner critic loves to put a magnifying glass over your challenges. A rough day at school? The magnifying glass rolls over and your inner critic says, 'You're never going to like this school; you should probably move.' Volcanic thoughts like this one need a reality check from the inner hero. Providing yourself with a compliment or waterfall thought helps bring everything back into perspective. But the inner critic has another trick up its sleeve; it doesn't like to recognise your successes. Instead, it puts a minimising glass over all the good things that are happening for you in your life. If you just did well in basketball, your inner critic might say, 'That was just a fluke; it will never happen again!' Knowing the tools your inner critic uses (the magnifying glass and minimising glass) can help you keep things in perspective.

Case study: Shrinking Veena's magnifying glass and minimising glass

Veena was one of those children who experienced a lot of sadness and self-doubt; it projected right out of her eyes and into anyone who came near her. You couldn't spend time with her without feeling the weight of her negative thoughts merging onto yours. Veena had no idea she had this effect on people, and if she knew, she'd have been heartbroken. Veena loved everyone and gave anyone she met a chance. She tried so hard to be relaxed and upbeat like her mum and dad, but nothing seemed to work.

When Veena did well at something, she assumed it was too easy for her or maybe she just got lucky. When she didn't do as well as planned, she saw it as evidence that she was truly hopeless and completely undeserving. You guessed it, Veena's inner critic had an overactive magnifying glass and minimising glass looking over everything she did.

Solution

Veena was already aware of her pessimistic thinking style—she could tell anyone in detail how negatively she viewed herself. What Veena needed was to learn how to combat her entrenched self-criticism. I suggested she start with mindfulness and distraction to get away from the negative thoughts that bombarded her all day long. They were even affecting her ability to sleep well.

Veena liked the idea of focusing on her senses any time she noticed her inner critic take the magnifying or minimising glass out. When these negative thoughts started to bombard her, Veena tried to redirect her attention towards something else she could see, feel, smell, taste or hear. By the time she had got to the third or fourth sense, she was much calmer. The negative thoughts were powerful, however, and it took her a lot of practice.

Veena also practised daily affirmations that encouraged her to view herself as increasingly capable and deserving of success. She learned to tell herself 'I deserve this achievement' and 'I'm good at a lot of things,' as well as other positive and balanced statements. I reminded her she didn't have to believe them *yet*—that would come in time.

Over the next few months, by just learning to ignore the thoughts and remaining mindful and positive, Veena lost that heavy look in her eyes and reported that she felt like a different person. While she still needs reminders, she has managed to get on with things at a healthier pace than ever before.

Mind map: Magnifying and minimising

Divide the board in two, and on one side write 'Magnifying glass' and on the other write 'Minimising glass'. Allow some time for you and your students to explore the effect these two ways of thinking play out across different scenarios.

Role plays

Students respond to the following role plays by either magnifying the problem or minimising their success; they don't need to work in pairs.

- You won first place in the swimming race.
- You get dropped from the school soccer team.
- Your friends went to the movies without inviting you.
- You got into trouble for something.
- You get straight As on your report card.
- You apply to be a student leader but don't win the vote.
- You are selected to represent your school in the athletics carnival.
- Your football team has dropped three players and you're one of them.
- You have lost the house keys and your whole family is locked out.

- After saving for months, you finally have enough money saved to buy the skateboard of your dreams, but when you go in to the shop, the last one has been sold.
- You find a $50 note on the sidewalk. When you take it into the police station, they tell you to do whatever you want with it.
- Your parents are going away overseas, leaving you at your grandparents for two weeks.
- Your two best friends are starting to spend a lot more time with each other.
- Some of your close friends are starting to hang out together on the weekends, and you've noticed they don't always invite you.
- You want a part-time job, but you never get past the first interview.

Magnifying the important things: Five a day

A daily practice to silence your inner critic is noticing and appreciating what you do well. This new practice (different from gratitude), focuses your attention on what your inner hero would see in you. Your inner critic wants you to believe you are not good enough. Your inner hero knows you are capable and successful.

Prove your inner critic wrong every day by paying attention to five things you did well—or five things that went well, because of you. You can do this in your head or by recording positive observations in your journal. The simple act of noticing your good qualities and capabilities is a calming and optimistic habit to form.

Practise this skill now, discussing how it felt. Perhaps set a goal to incorporate it into everyone's day.

Play and games

Compliments and heroes

To celebrate everyone's inner hero, allow the group to walk around the room. When you call out, 'Compliments and heroes', everyone pairs up with the person closest to them. Pairs then take it in turns to compliment each other from the voice of an inner hero. Maybe they point out the person's best qualities or how their presence and actions in the classroom make things better. Continue the game for at least five minutes to allow everyone an opportunity to experience many compliments.

Lesson 3.5

Lesson 3.5

Not taking things personally

New confident minds concept: Ignoring the inner critic so you don't take things personally

Your inner critic (use its name) wants you to believe that every bad thing that happens is because of something you did or didn't do. It wants you to take everything personally. You have enough confidence to ignore it. While it's crucial to take responsibility for your actions and acknowledge and repair mistakes, it's not helpful to listen to your inner critic when it's making you feel responsible for things that have nothing to do with you. Many things happen from one day to the next that are completely out of your control.

Brainstorm: Not taking things personally

Learning how not to take things personally can be tricky. It's essential for your students to think genuinely about how you might take some things more personally than others. We all have our sensitive areas where we are vulnerable to criticism. Try the following brainstorm, asking the questions below, adapting and building on them to suit the situation. It's best if you write the ideas on a whiteboard to keep a record of everyone's thinking.

- What might it mean to take things personally?
- What kinds of things do people tend to take personally?
- Why do you think what people say or what happens to you sometimes feels personal?
- How can you tell if it is or isn't personal?
- What might help you not take things so personally?
- How might you remember not to take things personally?

Quiz: Not taking things personally

The idea here is for everyone to come up with at least three reasons why the following scenarios shouldn't be taken personally. You can offer it as a group quiz or divide into it into role plays instead.

- One of your closest friends is having three friends over for a party without you.

- Your teacher hints that you might be selected for a student leadership role. You know your teacher likes you, but the next day she announces that a different leader has been chosen.
- Your friend doesn't want to walk to school with you anymore. He said he would, but now he's changed his mind.
- It's your birthday, but your best friend has forgotten.
- You and your friends have always barracked for the same cricket team. This year, your best mate announces he is supporting a different team.
- Your mum has brought your sisters new outfits. She didn't buy anything for you.
- You needed your dad's help to finish off your geography assignment. You reminded him yesterday and today, but when you go looking for him you find that he's helping your sister instead.
- Your best friend likes the new girl at school and is focusing all his time and attention on her.
- Three of your closest friends have started group chats on their phones but didn't add your name to the conversation.

Case study: Amelie learns she is not central to everyone and everything

Amelie constantly argued with her parents. Whenever they complimented one of her brothers or sisters, Amelie would start to sulk and say things like 'I do that too,' and 'You never notice all the things I do for the family!' At school, Amelie would misinterpret people's jokes and thought all her teachers hated her because they never looked happy to see her. When Amelie came to me, she was feeling very lonely and completely disconnected from her family and friends.

Solution

I knew that teaching Amelie to see things in a different light was not going to be easy. She was a complicated individual, and her thinking style was very rigid. Amelie was working with me using *The Confident Minds Curriculum*, and although her progress was slow, by doing the activities one on one as well as group work with her class she was gradually improving.

The main thing that helped Amelie to take things less personally was to become more self-aware about her thoughts and feelings in an attempt to be less reactive. Whenever people said or did anything that made her uncomfortable feelings grow, she learned to pause and ask herself, 'How am I feeling?' and 'What am I thinking?' This focus on self-awareness helped her get closer to understanding her own insecurities, as well as her perception that unless she was number one in other people's eyes, she was a nobody.

Amelie's parents and teachers worked hard to reduce their focus on praise related only to successful outcomes, replacing it with positive feedback and recognition of overall effort (as explained in the introduction). In time, Amelie's self-esteem began to grow and her outward expression and response to others became far less critical and competitive.

Play and games

It's personal, chasey

Write a number on each person's hand from 1 to 5 by lining the group up and counting them out until everyone has a number. One at a time, call a number which then becomes the one everyone has to chase. For example, if you call out 5, everyone with a 5 on their hand puts their hand up and on 'go' the group chases them while everyone else remains safe. Each time a number 5 gets caught, they have to sit down for that round. Allow plenty of time to cover all the numbers so everyone experiences 'It's personal, chasey.'

In the end, debrief about what it felt like have most of the group after just you and the others with the same number. Consider how hard it might be for people not to take some things personally.

References

Bernard, M. E., A. Ellis, and M. Terjesen. 2006. 'Rational-Emotive Behavioral Approaches to Childhood Disorders: History, Theory, Practice and Research.' In *Rational Emotive Behavioral Approaches to Childhood Disorders: Theory, Practice and Research*, edited by Bernard and Ellis, 3–84. New York: Springer.

Davidson, R. J. 2018. *The Emotional Life of Your Brain*. New York: Penguin Putnam.

Tod, D., J. Hardy, and E. Oliver. 2011. 'Effects of Self-Talk: A Systematic Review.' *Journal of Sport and Exercise Psychology* 33: 666–687. doi: 10.1123/jsep.33.5.666.

Charlotte Bolton

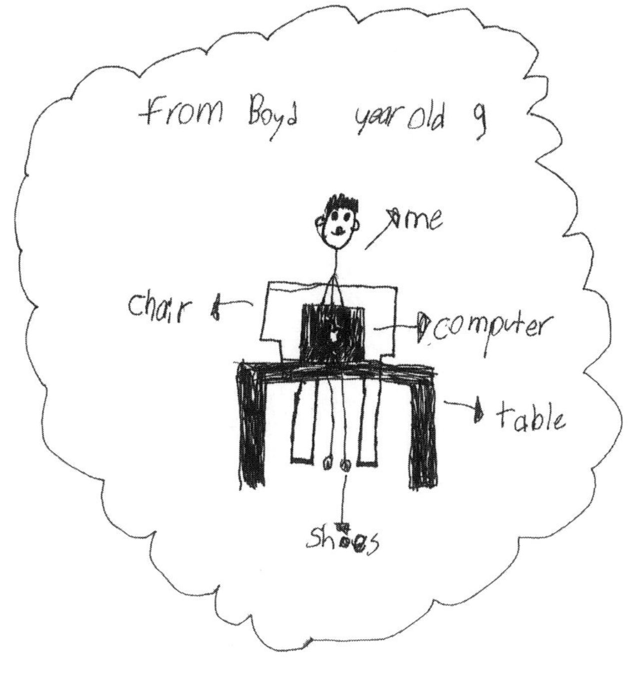

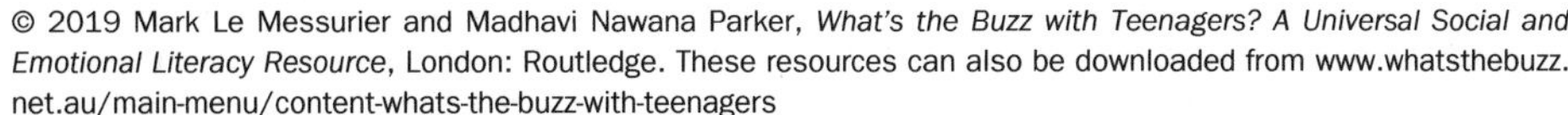

Soraya 13

Ellie 8 years old
are you OK?
?
Waaaa

Georgie

I feel much better now!

Emma, 12 years old

Kobe 5

Daisy a picture of Rosie

Mia

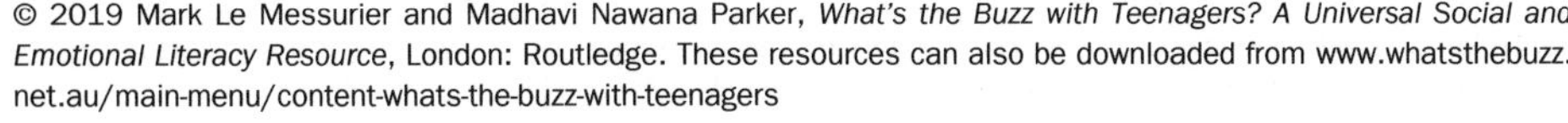

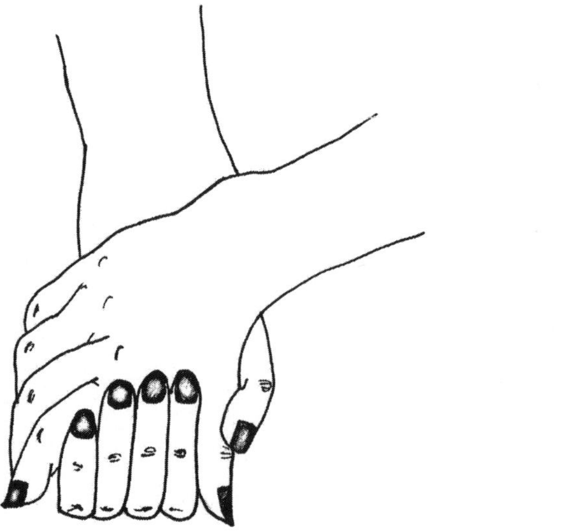

1, 2, 3, 4, 5
BREATHE
6, 7, 8, 9, 10
BREATHE AGAIN

By Maya Bentley
10 years old

I give up
I'm not good enough
Why am I so bad at this?

By: age:
Roszi 11

Soraya 13

Soraya Forbes

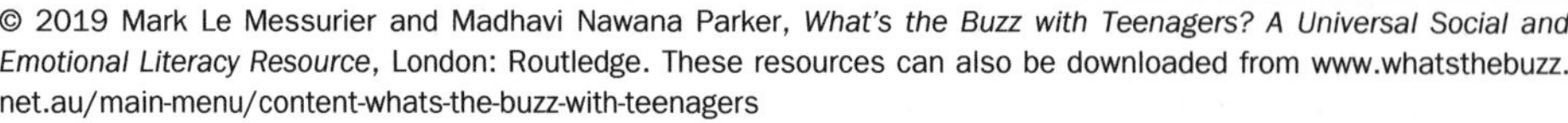

Sam The Ant
Once upon a time there was an ant called Sam. Sam was an ant, but he was not normal. He was a... TALKING ANT!
Hi Guys
1
It wasn't just talking that made him 'un-normal', he also knew how to drive a car!
WHAT?
2
Sam was amazing but not every ant agreed. Some ants teased him about being able to talk and drive.
*You talk and drive a car? **Ha ha ha!
3
One day Sam had enough of being teased so he went to see Madhavi ant and she told him the other ants are just jealous.
Thanks Madhavi!
4
The next time the ants teased him he said... "I can drive and talk and I am proud of myself!"
I'm proud of MYSELF!
5
The ants felt bad for teasing Sam and said sorry. Sam forgave them and they became Best Friends.
Best Friends CLUB!
THE END!
6

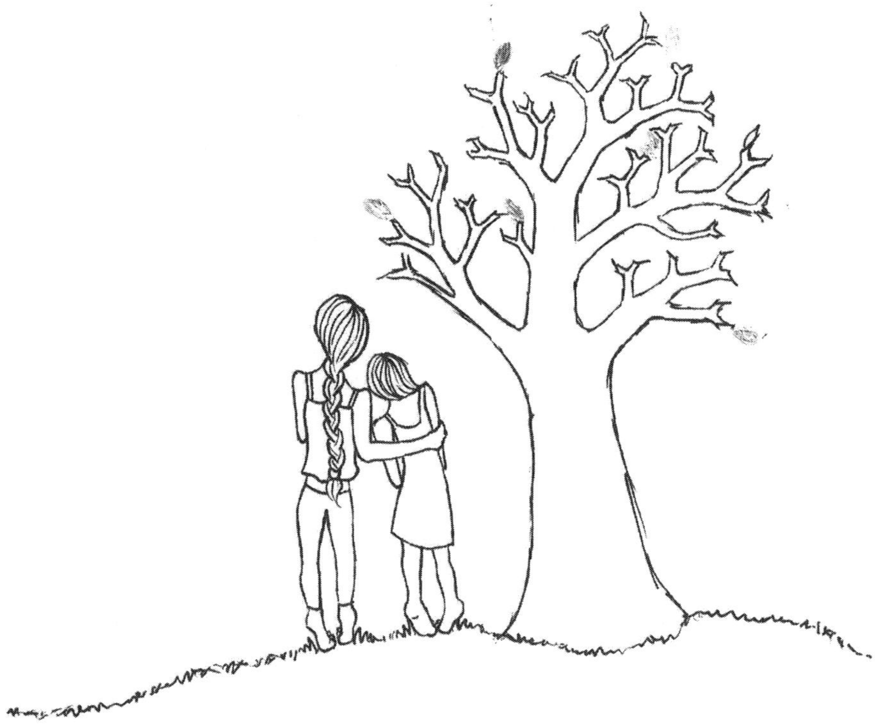

Soraya 13

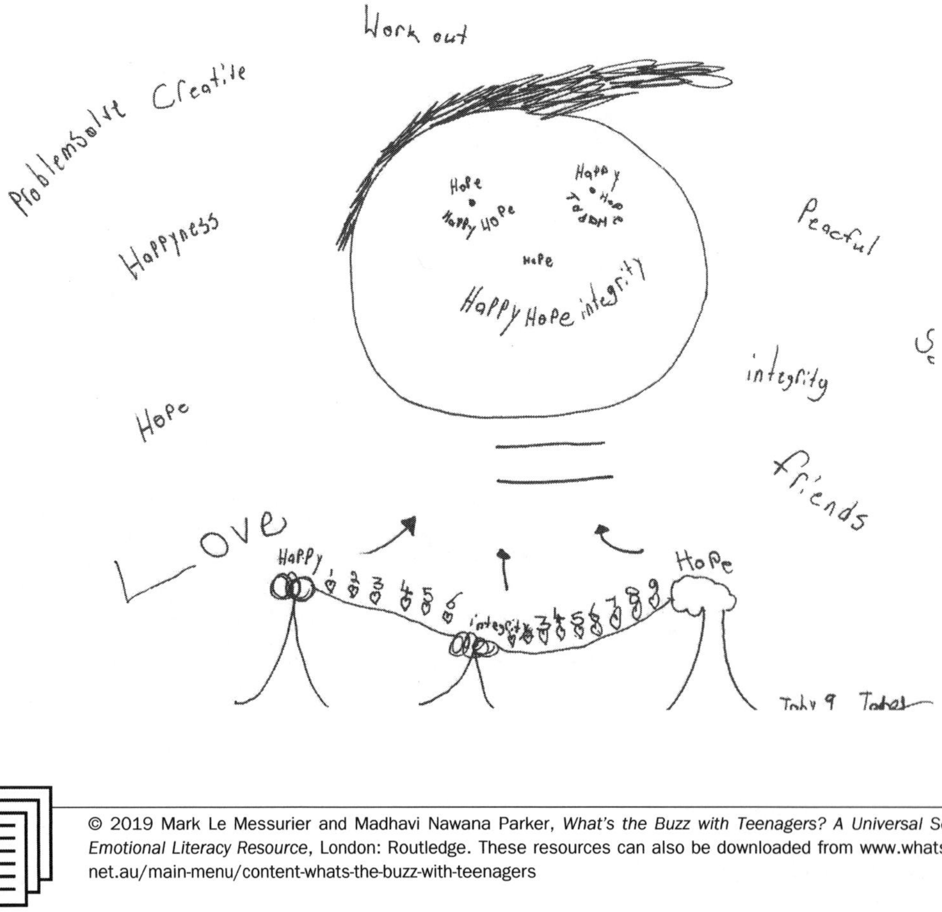

Work out

Problemsolve Creative

Happyness

Hope

Peacful

integrity

friends

Love

Happy Hope integrity

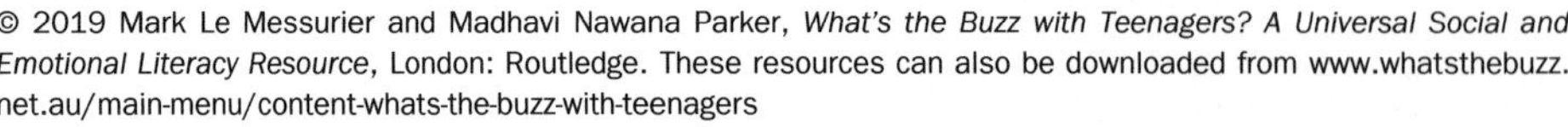

Toby Parker

Zach S

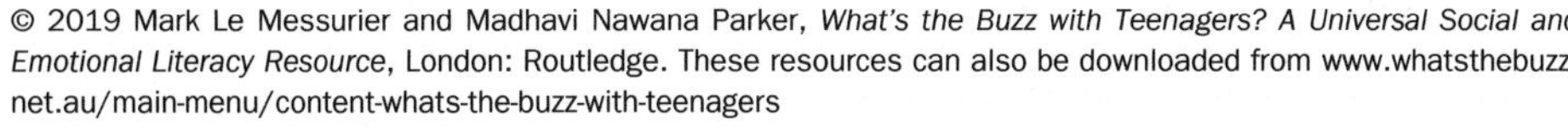

Zach
Parker

CHAPTER 4

Using emotional intelligence to disagree gracefully

Introduction

Disagreements between children can be frequent and intense. Ask anyone working in a classroom or raising a family if they've had a day that was conflict free. They are rare. Disagreements don't happen because young people intentionally want to cause trouble or upset each other. Their emotional intelligence is still in its infancy. As a result, they can find it hard to regulate their feelings, empathise with others and manage their impulses in socially responsible ways. With consistent teaching, guidance and encouragement, the frequency and nature of their disputes can reduce. Programs like *The Confident Minds Curriculum* target specific skills to build emotional intelligence explicitly so that, over time, young people can get better at disagreeing gracefully.

Disagreements take many forms throughout the life span. Young children might argue over turn taking and sharing, primary aged children disagree about what to play and whom to play with, while teenagers experience conflict over increasingly complex social dynamics and value systems. Adults are also susceptible to disagreements in their lives. Depending on their skills in empathy, compromise and emotional regulation, differences can either be worked through effectively or built up into entrenched conflict.

Developing a graceful style of disagreement takes emotional intelligence, a set of skills lying at the heart of well-being and healthy relationships. Without teaching these fundamental skills, conflict between children continues to build, and the environmental response is often punitive. When consequences for poorly managed conflict are focused on improving social skills, self-awareness and emotional regulation, students are better able to respond appropriately to disagreements.

Unlike the traditional intelligence quotient (IQ), emotional intelligence (EQ) can be learned and developed. Goleman (1995) Teaching young people early on that differences between people are normal but handling conflict respectfully is essential and can make a considerable difference to their relationships with others. Through focused attention, children are provided with an extensive skill base for dealing with disagreements later on in life in healthy and constructive ways. During intense disagreements, being able to put yourself in someone else's shoes is not only a sign of psychological maturity but a powerful way of remaining friendly, respectful and connected.

Specific personalities, thinking styles and emotional temperaments are naturally more inclined to make use of empathy. For those who struggle to empathise with others, explicit teaching coupled with caring environments, lots of encouragement and opportunities for practise will make all the difference. It's never too late to develop an appreciation of others' thoughts, feelings and motivations.

Teaching and valuing emotional intelligence in the classroom helps everyone stay calm, kind and empathetic towards one another, so that everyone has the best chance to learn in a peaceful environment. Once empathy improves, children's ability to compromise comes far more naturally. Without compromise, young people can get fixated on an all-or-nothing mentality, pushing their views onto others in their need to be right and win at all costs.

This chapter offers a range of ways to help you and your students gain mastery in disagreeing gracefully, respectfully and constructively by investing time and effort into emotional intelligence. Before beginning the first lesson, make sure your students have a basic understanding of how disagreement and conflict are defined.

Pre-lesson mind map: Exploring disagreements

Write 'Disagreements' on the board. Support students to explore the concept of disagreements: what leads to disagreements, how might it feel when someone disagrees with you, how it feels when you disagree with someone else, what each side might have in common and what might cause disagreements in the first place. Enhancing students' self-awareness through this initial mind map is essential before continuing on to the lesson plans. The reason for this is that many of us focus on the other person's behaviour when we disagree, rather than acknowledging that we too have initiated and maintained our fair share of arguments, keeping them going for longer than was actually necessary.

Lesson 4.1

Letting go of your fixed position

New confident minds concept: Letting go of the need to be right

Your perspective is how you view the world. It's defined by what you uniquely value and believe to be right and true. Developing a position through your own unique perspective, without being inflexible, is the challenge in this lesson. When you are excessively attached to what you think is correct and valuable, you are more likely to be agitated when someone else's position doesn't match your own. You may take the opposing person's differing position personally and feel threatened by it. This agitation can make you want to prove the other person wrong, hoping they will change their mind and see the error of their ways.

Taking opposing positions personally because you're too attached to your own point of view is emotionally disconnecting as well as a leading cause of entrenched conflict. It can stop you from making friends with people who see and experience the world differently. These are often the very relationships that extend you as a person, building your empathy and ability to collaborate with others on a whole new level.

Letting go of your hard-fought position doesn't mean you have to change your core values or beliefs. When you allow other people to see things from a different perspective and take a position you don't entirely agree with, you no longer allow your views to get in the way of disagreeing respectfully. When you disengage from an absolute need to be right and understand that alternative points of view are not a premeditated attack upon your personal identity or valued position, you will be calmer and less threatened when confronted by significant differences of opinion.

Case study: Kate opens her eyes

Kate was proud she'd become vegetarian. She chose to stop eating animals because she strongly believed that eating animals was wrong. Kate desperately wanted all her friends to think more carefully about eating animals too, expecting them to become vegetarian as well. She understood that it was unkind to benefit from someone or something else's expense. Although she loved the taste of meat, she couldn't ignore what eating it now meant to her.

Kate's fixed position was that eating meat is wrong, so she decided to spread the word. She was so attached to her own perspective that when people ate meat around her, she judged them as cruel, heartless and uneducated, and to everyone's angst, she didn't hesitate to let them know.

Before long, she was advocating for vegetarianism wherever she went. While she was passing judgment upon others' beliefs, she couldn't handle it when people didn't appreciate her moral and ethical position. Unfortunately, mild disagreements turned into heated arguments when she tried to convince everyone to stop eating meat. She took it personally when people said they were okay with eating meat, despite what she had just told them. She felt depleted after any interaction where she wasn't told she was right—or at least super kind and caring because of her vegetarianism.

One day, her closest and most trusted friends approached her. They kindly let her know people were getting annoyed with her unrealistic expectations. Kate immediately became defensive, throwing her arms into the air and rolling her eyes. She stared her friends down and said, 'I don't care what any of you think; right is right!'

Solution

Kate was having lots of trouble with her friendships since becoming vegetarian. The school was very concerned for her well-being, so I checked in with Kate to help her understand how being too attached to a fixed position was not only unhelpful but potentially harmful to her close friendships and the stability of her broader support network.

To begin with, I empathised wholeheartedly with Kate. Her beliefs were her own, and she was certainly entitled to them. There were many things about how she thought and felt that held value. What I wanted to help her understand was that although her values and beliefs were important, the way she was going about sharing them needed refining. Kate's need to control others' perspectives were unnecessarily divisive and made people who didn't share her beliefs feel judged.

I asked Kate how she felt when she was told what to think or how to behave. I asked her to consider the perspective of a meat eater. I explained how most people do what they do because they also think it's right. I encouraged her to consider how other people might feel when she told them their values and beliefs were wrong. I taught her that when she disagrees with someone, as long as she's overly attached to her position and over-identifies herself with a cause, she risks becoming fixated on the need to be right, limiting her ability to learn from other people's understandings and perspectives.

Kate agreed to practise her tolerance and understanding of a nonvegetarian position. After all, she was a meat eater herself up until a few weeks ago. She also tried to remind herself that it was unkind to make people feel bad for their values and beliefs. So the next time her friends had meat in their sandwiches, Kate took slow deep breaths and told herself, 'I understand that being vegetarian isn't for everyone; my friends are still great people either way and there's lots more things we still have in common.'

Journaling: My strongly held position

Allow time for students to become more aware of some of the strong positions we all take on a broad range of topics. Ask questions like 'What do you care most about?' 'What's your belief of right and wrong?' 'What might the opposing position be?' These are all ways to help students delve a little deeper into their strongly held beliefs.

Allow plenty of time for children to explore their positions, as many disagreements across the life span relate to the frustration experienced when two or more people don't share the same points of view and struggle dealing with their disagreement gracefully. By increasing children's awareness that others have equal rights to their own points of view that may be very different from their own, you are cultivating a more empathetic and sympathetic environment to help everyone get along better.

Avoid jumping to conclusions when you don't like something someone says or does

Quite often, someone else's unhealthy behaviour is not about you, it's about something that is going on for them. Brenner (2014) Keep in mind that while the disagreement happened with you, if you can't find your part in it, people can fall into the bad habit of projecting their stress onto others to alleviate their own pain. Whether this is right or wrong, you can't control another person's behaviour. Sometimes it's best to acknowledge this and move forward without reacting and adding fuel to the fire. The more you think and overthink a problem, the more likely you will end up creating a reel of unhealthy thoughts about that person and the situation. Often these thoughts are incorrect or at the very least flawed. Try not to go there.

Let go of the need to be right

Having proof that you're right in a disagreement and the other person is wrong will of course make you feel better. Being right feels good! Just keep in mind the other person feels exactly the same way as you about being right. Why not let them and agree to disagree. All you need to say is, 'I see your point. Can we agree to disagree and leave this behind us?' Forgiveness and understanding is much better for your health than holding grudges.

Create a space between yourself and your reactions

Knee-jerk reactions are only natural when you feel threatened by someone seeing things differently from you. When someone says something you don't like, it often feels personal, and this feeling of being attacked can sometimes lead to an unbalanced reaction. To create this space, imagine you are physically surrounded by something you find peaceful and beautiful. Perhaps a rainbow, a field of flowers or fluffy white clouds. Imagine that no matter what someone says or does, their words and actions can't enter beyond that space of peace around you. Within your peaceful space, you pause, breathe and centre yourself before responding. Counting to 10 in your mind while in this space can help you slow down too.

Role plays

To practise exploring how to let go of your strongly held position, offer the following role plays, encouraging your students to come up with their own examples as well. Remind students to incorporate their new understanding about not taking things personally, not jumping to conclusions, letting go of the need to be right and creating their own peaceful space to slow down knee-jerk reactions into their role plays.

- Your teacher believes it is essential that your classroom removes all general rubbish bins, replacing them with recycling only bins. She suggests that if anyone has rubbish that can't be recycled, they have to take it home and dispose of it there. You think the idea is unnecessarily burdensome and that people should be able to make their own choices about how they keep their environment clean. Your head feels like it's going to explode as you listen to everyone agree with your teacher.
- You don't like cleaning animal enclosures, but your teacher insists you help clean up the rabbit hutch. You remind your teacher you never asked for a class pet, so you shouldn't have to clean up after them. Your teacher is annoyed, and you feel strongly about your argument.
- You want to take your iPod with you to a friend's party. Your parents say it's bad manners and refuse to allow it. You're super angry and feel they don't understand that 'everyone' takes their devices to parties.
- You don't appreciate how your friends like going to movies. You'd rather hang out together at home.
- You don't like the colour your friend chose for your group work poster. You want him to pick something brighter because you think bright colours look better, but everyone else in the group likes it.
- There's a friend of yours who eats unhealthy food. You want him to stop before he becomes unwell. When you see him eating, you find yourself rolling your eyes and moaning and groaning. You want to tell him what you think. Your teachers have warned you, it's his choice and he knows what is and isn't healthy. Your teachers say he has a right to choose what he eats.
- Your teacher lets a different member of the class choose a game every Friday afternoon. You are tired of other people's choices and have got

into a lot of arguments lately about their decisions. You tell your teacher to choose you next, because you feel your ideas are much better than everyone else's.

- You want your parents to drive you to school, which is a 10-minute walk from home. They agree to do this on hot days and rainy days, but if the weather is good, they want you to walk. You are mad at them and think it's their responsibility to get you to school.

After the role plays, remind your students they don't have to agree with everybody's way of doing things, but they do need to be respectful of other people's thoughts and feelings.

Play and games

Let it go

Ask your students to think of something they identify with deeply. It might be a value, an opinion or a hobby or sport they care a lot about—anything of strong emotional value. Provide everyone with construction paper to make a paper plane. First, they need to write their name and their strongly held position on the paper. Next, they can create their paper plane however they like. For some extra fun, pop on some music (consider playing 'Let It Go' from the movie *Frozen*. Older students might find this cringe-worthy—which isn't a bad thing for sharing a laugh!).

Students line up outside or in a big indoor space. They pay a moment of attention to their strongly held position, and then literally let their belief go by sending their paper plane off in flight. Allow them some time to play with their planes, set distance goals if they feel like a bit of competition, and have some fun.

Lesson 4.2

Respectfully interacting with challenging personalities

New confident minds concept: Getting along with different personalities

Individual personalities come with such a broad variety of temperaments and strongly held positions that being agreeable all the time can be difficult. Most of the time, by detaching from the need to be right and acknowledging another person's point of view, self-control can be restored and conflict avoided. Sometimes, individual personalities for a variety of reasons may seek to make things uncomfortable or difficult for others. They might enjoy certain aspects of conflict, often pointing out other people's vulnerabilities or pushing their own beliefs onto others.

People who behave in this way may trigger an overwhelming need in you to defend and justify your own strongly held positions. Irrational or disrespectful behaviour by others can make you feel protective or aggressive, fuelling your need to prove them wrong. It's most helpful to your well-being if you can avoid the trap of believing they will suddenly change their mind and adopt your own values, attitudes and beliefs. Even if they did, they would rarely give you the satisfaction of letting you know. Being right all the time and proving others wrong is their craft. Ironically, while they'll be the hardest personality to practise with, they can provide you with the best 'training' for letting go of your strongly held positions. Try not to take their behaviours personally.

It's important to understand that people behave this way because of their own challenges in communication and emotional regulation. Behaviour that intentionally undermines other people's self-worth communicates significant unmet needs, highlights underdeveloped skills and exposes severe insecurities. Interpreting behaviour in this way doesn't mean you excuse it, but understanding it might help avoid unnecessary criticism of yourself.

Role plays

During the following role plays, students have a chance to practise acceptance and understanding of extremely different or difficult personalities. They also encourage students to rehearse letting go of their strongly held positions. Offer the examples below to help students get started or support them to create their own.

- You're proud of your design entry for the local community youth art awards. You want to tell your friend, despite knowing she highlights the negatives in everything you do. You're just so proud of your work that you can't imagine she'll have anything bad to say. She looks at your design for what feels like forever, says nothing and holds her face in a state of disapproval. You feel very upset, and start questioning if your work is any good.
- You just got your report card back. It's a huge improvement on last year's and your parents know how hard you tried. They make it clear they don't care about grades. Your sister is a straight-A student but doesn't put much effort into her work. She grabs your report card and looks it over with a shocked expression, shouting, 'I would cry all day if I got a report card as bad as that. Mum and Dad are going to be so embarrassed by you!' You feel devastated that she can't see how hard you've worked. Now you're worried your parents really are embarrassed by your grades.
- You adore your best friend and the two of you are really tight. You understand and accept each other, warts and all. You know you'll be mates forever. Your friend is a bit quirky, and no one else has bothered to get to know him properly. There's another student at your school who wants to be your best friend, but you worry he's not very kind or honest. Whenever you're around him, he tries to make your quirky friend feel small. It's hurting your feelings and all you want to do is defend your friend.
- The problem you have with a close friend that is when you do well in something, she doesn't want to hear about it. She changes the subject every time you talk about your achievements or the things you enjoy. You're pretty sure you don't do the same to her. You also find it frustrating that she only likes talking about herself.
- You're naturally shy and find it hard to speak up in big groups because you worry about saying the wrong thing and looking silly. You know this is your inner critic talking, but you're not good at ignoring it yet. Whenever you do get the courage to talk, one person in the group will either roll their eyes or unfairly criticise your ideas. It's hard not to take this personally.
- Your friend is a chronic interrupter. He doesn't mean anything by it and genuinely struggles to listen. You find it difficult to be around him sometimes, but you don't want to hurt his feelings by pointing this out. He is a good friend in every other way.

- Your best friend is only kind to you. When it comes to everyone else at school, she is a bully. She puts people down, starts arguments and spreads rumours that aren't true. You are confused about what to do and don't know why you like her so much when she treats other people so badly.
- Whenever you come up with an idea—like what you want to do when you leave school or where you'd like to go on holiday—someone in your class always says, 'Why would you want to do that?' It makes you doubt your own choices, even though you felt confident in them before sharing your thoughts with the group.
- There's a person you want to be friends with. You know it's for the wrong reasons; she is popular and everyone else thinks she's great. You've tried for years to get noticed by her. You compliment her, you smile whenever she walks past and you try to be friends with her friends. Someone else says to you, 'Why do you always suck up to Riah? She's never going to let you in.' How might you think differently about this and let go of your need to be liked by Riah?
- There's one friend in your group who never agrees with what anyone else says. Everyone's met at your house for your birthday. You're hoping to see a movie but haven't decided what to see yet. Your friends ask what you'd prefer, but when you let them know, one of your friends says, 'I've seen that movie. It was rubbish and there's no way I'm seeing it again.' You're used to this person not agreeing, but you're annoyed he's done it on your birthday. How might you handle his refusal to go?

Private journaling and mind map: Challenging personalities

It's time to get personal so students can explore who they struggle to get along with and why. Most people know who they do and don't get along with, but they rarely spend enough time identifying why that is the case. Exploring similarities and differences not only builds self-awareness but enhances our ability to empathise with other people's point of view. This approach can be helpful for everyone.

Ask students to take out their journals and identify a difficult or opposing personality. Everyone writes, 'My values and beliefs' at the top of the page. Remind everyone to be respectful by not writing the other person's name. While journal entries at school are intended to remain confidential, this can sometimes be hard to monitor. The idea is to spend time trying to see where the other person's point of view differs from our own. Make sure students understand they don't need to unquestioningly agree with others or reject their own beliefs, but to be able to get along with a wide variety of personalities, it's helpful to let go of thinking your worldview is the only correct one.

Play and games

Challenging personalities balloon lift

Give each student a balloon and ask them to imagine that the balloon represents the person they feel most different from in the world. Ensure students know this person shouldn't be someone who is hurtful towards them, just different. Play some energising music and ask everyone to keep their balloon from harm by gently tapping it up in the air so it remains afloat. This analogy for lifting others, even when you don't see eye to eye, is one way to extend their understanding of different or challenging personalities in a playful manner.

Lesson 4.3

Empathy: Putting yourself in someone else's shoes

New confident minds concept: Empathy

One of the most valuable skills in emotional intelligence is being able to put yourself in another person's shoes to consider the thoughts and feelings of others. Having empathy does not mean you have to agree with other people's perspectives. It just means you can see beyond your own thoughts and feelings and see things from their viewpoint.

The benefits of empathy include social harmony, better mental health and stronger relationships at school with teachers and peers, which contributes to better academic outcomes. The outcomes flow on to adult life too. Studies have shown people with empathy have greater personal and professional success, higher levels of happiness, better relationships and lower stress. Post and Neimark (2008)

Empathy is also crucial for emotional regulation. Pace et al. (2009) If you haven't developed healthy levels of empathy, you might end up in a regular state of intense and perhaps excessive frustration towards others because you can't see beyond your own mind and perspective. When you know other people have their own thoughts and feelings that feel important to them, it is much easier not to fly off the handle with every disagreement that you encounter.

Mind map: Empathy

It's time to get your students thinking about the why, what and how of empathy. Allow plenty of time to discuss and extend the conversation as much as possible. Empathy is a skill essential to building emotional intelligence, reducing egocentricity and frustration in disagreements. Write 'Walking in someone else's shoes (or empathy)' on the board. Allow plenty of time to explore the topic and what it feels like when you give it, receive it and don't get it.

Case study: Putting yourself in other people's shoes

Shehan struggled with empathy. At every turn, she would notice things in others she didn't like and would instantly feel annoyed. She saw them as less advanced than herself. Shehan's feelings of resentment bubbled inside her all day. When she couldn't hold on anymore, Shehan would explode.

Shehan would often say things she'd later regret, finding herself in constant disagreement with most people. By the time I began working with Shehan, she had few friends left at the school. Shehan couldn't understand why, and she continued to struggle managing differences of opinion gracefully. Her understanding of other people's thoughts and feelings was limited, and failing to see beyond her own point of view meant conflict was rarely far away.

I began by asking Shehan what it was like to be her. This is something I often ask my students. It not only gives me insight into how they see themselves, but gives them a chance to stop, reflect and develop greater self-awareness. Shehan became teary quickly, declaring she had no idea why people were so mean to her. She explained how everyone stirred her up and disagreed with her. She said the people in her school were very strange, and they saw things very differently from the rest of the world—the 'rest of the world' meaning Shehan herself. She was so immersed in her own worldview that if someone didn't see things exactly how she saw them, their point of view made no sense to her at all.

I knew developing Shehan's empathy was vital if she was going to learn to manage her feelings and maintain long-lasting friendships. Teaching empathy has its challenges. It's one thing to know that other people think and feel differently from you; it's another thing to understand and care about it. So I asked Shehan to tell me about a time she disagreed with someone. She began telling me about an incident that morning where she'd accidentally bumped into another student. They'd dropped their drink bottle and it had smashed right at Shehan's feet. Shehan's thoughts were that she didn't do it on purpose; the bottle wasn't hers so she left it on the ground. She made brief eye contact with the other girl, shrugged her shoulders and walked away without a second thought.

The other girl had said to Shehan, 'You could at least offer to help.' Shehan got mad and shouted, 'It's not my problem!' Another student came over and told Shehan to chill out. Shehan was so upset that she rolled her eyes and screamed, 'What's everyone's problem at this school!?'

I asked Shehan to tell me more about why she got so angry at the girl who'd dropped the drink bottle. Shehan replied, 'Well, isn't it obvious?' I smiled and said that from my perspective, it wasn't obvious and I needed her to help me understand. Shehan couldn't see the problem. She said that if she had done it on purpose, then she would have said sorry. Her hands were too full to help anyway. Shehan went on to explain that she wouldn't want someone to help her if she dropped her drink bottle because that would make her feel like she owed them.

Solution

Shehan and I sat down and drew a picture about what had happened. We spent time analysing each moment, breaking everything down to include each person's possible thoughts, feelings and motivations. Through this, Shehan was able gain new insight into the other girl's perspective and likely interpretation of the event. We guessed that the other girl might have wanted Shehan to say sorry and offer to help, even if it wasn't Shehan's fault. Maybe the girl had felt sad that her drink bottle broke, and given it landed right in front of Shehan, she might not have understood why Shehan didn't stop to pick it up. We continued to add as many possibilities to the picture as we could.

Role playing worked well for Shehan, and acting out the different scenarios that really annoyed her was especially helpful. She would spend time taking on the perspective of other people, stepping into their shoes to consider what thoughts and feelings they may be experiencing. With lots of practice, drawing examples, breaking down situations, role playing and taking on the perspective of others, Shehan's mind began developing the necessary connections for empathy.

As the weeks progressed, Shehan learned many other ways to improve and maintain her well-being every day. This included regular exercise, listening to lots of her favourite music, diaphragmatic breathing and trying to smile at people more often, all of which lifted her mood. Shehan continues to try and put herself in other people's shoes. More than anything, this helps her shift from inflexible anger and frustration towards calmer and clearer ways of solving problems and managing conflict. It isn't easy but with practice, Shehan is gaining a deeper and more practical understanding of empathy.

Role plays

For this series of role plays, students pair up and put themselves in another person's shoes. After they have explored the following examples, it might be helpful for students to share a personal story and role play these with a partner where the focus is on responding with empathy.

- Julius struggled with learning. He was in a class where everyone seemed to find things easy. He rarely put his hand up to ask for help because this made him feel embarrassed. He didn't want other people to think he wasn't smart. Show how a friend or teacher could put themselves into Julius's shoes so they can better understand his thoughts and feelings. Let Julius know that it's okay to find school work difficult and that asking for help is not a sign of weakness.
- Gemma proudly walked into school holding a science project she had spent weeks developing. When it came time to stand up in front of the class and present her work, she froze and couldn't speak. To make things even worse, her hands began shaking and she started to cry. Some of the other students start giving her a hard time. Consider how Gemma might feel in this situation. Show how you might stand up for Gemma in a polite and empathetic way to help her feel better.
- Your family travels a lot, as do many of your friends' families. One day your group is talking about how beautiful Paris is. Only one member of your group hasn't visited Paris before. In fact, she hasn't ever been overseas. The look on her face tells you she is struggling to be part of this

conversation. Think about how she might be feeling in this conversation. Show how you can empathically turn the conversation around so she doesn't feel small and left out.

- It's swimming carnival. You and your best friend love swimming and have planned all the events together. The night before the carnival, your friend breaks her arm and can no longer join in. What can you do during the carnival to show her empathy?
- You're the only person in your class that doesn't own a mobile phone. You find it embarrassing. Show how one friend might make you feel better by empathising with your situation and offering you encouragement.
- You just got a new puppy and you've never been so excited in your life. On the day you bring it in to school, one of your friends tells you their dog just died. Think about how she might be feeling. What can you do to help her feel better?
- There has been some terrible news overseas. You're not directly affected, but you feel really upset. What can you do to reach out and show empathy from so far away?
- A new boy at school is really struggling to make friends. You have tried to get to know him but have found it hard to get along with him. He often says and does things that are awkward, like correcting people when they aren't wearing their school uniform properly or commenting on what you eat for lunch. How can you show empathy?
- Your friend really struggles to play basketball. He almost always misses the ball. He often passes the ball to the wrong team and everyone says he lets the team down. He really is trying his very best. How will you show empathy for him as well as your other friends in the team?

Play and games

The hardest thing in my life...

Stand the group in a circle. Whoever feels comfortable takes it in turns to stand in the centre of the group and briefly share something that they find really challenging or frustrating. The group responds by listening, nodding and offering empathy and encouragement. Be prepared to go first so you can role model courage to be open and honest about challenges.

Note: Listening to other people's stories of hardship without competing by adding your own is one way to build empathy. A similar effect is noted when young people are exposed to books about experiences different to their own. Reading books and storytelling continue to prove their worth in the development of healthy social emotional literacy. Chiaet (2013)

Lesson 4.4

Handling uncomfortable feelings during disagreements

New confident minds concept: Staying calm during disagreements

Being able to handle your feelings in stressful situations is an integral part of your emotional intelligence. When you disagree with someone, it can be hard to process your thoughts and feelings. Why wouldn't you feel bad when someone is not thinking or feeling the same as you are? A big part of improving how you handle disagreements is managing your own feelings, so that your thinking stays calm and clear. While chapter 5 will explain many ways to better manage your emotions, this lesson will help students learn how to specifically cope with their feelings when they are in a challenging disagreement.

Mind map: Calming strategies for disagreements

Write 'Calm disagreements' on the board. Create a mind map to explore all the ways people might stay calm during a disagreement. You might offer ideas like counting to 10, having a drink of water, moving away from what's bothering you or slowing your breathing down. Let them know what strategies you use too.

End the mind map exercise with a reminder that cooling down and being calm gives you the best chance of keeping your thoughts clear so disagreements don't turn ugly.

Role plays

- Your teacher is upset to find the air conditioner was left on over the long weekend. It's your job to keep an eye on this. You are sure you turned it off, but she won't listen to a word you're saying. She is so angry about the wasted power that she is started to say things about you not caring for the environment. You're feeling hurt. Show how you might stay calm, despite the injustice.
- You see a group of bullies harassing a new student in the first grade. You are furious. You know handling anger is not your strength yet, but you can't ignore what's happening either. What might be a calm response?

- When you're talking to your family about something you care about, everyone ridicules you. You feel anger building up inside. You have tears in your eyes. All you want to do is yell at your family for being so mean to you. How could you let them know about how you feel without losing your cool?
- You have left your homework at home and your teacher is disappointed in you. He raises his voice, which adds to your sadness and embarrassment. You want to tell him you're sorry and you've learned your lesson. You also want to ask if you can talk about it another time, like after school when no one else is listening. How will you do it?
- You and your friend can't agree on what movie to see. Your friends are getting pretty rude about your taste in movies. How will you calmly handle it?
- You and your sister want pizza for dinner, your brother and cousin want spaghetti. How will you all discuss it calmly?
- You were looking forward to a weekend at home relaxing after a hard week at school. The rest of your family want to go on a day trip. How will you express your feelings without starting an argument?
- You are mad with your friends for not doing their share of the art project. It's due tomorrow. How could you sort this out calmly?
- Your mum is angry at you for leaving your new sneakers at the oval. You go back to find them, but they're gone. When you tell your mum, she starts shouting at you. You want to scream right back. You feel like she's being unfair—you didn't mean to lose them, you just forgot. How will you communicate calmly and make this better?

At the end of the role plays, talk to your students about the importance of planning ahead to stay calm in a disagreement. Starting the school day with a mantra like 'I will try to stay calm no matter what' has helped many young people be proactive in their stress management right from the start of their day.

Mind map: What gets in the way of staying calm in a disagreement?

Staying calm when you're not getting along with another person is easier said than done. Many things can get in the way of being calm. Help your students think about why this might be. Help them build their self-awareness to increase the likelihood they will learn this skill in depth over time.

At the top of the board, write 'Barriers to staying calm'. Don't forget to share your experiences too.

Play and games

Handling your feelings game

Excitement and humour can be as hard to regulate as anger and sadness. It's time to have some fun. Taking turns, one person at a time stands in front of the group. Their goal is to keep a straight face and not laugh, no matter what. One by one each person comes up to them and either tells a funny joke or does something to try and get them to laugh. Allow each person to be at the front for at least a minute or two. The aim is to get them to laugh. Another variation is to remind your group about what they learned in the healthy relationships chapter on mirror neurons. Ask them to work in pairs, with one student smiling nonstop, and the other working hard not to smile back.

Lesson 4.5

The art of staying respectful when you disagree

New confident minds concept: Respect, no matter what

There are many levels to disagreeing respectfully. Now your students are better equipped to disengage from their strongly held positions, empathise with others and stay calm under pressure. They are ready to focus their attention towards maintaining respect for others, even when they don't see eye to eye.

Offer the following framework on a whiteboard (or print it out as a tip sheet). Invite a variety of opinions as you go through each point. Add anything new that might lead to constructive resolution of disagreements. The framework is yours to adapt to suit your needs and values.

Respectful disagreements framework

1 Calm yourself before you say or do anything, so you have the best chance of being heard and saying what you mean without upsetting anyone. Ways to be calm include tuning into your senses instead of your thoughts, taking slow deep breaths, shaking off uncomfortable feelings by stretching your body or moving around, having a drink of water and anything else that helps.

2 Put yourself in the other person's shoes. You don't have to agree with their thoughts and feelings or like what they have to say. Just take a moment to step out of your own thinking and understand what might be going on for them. By doing this, you are showing empathy, which helps you get along with other people better.

3 Kindly let the other person know that you want to sort things out. When you do this, it shows you care about the problem. You might say, 'I want us to figure this out together' or 'I want to understand what's going on,' 'Your friendship matters to me more than being right, can we please talk?'

4 Get ready to listen, even if you don't like what you're hearing. You can't expect someone to listen to you if you don't listen to them first. To get the conversation going, you might ask, 'Can you help me understand how you're feeling?' and 'What would you like to happen next?'

5 When it's your turn to speak, calmly talk through how you're thinking and feeling.

6 Ask if they have any ideas to solve it. Ask if they'd like to hear your thoughts.

7 Always aim to end on a friendly note. Say, 'Thank you for listening' and do something that makes everyone feel good about themselves.

Remember, even the very best of friends disagree or say hurtful things on impulse sometimes. Don't end a friendship just because you have made some mistakes along the way. Burning friendship bridges is something a lot of people regret later on.

Role plays

In the role plays that follow, students try to remain calm with the person they disagree with by using the suggested framework. Remind them to put themselves in the other person's shoes and express their thoughts and feelings calmly and respectfully.

- Your parents won't let you have a mobile phone until you have enough money to pay for it yourself. You feel like you're the only person left in the whole school who doesn't have their own phone. You bring it up with your parents again. They respond with 'You're just not ready and it's not happening, like it or not.' You don't feel like they understand.
- Your brother said he fed the cat, but you're positive from the sound of its clawing and meowing that he hasn't given it anything. It annoys you when he says he's done something he hasn't, and you're pretty sure the cat is hungry!
- Twenty dollars is missing from your wallet. You have good reason to know who did it. How might you talk about it with this person, when you know they will deny taking it?
- Your teacher has given you a bad grade for an assignment. She has written, 'More effort next time.' You put everything you had into this assignment. You want to confront your teacher because you think she needs to know how you're feeling. You're super angry.
- You are frustrated your school still has more rubbish bins than recycling bins. You are part of the student leadership team and the only member who feels strongly about this. Everyone else laughs when you bring it up, saying, 'You can't change the world—this is small compared to the other problems we should be solving!' Show how you would communicate your thoughts and feelings calmly and respectfully.
- Your parents believe you did something that you didn't. You're upset and so are they. Show how you can calmly express your thoughts and feelings to reach a solution.
- Your family wants to go on a camping trip in a tent. You disagree and want to stay in a hotel. Camping is not your thing. How could you communicate this respectfully?
- You have four siblings and they all want to watch something different for family movie night. The arguments are starting to get really loud. Show how you will involve yourself in the discussion calmly and disagree respectfully.

Journaling: Self-talk for respecting others and disagreeing gracefully

Remind your students that the quality of their thoughts will predict how they feel and react. With your guidance and encouragement, students think of self-talk examples to help them stay calm, respectful and empathetic when there is a disagreement.

For ideas, start here.

- 'We might both be right.'
- 'This means as much to them as it does to me.'
- 'Friendship is more important than winning an argument.'
- 'The Golden Rule never fails.'
- 'I'm a nice person. I can be respectful.'

Play and games

Smile time

Seat the group in pairs. Each person thinks of someone they disagree with. Without saying who the person is, they look at their partner and pretend they are the person they are in conflict with. Set a timer and see which pair can last the longest staying calm and smiling reciprocally as they disagree with each other in an imaginary argument. It's crucial their thoughts should be about the person they struggle with, not the person in front of them. This game usually ends in lots of laughs, and it might be hard to find a winner as few pairs end up genuinely frustrated or angry. Smiling and being playful about complicated people in their lives provides gentle practice without any pressure.

Lesson 4.6

Win-win instead of win-lose: Teaching compromise and meeting halfway

New confident minds concept: Compromise (win-win)

Empathising with others and knowing how to step outside of your own thoughts prepares you for compromise, a fundamental emotional intelligence skill for disagreeing respectfully.

Most disagreements involve two or more people with a strong desire to prove that they are right. Strong thoughts about getting your own way lead to intense feelings that can damage even the strongest of friendships. Usually, at the heart of any disagreement is the thought 'I've got to win!' or 'I have to prove I'm right!' When you move away from win-lose outcomes towards compromise, you create a win-win opportunity. Every time a young person practises compromise, they are building their empathy muscles.

Compromise self-talk

Discuss the self-talk statements that follow and brainstorm your own. Explain how stepping out of 'me' and 'win' can give everyone a better chance at solving disagreements respectfully and staying friends.

'I don't agree, but I'm fair and respectful.'

'I don't have to prove I'm right.'

'I don't have to win every time.'

'Things can still work out, even if it doesn't turn out exactly how I planned.'

'We can both get some of what we want. If I get all of what I want, that's probably not fair on the other person.'

'When everyone is calm, I'll ask to talk it through, so we both get some of what we want.'

As a group, discuss how each thought could be communicated. For example, 'We can both get some of what we want. If I get all of what I want, that's probably not fair on the other person,' can be communicated like this: 'I can see this matters a lot to you. I want this to work out. Can we figure out together if we can meet halfway?'

Aim to get a long list of constructive comments students can use during a disagreement that reflect the compromise mindset. Placing these on a poster can help remind everyone that communicating through empathy, mutual understanding and compromise is a healthier way towards a resolution than getting stuck on being right and winning the argument.

Role plays

Now that your students have a good understanding about how to disagree respectfully by considering a win-win, it's time to practise. Keep some reminders on the board to make sure everyone is trying out their new skills.

- You don't want to walk your little sister to school anymore. You want to meet your friends instead and walk with them. She wants you to walk her and so do your parents.
- You aren't allowed to check your mobile phone after 7:00 p.m. at your house. After 7:00 p.m. is when all your friends are texting each other and you're feeling left out.
- You want to make an iMovie when your friend comes over, but he wants to play with your dog instead.
- Your friend thinks you're not spending enough time with him. He thinks you're getting 'obsessed' with a new friendship group and he's pretty upset.
- You don't want to walk the dog anymore. You love your dog, but you are struggling to keep up with your sport, homework and time to relax. How will you bring it up with your parents (who don't want to walk the dog either)?
- You have outgrown the decorations in your room. Your parents have said they don't have enough money to update it yet. You're frustrated. What could you say and do?
- You are so tired of being on dishes duty in your house. You understand everyone needs to pull their weight and do jobs. The thing is, you haven't had a change for years! How will you respectfully discuss this with your family?
- When you get home from school, you have a lot of jobs to get done. Now you're older, you have a lot more homework. Plus, you have learning difficulties. Everything takes more time and effort for you. You're feeling emotional and exhausted. How can you find a win-win? You know your parents work hard and genuinely need all the help they're asking of you.
- Your family always has dinner at the same pizza bar because it's 'everyone's' favourite. The truth is, you don't like pizza. You love dinners out with the family, but how will you get a win-win when the rest of your family aren't into the food you like?
- The rule in your house is no TV during the week. You feel like you're missing out on what everyone is talking about at school. What's a win-win solution you could negotiate with your parents?

Give me three!

It's hard to see past your own nose in a disagreement. Most people can only think of one solution—which is usually the outcome they want. While it won't always be possible, help young people come up with three possible solutions to their disagreements. They can do this together with the person they disagree with or on their own, depending on their abilities. The main thing is, they get accustomed to finding more than one possible solution.

Final points on disagreeing

Ask questions to clarify intention

In the right context, with the right person, after a hurtful statement or action students could ask the other person, 'Do you realise what you just said/did?'

Being impulsive is common in childhood. It's not uncommon for young people to say or do things they regret. To break an impulsivity circuit and get the other person thinking, young people can try 'answering back' in a way that nudges the other person's self-awareness. Be aware that not all children are skilled enough to ascertain when it is and isn't appropriate to use this response. Share this tool carefully. At the moment of emotional hurt, the child asks the other child, 'Do you realise what you just said?' or 'Do you understand what you just did?'

Communicating like this can help both parties move forward from the tricky moment and potentially grow from it. This statement won't always be useful and will depend on what's happened and who was involved. In the right situation, it can create lively conversation, build social-emotional literacy and bring accountability to the table.

Understand misunderstanding

According to the Cambridge Dictionary, 'Misunderstanding is a failure to understand, or an argument resulting from the failure of two people or two sides to understand each other.'

Share this definition with your students, inviting their thoughts and opinions. Ask them to think of a time they had a disagreement stemming from a misunderstanding. Remind them how important it is to communicate with each other gently and to step into each other's shoes when things aren't agreeable.

The Golden Rule in disagreements

Teach others how you like to be treated—if you don't like it happening to you, don't do it to others. Finally, remind your students about the Golden Rule. When someone feels strongly about their beliefs, it's crucial to treat them respectfully, no matter how much you disagree with them or feel you're right. Ask your students how they like to be spoken and listened to when someone disagrees with them. Ask if it would be fair to offer the same to others. From this discussion, as a group, agree on a set of ways to use the Golden Rule during a disagreement.

References

Brenner, A. 2014. 'How to Stop Taking Things Personally: Learning How to Hold Your Space and Keep Your Power.' *Psychology Today*, August 26.

Chiaet, J. 2013. 'Novel Finding: Reading Literary Fiction Improves Empathy.' *Scientific American*, October 4.

Goleman, D. 1995. *Emotional Intelligence.* New York: Bantam.

Pace, T. W., et al. 2009. 'Effect of Compassion Meditation on Neuroendocrine, Innate Immune and Behavioral Responses to Psychosocial Stress.' *Psychoneuroendocrinology* 34, no. 1: 87–98.

Post, S., and J. Neimark. 2008. *Why Good Things Happen to Good People: How to Live a Longer, Healthier, Happier Life by the Simple Act of Giving.* New York: Broadway Books.

CHAPTER 5

Optimism: How to pay attention to what's going well

Introduction

Healthy, balanced optimism helps build a sense of contentment. People who acknowledge what's wrong but maintain an ability to remember all the things that aren't wrong, are better positioned to maintain composure and proceed with a steady head in even the most challenging situations. Balanced optimists are more likely to differentiate between a genuine crisis needing an urgent response and an everyday challenge that is a normal part of life. They practice staying calm and focused, maintaining hope until the difficulty is resolved.

People with a confident and optimistic outlook often make great friends. They recognise and expect the best in others, focusing on people's strengths, instead of judging them for what they cannot do. Fault finding in optimists is less common, and they tend to carry a softness about them as they sustain hope and find the good in what's around them. By bouncing back from adversity and accepting rather than resisting obstacles, optimists search for opportunities and learn from their mistakes. Optimistic individuals maintain a healthy sense of hope and confidence in their own and other people's ability to master what it takes to solve problems and move forward.

Optimists are not blind enthusiasts who think everything works out no matter what. They remain rational and realistic. Optimistic individuals know that things do go wrong, the world isn't always fair and there are genuine emergencies that need resolution. Acknowledging their limits and tuning in to the reality of a situation, people with an optimistic outlook intervene only when absolutely necessary. Their capacity to stay calm through balanced analysis and a positive outlook is a valuable skill, and one that gives them an advantage over others in times of crisis and conflict. 'Optimists do acknowledge negative events, but they are more likely to avoid blaming themselves for the bad outcome, inclined to view the situation as a temporary one and likely to expect further positive events in the future.' Iyer (2017)

Optimism is a thinking style that can be developed, even in the most resistant pessimist. Neuropsychologist Rick Hanson (2016), notes in *Hardwiring Happiness* that people naturally emphasise negative things they experience. After a few more challenging times, a person risks becoming so sensitive to hardship that they enter into a state of hopelessness and helplessness. However, according to Hanson's research, this state of learned helplessness has little to no effect on long-lasting memory systems in your brain. Hanson suggests that with focused attention and practice, your brain can learn to give both positive and negative experiences equal weight.

If you're still not convinced and need more information to encourage this skill in your home, school or workplace, optimists are more likely to live longer, healthier lives and are significantly less prone to depression and anxiety. Optimists also show lower stress levels with higher motivation and resilience. Seligman (2006)

People who communicate with overall optimism are often sought after in schools, workplaces and social groups. Their balanced confidence in others and hope for the future make them great companions—everyone hoping, perhaps, that some of their enthusiasm will rub off on them. Before proceeding, understand that learning optimism takes time. By nature, people are wired to hone in on what's wrong in their world, and many people have a natural tendency towards general negativity. Be kind to yourself as you carve out a more flexible thinking style. By using the tools throughout this chapter, optimism can become a natural part of your confident mindset.

Lesson 5.1

What is optimism?

New confident minds concept: Optimism

People with an optimistic attitude don't overlook what's going wrong but tend to focus on what's going right, while seeking solutions for what isn't. They understand the value of hope, presence, gratitude and social connection. Trusting themselves and others to reach a balanced and healthy outcome, they understand they are not the only person who faces challenges. Twists and turns are part of everyone's life. Resisting their presence fuels frustration because it makes you think, 'This should not be happening to me!'

Optimistic individuals have learned to choose their thoughts and words carefully. The way you see a situation, right down to the wording you use to describe it, affects how you feel and how much you are able to enjoy life. Optimists have developed the habit of exchanging destructive, pessimistic words for confident, optimistic ones. Instead of 'I have to,' optimists learn to say, 'I get to.' When tragedy strikes, optimistic people direct their attention towards what they can do to lessen the impact of a crisis. People with an optimistic outlook appreciate that human beings overall have the capacity to demonstrate more kindness towards each other than cruelty.

Optimists use their strengths to make a difference. They take full responsibility for their mistakes and try to do something constructive to make things better, without losing hope in themselves or others. Highly critical or pessimistic individuals tend to generate and maintain a negative outlook even when life is going along quite steadily. Optimists have learned the world has its challenges but isn't as horrible as it's sometimes made out to be. In fact, many historians and researchers argue that the world is a far safer and cohesive place than ever before. Pinker (2018)

Optimism isn't about putting on rose-coloured glasses or making everything seem perfect when it's not. Negative events are an unavoidable part of life. When optimists notice them, they keep them in perspective, take action where necessary or stay calm and wait it out. A healthy amount of scepticism is still important to help us avoid unnecessary risks or untrustworthy people. The difference is that people with an optimistic perspective have a balanced lens to help them make confident everyday decisions without unnecessary anxiety.

Case study: New ways to look at challenges

Jemma and Alison were desperate to be in Club Netball. However, much to their disappointment, neither won a place. Jemma, who was known for her optimism, understood that there was fierce competition, with eight players trying out but only three spots available on the team. Jemma told Alison she was happy with her own efforts, believing she did well even though she wasn't selected. She said she would ask their coach what she could improve on to better prepare for next season's try-outs. After her initial disappointment, it didn't take long for her joy and enthusiasm for netball to return.

Jemma pushed through her disappointment, focusing only on the situation in front of her. She remained hopeful and confident there would be things she could do to improve her situation. She avoided taking things personally and didn't exaggerate her own lack of ability or accuse the coach of making the wrong decision.

Alison, on the other hand, was furious. She accused her competition of being arrogant and showy. She focused all her attention on things being everyone else's fault and completely out of her control. She burst into tears and said, 'I'll never make Club Netball, I hate netball, the coach is useless and I'm not playing it this season for school either!'

Solution

While I wasn't directly involved in the solution, the coach had this situation covered. He was an impressive leader who inspired the students to try their best. He had very little time for catastrophisation and knew how to give constructive feedback without undermining children's belief in themselves. He observed from the sidelines for a while, then apologised to both girls for listening in on their conversation. He expressed his appreciation that the girls came along and tried out for the team. He then spoke to Alison, and the conversation went something like this:

'Alison, I understand how much you want to get into the club, but there are only three spots open this season. Right now, just like you, some players have missed out. I wonder if your situation is any different to what they are going through?'

Alison paused, not ready to answer but willing to listen, she shrugged her shoulders and looked at the coach to let him continue. He asked, 'Can your netball skills improve if you quit?' Still silent but wanting help, Alison shrugged her shoulders again. So the coach continued, 'How might you feel after you've quit netball for the season?' The coach then reminded her that focusing on the negatives would only bring about uncomfortable feelings that contributed nothing to solving the problem or improving her netball skills. He finished by pointing out her strengths and helping her set a goal to make the team next time. They mapped out how she might get there, and he assured her he would be at her side to encourage her along the way.

Mind map: Optimism

In the centre of the whiteboard write, 'Optimism' and draw a circle around it. If necessary to prompt discussion, ask your students the following questions:

- What is optimism?
- What kinds of thoughts do optimists have?

- How might optimism be helpful?
- How might optimism be unhelpful?

Group discussion: Optimism

Ask your students to consider the following scenario. Discuss how the outcome might differ for an optimist vs. a pessimist:

You're climbing to the top of Mt. Everest. It's your life's dream and you have trained for months. A few hours after leaving base camp, you reach for your camera to capture a view like none other. You realise your batteries are flat and you're not only going to miss capturing this moment but all the moments that follow. Show how an optimist and a pessimist might approach this situation.

Exchanging 'have to' for 'get to'

Most people have obligations that are not always pleasurable. Day-to-day experiences revolve around a combination of rest, fun and things we *have* to do. If life was all fun and games, perhaps we would feel less content, as there would be fewer opportunities to appreciate the emotional contrast between things going smoothly and the unavoidable bumps in the road. Maybe it's the colourful blend of obligations and pleasures that help us feel more grateful.

When thoughts like, 'I have to' flood your mind, you're likely to experience frustration. When your mind is dominated by 'I have to do this and I have to do that,' you enter a state of pessimism and resistance. Struggling against the inevitable is exhausting and makes everything harder to push through. Remember, your thoughts affect your feelings.

One way to breathe optimism into daily tasks is by saying 'I get to' when you would otherwise say, 'I have to.' For example, instead of 'I *have* to clean my room,' you might say, 'I *get* to clean my room.' Instead of 'I *have* to go to school,' think, 'I *get* to school.' Your students may be thinking, why on earth would anyone want to go to school? However, these same students may be surprised to learn that 264 million school-aged children around the world don't have access to education. UNESCO (2018)

Brainstorm: 'Have to' or 'get to'?

Divide your whiteboard into two columns, one titled 'Have to' and the other 'Get to'. As a group, brainstorm and record obligations that are often attached to 'I have to.' Next, against each of these responsibilities, write an alternative 'I get to' statement in the opposing column. Remind everyone that they don't have to believe it's an 'I *get* to' yet. Saying it often fires and wires your brain's neural connections enough for the thought to feel real over time.

As a class, you can have some fun and ban the term 'I have to,' adding a challenge to replace it with 'I get to.' This can be a great source of laughter, especially when topics and tasks that are hard to rationalise with optimism arise.

Choosing your words carefully: Dropping the words, 'always', 'nothing' and 'never'

When you're feeling cynical or pessimistic, your mind tends to make small challenges seem extremely large. One problem, big or small, feels self-defining and everlasting. Words like 'always', 'nothing' and 'never' become dominant, and because your thoughts affect your feelings, how you feel changes instantly. Words are powerful, and a typical dialogue from a pessimistic mindset goes something like this:

'This kind of thing ALWAYS happens to me. NOTHING goes right for me at this school. I'll NEVER make any friends.'

Allow time for students to think about when they fall prey to the 'always, nothing and never' thought pattern. Remind them, they can always choose another thought. Support yourself and your students to flip your thinking to a more optimistic outlook by selecting different, more optimistic words. A poster in the room can act as a reminder. You will find a free download to help your students choose more helpful thoughts at www.positivemindsaustralia.com.au.

Role plays

The following role plays give everyone a chance to try out new words that are more likely to produce calm and optimistic thoughts and feelings.

- Your friend has dropped your phone for the third time this month and yet again, there's a crack on the screen. You feel like he 'always' drops your most valued possessions. He 'never' apologises, and 'nothing' seems to change!
- You were excited to take a bike ride with your dad, but right before you leave, some family friends unexpectedly drop in and the ride is cancelled. Right now you feel that all the best plans never work out.
- You missed out on your friend's Easter egg hunt by five minutes because your family is always running late.
- You're bored at home and there's nothing to do.
- Your camping trip with Mum has just been cancelled because you have the flu, and you're worried you'll never get the chance to go again.
- You dropped your best crystal down the sink and there's nothing you can do about it.

- School ended half an hour ago, but no one has come to pick you up. Your parents are often late, but this feels too late, even for them! Now you're worried they will never come.
- You lost your favourite drink bottle. Now you'll never find another one as good!
- You can't find anyone to hang out with at lunchtime and you're left wondering, why does this always happen to me?
- You don't understand the lesson. You feel like you never understand what the teacher is talking about.
- You just arrived at a party. The first game is Pass the Parcel. The game comes to an end and you didn't get to unwrap a single layer or win a prize. It feels like you never get to win anything.

Play and games

Finding positives in negatives

Give everyone a moment to think of something that has challenged them lately. Remind them when it's time to play that they must not share something that is too personal. If they are unsure, suggest that they check in with you first. Be a great role model and share something you've recently found difficult. Ask your students to suggest three positive things that could come out of it.

As an example, if your car broke down and was sent off for repairs, three positives might be:

1 Walking to work and getting some exercise.

2 Catching the bus and meeting new people.

3 Saving money on petrol and not having to worry about parking.

Split everyone into pairs and provide them with a piece of card or construction paper. Each person takes turns to share their problem while the other listens. Once they've had a go at explaining their predicament, they both get to write a cheer-up card for each other, pointing out some positives that could come from their challenge.

Lesson 5.2

Productivity and capability in hardship

New confident minds concept: Tuning into your capabilities and productivity during hardship

Instead of helpless, hopeless or 'why me' thinking, optimists acknowledge their feelings so they can maintain their focus on personal strengths and capabilities in order to be productive in the midst of hardship. They maintain hope, develop skills and invest in the future to meet their challenges. Addressing problems in this way maintains healthy and constructive thought patterns, while increasing optimism at a time where hopelessness might otherwise dominate. Bailis and Chipperfield (2012)

Individuals with an optimistic outlook avoid viewing themselves as powerless and incapable. Making use of their strengths and support networks, they actively contribute to the outcomes they seek. For young people without these networks, schools are wonderful places to offer such mentoring so that everyone has a chance to benefit from the power of social connection.

Journaling: Hardship

Ask your students to take out their journals and record a short list of hardships they've experienced at home or school. Give them plenty of time to follow this by identifying personal strengths, talents and attributes that might help them be productive during hardship. End with a discussion about how hardship is part of everyone's lives, but you don't need to be identified by your hardship. There's usually something you can do about it and if you are stuck for ideas, you can ask for help from a trusted adult or friend.

Case study: I can do hardship

Liesl had just turned 13 and wanted desperately to get along with everyone, but she was often in conflict. I asked her to get everything out of her mind by writing a hardship list, just like the one you and your class are about to create.

Liesl's hardship list:

- I'm always in trouble with my science teacher. She is completely unfair and really mean to me.
- My sister and I fight all the time. She is a complete pain and I hate her.

- I want more pocket money to buy new clothes.
- My parents don't understand what it's like to be a teenager.
- I have no energy after school for homework and chores and I shouldn't have to do them.
- This school is not how I thought it would be.
- I haven't made any friends and I want to leave and go somewhere else.

When Liesl first started seeing me, she was extremely pessimistic. For Liesl, a list like this was further proof of how unfair life was. She saw herself as being wounded by a school she believed to be 'hopeless' and a family she felt didn't understand or care about her.

Solution

I met with Liesl's parents and while they had some parenting strategies to improve upon, it was primarily Liesl's negative thoughts, her limited self-awareness and difficulty staying calm under pressure that was spoiling her enjoyment of home and school. One of Liesl's first tasks was to write the word 'capability' on one side of a folded page and 'productivity' on the other. I reminded her to be honest and take full responsibility for her part in the disputes. Self-awareness was not one of Liesl's strengths, and she typically blamed others for her problems. Overall, her pessimistic mindset needed gentle challenging, and Liesl understood that focusing on her strengths and capabilities was part of the deal. During our time together, Liesl received lots of empathy about her experiences, as without this acknowledgement, she risked not feeling heard or understood.

- Science is the hardest lesson. I zone out and act up because it's either that or staring at the page clueless. I'm going to apologise to my teacher and ask for help.
- I'm kind. I'm going to pretend my sister is my best friend. I'll see if that helps me bring out the positives in our time together. I might talk to her about what's going on between us; she might be feeling upset too.
- If I do chores, Mum and Dad have promised to let me take on bigger responsibilities around the house for more money. I'd rather do that than a part-time job because I'm behind in my school work as it is.
- I can walk the dog after school. It's good for the dog and good for me. I don't exercise enough and if I do, I might feel more energetic. I'll put my Fitbit on and set a daily challenge. I'll reward myself when I get back by snuggling up to my dog and reading a magazine.
- I'll phone my friends from my old school. I haven't been doing that lately. I'll join a club at my new school and see if I meet people that way. I have been feeling so nervous I haven't really talked much to anyone. I'll try my best to look at people and smile.

The purpose of this activity was to identify Liesl's personal attributes that had helped her be productive in times of hardship. This part *was* about making it personal (in a good way!). Over time, Liesl and I recorded her various strengths and the actions taken that helped things work out for the better. This helped her identify the personal attributes that helped her be productive in hardship.

- I spoke face to face with my science teacher instead of talking behind her back. I stayed friendly and open. I asked for what I needed.
- I'm naturally good at finding things to like in other people. My shyness and fear got in the way at my new school, but I'm getting back into the swing of being friendly. Even my sister is feeling more positive towards me.
- I'm efficient when I get started on things. I 'm good at helping once I get going.
- I made an effort and exercised. Once I put my mind to something, nothing stops me. I'm hard working. I also care about my dog. He loves me and when I realised how much fun he was having going for a walk, I knew I was taking good care of him.
- I am a positive and friendly person. I have been more aware of the things I like about my new school, just like I did when I first started at my old school. I am friendly and funny, and I've been brave enough to show this lately and it's making a difference.

As you can see, the process of being capable and productive isn't a breeze. Sometimes it's much easier to lapse into a helpless mode and give up. When you keep going, you build optimism as well as evidence that you are a capable agent, exerting choice and control over your life.

Play and games

Tug of war

Using a strengths focus, students divide the group by looking at each other's capabilities, separating everyone into teams of similar skills and experiences. Use a rope or long sheet for students to pull against their opponents and let the fun begin.

Lesson 5.3

Staying optimistic and not getting personal when you don't get along with someone

New confident minds concept: Maintaining optimism and not getting personal in conflict

People with an optimistic outlook are gifted at finding the best in others and communicating differences of opinion respectfully. An optimist's overall focus is on people's likeable qualities rather than their disagreeable ones. They have learned to seek out the best in everyone. When they don't see eye to eye with someone, or when values or qualities don't match their own, an optimist doesn't take things personally or inflate their own ego by making the other person feel bad. This places them in the best position to get along with a broad range of people.

There's an art to disagreeing with someone, without the need to attack who they are as a person. The polarised extremes of 'right and wrong', 'good and bad', 'better and worse' ultimately lead to disconnection, increased conflict and a pessimistic outlook. This doesn't mean we ignore harmful or disrespectful behaviour. It's about maintaining open and respectful communication even when you're unhappy, without being negative, judgmental or hurtful. You can point out what's not working in a situation without making it personal.

Journaling and quiet reflection: Not getting personal about differences

Encourage your students to think about someone they don't appreciate or find easy to understand; someone they feel might be 'wrong' or 'misled'. Journals can be a great place for students to record their thoughts or just offer quiet reflection. While they consider this person, help them answer the following questions:

- How is this person similar to me?
- What might we have in common?
- What could be important to them?
- Is it possible they see *my* way of doing things as strange or wrong?

This empathetic process of stepping into another person's shoes helps build optimism and a sense of connection and understanding.

Brainstorm and mind map: Having differences without getting personal

Discuss how differences in values, behaviour and perspective can feel uncomfortable. People feel protective about what they believe in. Remind students that if they are feeling upset, it's likely the other person is too. Communicating your thoughts and feelings in a way that's fair, reasonable, respectful and not personal will give you the best chance of making and keeping friends.

Allow time to brainstorm and mind map not getting personal about other people's character or values simply because you disagree with them. Hopefully by the end of the discussion, your students will be one step further away from taking differences personally or feeling the need to overcorrect or punish differing points of view.

Role plays

Breaking into pairs, allow students to role play effective communication for the following problems. Their goal is to resolve the issue without getting personal or insulting the other person's character, values or personality.

- Without warning, your best friend regularly cancels plans to catch up on the weekend. It's really frustrating and hard to make other plans when she gives such short notice. You feel like she's inconsiderate.
- You feel like your parents treat you unfairly and expect too much from you. You go to speak to them about it.
- Your sister has dropped your mobile phone and put a massive crack through it. You're furious. You feel like she never takes care of your things like you take care of hers.
- Your aunty promised to be at your awards ceremony. She completely forgot and didn't turn up. This isn't the first time this has happened and you decide to talk to her about it.
- You have your group presentation today. You and your friends agreed to bring along specific props. When you arrive at school, you realise you are the only one who remembered to bring anything.
- Your parents are super busy at the moment. You feel like they're not giving you any attention and you're really missing them. Sometimes you feel like they care more about their work than you.
- You're really into animal rights and have become vegetarian. Your best friend tells you being a vegetarian is a dumb idea. You think eating meat is a dumb idea, but you don't force your beliefs onto anyone. She won't stop paying you out. How will you turn this conversation around?

- You need your twin brother's help with maths. You have a great relationship and always make time to help each other out. Lately when you ask for help, your brother gets really mad and tells you he's too busy. You are never too busy for him.
- Your sister put an embarrassing photo of you up on Instagram. You think she is careless and immature. You go to discuss it with her.
- Your brother took $10 out of your pocket money. He put a note saying, 'I owe you $10' and he usually pays you back, *but* you really wanted to buy takeaway with your friends. You're not impressed he didn't warn you and you feel like he's being really selfish.

At the end of the role plays, congratulate the group on finding creative solutions for challenging problems, without getting mean or negative.

Play and games

Drop the blame game

This game provides practice for accepting that sometimes things don't turn out as planned. People don't always do what they said they would, and people might treat you unfairly. Blaming others and taking everything personally will only increase your angry thoughts, making you want to prove yourself right and the other person wrong.

Everyone stands together in a circle with a ball. As you call from the list of things that went wrong, whoever is holding the ball has to come up with a positive explanation for it. Whenever the ball gets dropped, the person who dropped it needs to invent an explanation that blames themselves, others or the world for what went wrong! This list is deliberately short so you and your students can get creative and develop your own list of challenges.

- I came to school with no lunch.
- I lost my keys.
- I broke my favourite watch.
- I dropped my dad's mobile phone.
- The dog ate my sneakers.
- I forgot to bring my uniform in from the line and it got soaked in the rain.
- I turned up to casual day in my school uniform.
- I didn't make the basketball team.
- I failed my maths test.

At the end of this game, ask your students, 'I wonder if blame made anything better?'

Lesson 5.4

Carving out an 'I'm not helpless, hopeless or powerless' dialogue

New confident minds concept: I am hopeful, powerful and capable

Life isn't always straightforward or fair. People and events will often take you by surprise with very little warning. It's only natural to feel discouraged, lose hope and wonder, 'Why me?' Few people remain entirely calm, proactive and confident when a curve ball comes their way and some curve balls are excruciatingly painful and these naturally take a longer time to accept and respond to confidently.

When challenges arise, a sense of helplessness, hopelessness and powerlessness stops optimism in its tracks. When life gets messy, it's crucial to stay focused on your own capacity to make what happens next better. When children feel empowered, seeing themselves as capable no matter what, their emotional well-being, resilience and level of optimism improve. Seligman (2007)

Group discussion on avoiding helplessness, powerlessness and hopelessness

To help a person feel a sense of capability during a time they might otherwise be feeling hopeless, Martin Seligman (2007) suggests asking this thought-provoking question:

'Is it possible that there are some ways you could change the outcome with some personal effort on your part?'

Ask your students to reflect on something that has gone wrong in the past or a challenge they are currently dealing with. Now ask the following questions:

- What kind of thoughts do you have about this?
- Do you find yourself asking, 'Why me?' or 'This is unfair!'

These questions are only natural. In the midst of a challenge, it's normal to feel like you're the only person on earth going through something big. The reality is that loss, suffering, uncertainty and conflict are all part of the human experience. Not letting the troubles define you is the challenge.

Cap the reflection time by linking back to Martin Seligman's (2007) points above, using the following questions:

- Is there anything you can do to turn this situation around?
- What kind of thoughts do you have when you ask yourself, 'Why not me?'

These questions can help you feel more connected with humankind and less caught up in your own mind. When overwhelmed by personal suffering, you can quickly lose perspective and fall into the helpless, hopeless and powerless mentality. Asking, 'Why not me?' brings you one step closer to understanding that your experiences are no different to most others. This approach helps avoid the helpless and hopeless thinking pattern that can quickly overtake a person's thoughts.

Whatever you're going through, no matter how difficult it is, someone else, somewhere else is more than likely going through the exact same thing. No one is exempt from hardship. Once everyone has had a chance to think this through and discuss it if appropriate, it's time to practice these skills in a role play. Where appropriate, students can use a personal challenge they are experiencing right now.

Role plays

Role plays can be resolved using the following question, adapted from Martin Seligman (2007).

'What can you do, in your power, with your effort and skills, to make a difference to how this turns out?' or for younger students, 'What can you do to help this situation turn out for the best?'

- Your best friend is mad at you and you have no idea why. When you ask them if you can talk, they make it super clear they do not want to speak to you about it.
- You're finding it really hard to study for your maths test. You really don't understand the work at all.
- You don't want to be at school camp. All the activities are out of your comfort zone and you're feeling really nervous.
- You left your brand-new jacket behind at the airport. You don't have another one and your family takes ages to save up for this kind of thing. You don't want to tell your parents.
- You want to join the swimming team, but you can't keep up with the high standard of swimmers. You worry they're all getting into the team because they have their own pool at home and you don't, so you can't practise.

- On your way to school, you realise you've left your homework book in your bedroom.
- You eagerly watch as the lunch orders come into class. You have been waiting for that hot dog all day. The orders get delivered—but yours isn't there. You're disappointed and extremely hungry!
- Your little brother has been growing a tomato plant, lovingly attending to it every day. You walk past the plant and accidentally knock the first tomato off. Your brother's face looks like it's going to break with sadness.
- Your parents won't let you get a social media account. Your friends all use it to stay in touch.
- You're bored and your parents are busy. It's only the start of the school holidays.

Congratulate the students at the end of their role plays for their creative input. Pessimism feeds off hopelessness, while optimism thrives on hopefulness and capability. There's almost always something you can do to make life flow better. The role plays were a reminder of this. Meeting challenges with questions and calling upon self-reflection and optimism stretch most people out of their usual thinking patterns.

During tough times, encourage your students with positive feedback like, 'You're a capable person. I know it's hard, but you have everything it takes to get through.'

Play and games

Limbo

Put on some music. This game provides a chance for your students to continue building their sense of capability in a fun way. Hold a pole, old broomstick or anything that resembles a limbo stick. In tune, everyone has a chance to limbo under the stick until you have only one person who can achieve it—the winner.

Lesson 5.5

Drop the controls

New confident minds concept: Letting go of trying to control your environment and circumstances

A common source of frustration is trying to control your environment and everyone in it. If you hold standards for others that are higher than reasonable, you're almost always going to be disappointed. To maintain optimism and a confident mindset, you need to acknowledge what you can and can't control.

Journaling: Reflecting on upsetting situations

Ask your students to write a list of upsetting situations in their journal. They can share them with others if appropriate. Be willing to share your own too.

Brainstorm together what parts of these tricky situations are within your control and which aren't. In what ways can you take some power? For example, if you lost your part-time job three months short of saving up enough money for a new iPad, you may be tempted to be mad at your boss, deciding then and there that you'll never get that iPad (pessimistic thinking). Alternatively, you can think, 'I'm not the first person this has happened to and I won't be the last. I still want that iPad, so I'll look hard for a new job. I'm going to get plenty of exercise to help me stay calm and keep everything in perspective.'

Shake it up challenge

Doing the same thing over and over again can stifle your energy and enthusiasm. One way to grow, is by adding variety to shake things up. Ask your students to think of one thing they do exactly the same every day. Now ask if there is one aspect they can change in that familiar routine. For example, if you ride your bike a certain way to school, is there a different way you could travel? If you have your bedroom set up in one way for a while, could you move some things around to change the setup?

Adding these small changes can be energising, creating an excellent foundation for enthusiasm and optimism about your environment and daily rituals.

Role plays

Respond to the following role plays by showing how you will let go of control and go with the flow instead:

- Your friend rarely does his share of work in group assignments. Every time you tell him it's not okay, he doesn't seem to care and nothing changes. How can you let go of the controls and compromise?
- You want to play really active games at lunchtime with your friends. They want to sit around talking.
- You like your family to spend the weekend at home relaxing, but your family enjoys going out. How can you let go of the controls and compromise?
- Your little sister is a slow walker. She's only just started school, and it's your job to walk her into class and help her settle in each morning. Her lack of speed is driving you mad.
- You love to organise parties and have great ideas for catching up with friends. You were planning on hosting an Easter party at your place, but your best friend offered to host one instead. Much to your disappointment, she has entirely different ideas about how to have a party.
- You find your little brother embarrassing. You have new friends visiting today and all you want is for your parents to take him out somewhere, but you know there's no way they'll agree.
- You are really disappointed with the teacher you have this year. He is kind enough, it's nothing personal, but you really wanted another teacher.
- Your parents have planned a family holiday to the beach. You are furious and have a habit of taking your feelings out on other people. You plan to tell your parents you want a holiday somewhere else.
- Your best friend has become friends with a new kid in class you think is mean. You want your friend to know just how mean you think she is.
- You want to watch a movie tonight and know exactly which movie you want to see. When you sit down with your family, they have different ideas. Usually, they agree with your choice, but tonight, they are making it clear they want to watch something else.

Play and games

Blindfolded trust walk

This game is all about letting go of control and building trust. Students work in pairs (groups of three work fine too). Taking turns, each person is blindfolded and led around the room. The person without the blindfold gently guides them around obstacles, encouraging them along the way. At the end of the activity, take a moment to discuss what it feels like to let go of control and hand over trust to others.

Lesson 5.6

Increasing optimism by seeing the funny side of situations

New confident minds concept: Finding humour in difficult situations

One way to keep things playful during difficult situations is by finding a funny side. It's easy to get caught up in anger and frustration when things get tough, but these feelings fuel negativity and don't help you move forward or act constructively. Sometimes you just have to laugh. This isn't about putting people down or paying them out, it just means you look for the funny side of what's going on. Sometimes it's important to avoid taking things unnecessarily seriously.

Maintaining your sense of humour is an effective alternative for getting stuck in negativity, wishing that frustrating situations or people would change. These unrealistic expectations usually make you feel even more upset and do nothing but strengthen your brain's neural pathways for pessimism and helplessness.

Judging others for their behaviour, being angry about their values and beliefs or wishing them out of your life rarely gets you anywhere. Having a quiet laugh about the absurdity might just be what you need to get stress out and move forward.

Mind map: Using humour in challenging situations

Write 'Challenging people' in the centre of the board. Encourage your students to think of funny ways they could look at challenging or frustrating people or situations. End by reminding them that anger and a desire to control others will only burden them with stress and anxiety. Tell your students to have a laugh, let it go, and if the situation is really overwhelming then ask for help from a trusted adult.

Role plays

Ask your students to break up into pairs and role play the following scenarios. Alternatively, you can use the role play scenarios to start some conversations and do some problem solving. The idea is for students to approach the problems with respectful humour.

- You've arrived at camp and realise you haven't brought your pyjamas.
- Your mum has turned up to school in her workout gear, which happens to have a massive hole in the leg. Your mum has made it really clear to you

that she doesn't care about what others think. You, on the other hand, feel incredibly embarrassed.

- There's a kid in your class who is continuously spreading rumours about you. It's gone on for a long time. Despite the school working hard to make things better, nothing's changing. The rumours are ridiculous and no one believes them anyway, but you still feel really upset.
- Your sister continually accuses you of doing things she is actually doing. For example, last week, she told your parents you weren't walking the dog. You always walk the dog when it's your turn. She's the one who doesn't!
- A kid down the street is really fascinated by you. He has started to dress like you, and he's even started to talk like you. He is begging his parents to change schools so he can go where you go to school. You find this so annoying and you can't stop thinking about it.
- Your teacher calls you by the wrong name. She taught your older sister last year and she keeps using her name instead of your own. You think that using someone's proper name is really important.
- Your mum forgot to pick you up from school. When you phone, she is at the gym and apologises to you for losing track of time. You have loads of homework to do, it's stinking hot and you're really mad.
- Your dad is really into a style of music you don't understand. You know he loves it, but you want him to turn it off the second he turns it on. You think he should only play music *everyone* likes.

Play and games

Just for laughs

Have some fun as a group watching age-appropriate funny clips or telling a round of jokes. Enjoy at least 10 minutes of laughter together.

Lesson 5.7

Lesson 5.7

Keeping things in perspective: Bad times don't last forever

New confident minds concept: Have optimism for your future and remember, bad times don't last forever

When you're really struggling with a difficult situation, it can be hard to imagine how you will get through it. Tough times *are* tough, but if you think about it, I'm sure you've made it through some very challenging experiences so far. Remember that next time you face an obstacle.

There will continue to be moments when you feel the weight of the world on your shoulders, but remember, the weight lifts over time by talking to helpful people, practicing optimistic thoughts, having fun, being creative and choosing to do lots of positive and helpful things.

Role plays

In pairs, each person takes on one of the following problems or makes up one of their own. Each student reminds their partner that tough times don't last. Throughout the role play and in their own words, their task is to encourage their friend. At the end of the role play, allow a moment for students to think of a self-talk statement they can use next time they're experiencing something tough. Remind them how cheering themselves on and thinking confident thoughts means their negative emotions will be easier to manage.

The purpose of an activity like this is to remind everyone that challenges are temporary. Individuals with pessimistic thoughts have a tendency to see every setback as the end of the world. Optimists know things don't stay tough forever. They understand there are things that can be done along the way to move things ahead in a steady manner.

Before you begin, remind your students that once a problem has occurred, mulling it over or wishing it away does not change the fact that it's happened. Instead, encourage your students to refocus their energy into a more hopeful and optimistic attitude. Rebuild confidence by looking at what is working well, and engaging in other things.

- I'm embarrassed I failed my test.
- I had no one to hang out with at lunch today.

- My parents are furious; I just broke the TV.
- I have so much homework to do.
- My sister is ignoring me ever since I read her diary.
- My ankle is killing me after I fell off the trampoline.
- It's so hard finding the right classrooms in my new school.
- I can't remember where I put my pocket money.
- I'm bored.
- My teacher told me off for talking in class again.
- My bedroom is a mess and I can't find anything.

Play and games

Enjoying nature while waiting for tough times to pass

Take the group outdoors for nature watching if weather permits (you can do this by looking out a window as well). Help everyone notice what they see around them: the clouds, the leaves blowing about or the birds flying past. Allow time for students to sit in quiet reflection about all the beautiful things nature offers, without expecting anything in return. Practice being grateful for what's around you every day, and remind students that focusing on the present during a challenging time helps to keep things in perspective. The beauty of nature refreshes most people and rarely disappoints.

Final tips for building optimism

Write a positive note to another person every day for 21 days

Happiness researchers have found that daily optimism practice helps build the neurological pathways for hope. You can start a whole class or school habit of spending two minutes each day writing a short note, email or card to another person, telling them what you like and appreciate about them. As you do this, you consciously focus on what you like in others, which is crucial for healthy relationships. At the same time, you are spreading and receiving optimism. After 21 days of doing this, optimism and social connection have been found to increase significantly. Achor (2018)

Vaccinate against pessimism—it's contagious

If you've ever sat in a room full of babies and toddlers, you can see how much emotions can be contagious. When one baby starts to cry, it's not long before the rest burst into tears. Positive and negative feelings can be easily passed on from one person to the other.

Dr Nicholas Christakis and his colleagues researched the contagion of emotion over a 32-year period. Their research found that happiness may be a collective phenomenon. He argued that having happy friends, spouses and neighbours living nearby increases your happiness too. Coviello, Christakis et al. (2014)

Make sure your students are consciously aware of who the happy and optimistic people are in their lives. Discuss how they feel after spending time with them. Turn their attention towards the people in their lives who have a more pessimistic outlook. Remind the group that people who are generally good at finding fault or expert at noticing negatives are likely to experience a lot of destructive thoughts and feelings that may inevitably rub off onto others. Ask students, how might they feel after spending time with people like this? What can they do to shake that feeling off and keep their thoughts and feelings in perspective?

Perhaps offer a mind mapping or brainstorming opportunity to explore the theory that emotions are contagious. Do they have any evidence of this from their own experiences? Do they feel prepared to start spreading optimism—being ambassadors for confidence? Could they include more optimists into their friendship groups?

Focus and reflect back on the good times

People with an optimistic outlook not only look on the bright side, but they also look back on the bright side as well. This means they enjoy reflecting on the great moments that have already happened, as well as the great moments they hope to see in the future. This doesn't come naturally for most people, so you need to make a conscious effort to do this.

One way to build this habit is to do something special when you're out and about that will make a moment more positive and memorable. Take a photo of the best moment, try something new, aim to smile at everyone you pass or carry a journal with you to write or draw about your experience. Additions like these add value and joy to everyday experiences.

Gratitude journals

Recording daily what's gone well and what you're expecting will go well helps build pathways for an optimistic mindset. Most people have read about the benefits of practicing gratitude every day. If your students haven't already started one, include a gratitude journal as part of your daily practice.

Gratitude increases optimism and lowers the risk of poor health outcomes such as cardiovascular disease. Kim et al. (2016) Finding three things each day that went well draws people's attention towards good things and increases optimistic thoughts within 21 days. Achor (2010)

Role model optimism

Children and young people are watching and listening to adults all the time. In particular, they notice how adults respond to challenges. Doing your utmost to model optimism is one of the best ways you can cultivate a confident mindset. When you can, point out what's going well in your life. When tragedy strikes on the news, don't get caught up in the constant stream of criticism and negative bias. Instead, turn your attention towards the people who are doing the right thing by others. Look for examples of people helping each other out in times of crisis. When you're feeling overwhelmed, don't stop the self-talk at 'I'm exhausted.' Try adding something like, 'I'm grateful I have enough work to make me feel exhausted.' You don't have to believe what you're saying—stating it has an impact on the neurological pathways and helps strengthen a sense of optimism where it might otherwise be absent.

Next time you have a regret, explain it in simple terms and don't make it bigger than is necessary. For example, if you get a speeding fine, a pessimistic dialogue might sound something like, 'I can't believe I got a fine! It's so unfair how they set up the speed cameras on the downhill slope. This kind of thing happens to me all the time.' When a young person hears this, they absorb the words and the attitude. This kind of dialogue is not useful; it only builds anger and resentment. As an alternative, you can use more optimistic language, which may sound something like, 'I got a speeding fine today. I wasn't paying enough attention to how fast I was going. I haven't had a fine in a long time. It's okay, everyone makes mistakes. I'm going to forgive myself, pay the fine and move on!'

Outweigh negative self-talk by asking for 'five'

It's easy to come up with negative thoughts and explanations for the things that go wrong. It takes more creativity to come up with positive reasons. Next time a student is complaining about their circumstances, after acknowledging their feelings, help them tune in to what is going well. A playful 'Give me five!' challenges them to come up with five useful or good things about what has happened, five hopeful explanations for the situation or five things they have learned from it. If they can't do this yet, 'Give me five' can simply mean 'Give me five things that are going well in your life right now!'

References

Achor, S. 2010. *The Happiness Advantage: The Seven Principles of Positive Psychology That Fuel Success and Performance at Work.* New York: Currency.

———, 2018. *Big Potential: How Transforming the Pursuit of Success Raises Our Achievement, Happiness, and Well-Being.* New York: Currency.

Bailis, D., and J. D. Chipperfield. 2012. 'Hope and Optimism.' In *Encyclopedia of Human Behavior*, 2nd ed., edited by V. S. Ramachandran, 342–349. San Diego: Academic Press.

Coviello, L., Y. Sohn, D. I. Adam, C. Marlow, M. Fransceschetti, N. A. Christakis, and J. H. Fowler. 2014. 'Detecting Emotional Contagion in Massive Social Networks.' *PLOS One* 9, no. 3: e90315.

Hanson, R. 2016. *Hardwiring Happiness: The New Brain Science of Contentment, Calm and Confidence*. New York: Harmony Publishing.

Iyer, A. 2017. *Become a More Optimistic Version of Yourself.* Dallas: University of Texas, Southwestern Medical Center.

Kim, E. S., K. A. Hagan, F. Grodstein, D. L. DeMeo, I. De Vivo, and L. D. Kubsansky. 2016. 'Optimism and Cause-Specific Mortality: A Prospective Cohort Study.' *American Journal of Epidemiology* 185, no. 1: 21–29.

Pinker, S. 2018. *Enlightenment Now: The Case for Reason, Science, Humanism, and Progress.* New York: Penguin.

Seligman, M. E. P. 2006. *Learned Optimism: How to Change Your Mind and Your Life*. New York: Random House.

———. 2017. *The Optimistic Child*. New York: Random House.

UNESCO. 2018. *Accountability in Education: Meeting Our Commitments*, Global Education Monitoring Report.

CHAPTER 6

Problem solving and decision making: Building capability and independence through a sense of agency and self-efficacy

Introduction

Setbacks are both frustrating and inevitable. Building a sense of agency (knowing you have choice and control over what happens next) and self-efficacy (knowing you have attributes to help you influence your life), contribute to a confident mindset. Bortolotti (2018)

A sense of agency is associated with better health, overall satisfaction at school, academic performance, confidence and stress management. Bandura (2001); Chemers, Hu and Garcia (2001)

Agency is also a protective factor for anxiety and depression. As Bandura (1988) pointed out early in his research, a belief you don't have control over the situation and can't manage potential threats increases helplessness and hopelessness, feelings directly related to anxiety and depression. Self-awareness, hope and using your character strengths in balanced ways contribute to healthy optimism and flourishing. Peterson (2006)

A sense of choice and control in your life are imperative for problem-solving and decision-making skills. Thinking that life happens *to* you, not *with* you is a slippery slope towards helplessness and hopelessness, lowering confidence in your role as an active agent across the life span. Developing a sense of agency helps build an optimistic outlook and the confidence that no problem or decision is too big to manage.

Self-efficacy is another part of the problem-solving process. Self-efficacy understands that not only do you have choice and control in your life, you can also influence the outcome of your problems by using your capabilities. Self-efficacy and a sense of agency are the 'dream team' for being an active participant in the direction your life takes. The quality of a resolution links directly to our sense of agency and self-efficacy. Together, they increase our ability to bounce back from adversity and recover from traumatic events, including natural disasters, terrorism and sexual and criminal assaults. Benight and Bandura (2003)

To develop a sense of agency and self-efficacy, it's an advantage to know your strengths. Programs boosting self-awareness and development of character strengths have shown improvements in self-esteem, life satisfaction and performance. Freire et al. (2018)

This chapter teaches, strength- and solution-focused thinking to help young people understand they are not helpless, weak or incapable. By tapping into our strengths and capabilities with a sense of optimism, problem solving and decision making can progress in a confident direction.

Take your time and be patient as you build one of the more complex aspects of a confident mindset. A sense of agency and self-efficacy are part of a long-term process. You are learning a complex yet achievable set of skills that will evolve across your lifetime through increased self-awareness, maturity and lots of practice.

Lesson 6.1

Feeling capable

New confident minds concept: I am capable

Someone who sees themselves as capable will respond to problems with optimism and courage. They will make decisions with confidence and clarity. Capability can build when you focus on your unique character, values and strengths.

Activity: Identify character strengths and values

You can help your students improve self-efficacy by focusing on character strengths and values. A person with even the most complex challenges carries a unique set of assets related to their authentic self. Helping young people develop a sense of optimism in who they are as a person, despite their share of difficulties, builds self-confidence and supports a balanced perspective.

A valuable method for assisting young people in figuring out what they are naturally good at is by assessing their strengths. From the age of 10 and up, students can take a strengths survey at www.viacharacter.org. By answering a few simple questions, they receive results to explain how their character strengths rank in order from 1 to 24. Younger students can visit www.positivemindsaustralia.com.au to download a set of Strength Cards describing a broad range of character strengths. Students can choose the ones they identify with from the pile.

Both of these activities focus on character, reflecting the quality of a person's heart and mind. Focusing on character is important because traditional means of success usually omit a child's character and values, focusing instead on achievement-related strengths like grades, sporting prowess and popularity. The downside of basing self-worth only on external achievements is that when self-confidence stems primarily from comparing yourself to others, it tends to bottom out when you're not at peak performance. Character strengths are steadier concepts because they are part of who you are on the inside.

Journals can be a great place for students to record their results, or perhaps make a poster as a reference point for recognising and documenting children's capabilities. Allow some time for students to reflect on when, where and how they are most likely to use their strengths. When they experience a problem, prompt them to return to their list and ask which of their strengths might be helpful. Collating a class's strengths into a bar graph is another way to celebrate the diverse range of abilities amongst your group. Research has consistently shown that using your strengths and talents is energising and essential for your well-being. Harzer (2016)

Case study: There are often more strengths in a person than difficulties

Jackie's parents always worried about him. Every difficulty his parents ever had as youngsters rolled into their one and only child, Jackie. He struggled to learn, had few friends and hated trying new things. When playing sport, if not injured from motor clumsiness, Jackie would become easily distracted, losing focus on the game.

Jackie's parents were puzzled why his teachers never seemed overly worried. When raising their concerns with the school, Jackie's parents were told that he was doing fine. Their increasing anxiety led to them visiting specialist after specialist. While the family gained many helpful ideas about improving skills that were slow to mature, Jackie showed little interest in the sessions.

Jackie came in from recess to find his parents seeking my advice on how to help him develop his social skills. Jackie ducked his head into the classroom and asked, 'Why are you here?' They explained to Jackie that I was here to help him manage his feelings and make new friends. Jackie flew into a rage, chucking his lunch box across the room. 'I hate my life!' he shouted. Then he looked at his parents and cried, 'I hate you both. I wish I was never born!'

Jackie's mother burst into tears and grabbed him lovingly in her arms. 'I know you're hurting. It's okay.' While her words were comforting, Jackie's rage only intensified. For the next few days, Jackie remained deeply unhappy and completely disengaged. These behaviours were something his parents and teachers had never seen before.

Understandably, Jackie's mum was quick to look for answers and her first reaction was to blame. 'How could you ignore his problems for so long?' she asked the principal. She focused all her attention on the rage Jackie had shown earlier, and the change in behaviour during the days that followed. The school maintained they had never viewed Jackie as a child who experienced significant difficulties. They understood that he was clumsy at times, struggled with handwriting and a little quirky in his interactions. However, from their perspective, none of these characteristics impacted significantly upon his general well-being or self-confidence.

Solution

I sat next to Jackie, who refused to look at me. I took out a set of Strength Cards and let him know I'd heard that he was creative and funny, and that it was my job to find out what other strengths he had. Jackie gave me a sideways glance, and together we went through the cards, Jackie nodding each time he felt a card described him.

Later, I spoke to Jackie regarding what he'd said about hating his life and how I hoped to help him with that. Jackie sighed, rolled his eyes and restated, 'I hate my life.' He said his parents were always asking him a million questions about whether or not he was okay. Jackie was 10 now, and he'd been listening to these questions as long as he could remember. 'Well, *are* you okay?' I asked. Jackie paused a while, then answered, 'I thought I was okay. I'm not great at lots of stuff, but I keep trying and I'm always getting better. Besides, I have other things I'm good at. I like who I am. I never hurt anyone. I try hard at school and I listen to my parents. At lunchtime I like being alone, but mum thinks I must be lonely.' Jackie burst into tears, burying his head in his hands.

The school had the advantage of understanding Jackie's strengths and could see that he had a strong sense of agency and self-efficacy. Jackie had a 'can do' mindset. He didn't blame himself or others for his difficulties. He appreciated that they were part of life. Jackie enjoyed his time at school and found meaning despite the challenges he sometimes faced.

With a smile, I congratulated Jackie on just being himself. 'Jackie; if there were more people in the world with your brain, we'd have a much happier world. You're one in a million. You don't need fixing or changing, and we are extremely lucky to have you just the way you are.'

I called Jackie's parents later that day. I explained the reason no one worried about Jackie was that they were confident Jackie was already living and learning to his full potential. I explained the value of agency and self-efficacy, and how I believed this was a more accurate indicator of Jackie's success and general health than what reading level he was at, how well he held a pencil or how fast he could run.

While it took time for his parents to relax enough and accept Jackie for who he was, without thinking every challenge needed intensive intervention; in time Jackie returned to his contented self. Jackie's parents agreed to let him flourish in his own time, and Jackie eagerly welcomed a break from all the therapy. While the interventions had their benefits, there was no rush to cover everything all at once.

Note: For many young people, early intervention is essential, and for some, therapeutic interventions are necessary throughout life. What's important is to find a healthy balance, while building internal mechanisms like a sense of agency, self-efficacy and strengths awareness for coping with life's challenges.

Role plays

Students develop their own role plays in pairs or small groups, focusing on the strengths they have identified in themselves to find solutions and resolve a problem they are currently facing. Here are a few ideas to get everyone thinking:

- You are struggling to keep on top of your homework.
- A girl who doesn't like you, follows your social media account and leaves mean messages on your posts.

- Another person in your class keeps asking if he can come over on the weekend. You've had him over before and didn't like it. He throws your stuff around if you don't play things exactly how he wants you to, and he was rough with your pet cat. One weekend, without warning, he arrives at your house saying that your parents wanted you to hang out together.

Building your character strengths

While the primary purpose of this lesson is to help students identify their current strengths, research shows that by implementing a whole school approach where the development of social emotional learning is valued and immersion in supportive relationships sustained, student strengths naturally expand. Lavy (2018) By focusing on identifying strengths, you're not only celebrating existing strengths in your students, you're helping them to build and refine new ones.

Strength of the week: A whole class/school approach to building character

You can approach character strengths development as a group by choosing a 'strength of the week'. Once you have identified the strength you would like to focus on, write it on a bright piece of card, discuss the strength and how to bring it into action, supporting each other to use it as often as possible.

For guidelines on what you might like to focus on, strengths found most desirable in a friend were honesty, humour, kindness and fairness. Those most associated with peer acceptance were perspective, love, kindness, social intelligence, teamwork, leadership and humour. Wagner (2018) The remaining strengths are valuable in other areas of life as well, so remember to include those too.

Play and games

My talents and tricks

Give everyone a chance to think of one of their talents. Whether it's a somersault, handstand, dance, wiggling their ears, speaking another language or remembering useful facts, make sure everyone gets a chance to show their talent to the others and have it appreciated and celebrated. If someone in the group can't think of a talent, do what you can to help them find one.

Lesson 6.2

Other people are not to blame for my problems

New confident minds concept: Avoiding blame, accepting responsibility and being active in problem solving

When things don't go according to plan, many people look to find something or someone else to blame. Take the example of receiving a speeding fine. Instead of thinking, 'I sped, I have a fine, end of story,' you're more likely to be mad at the police, the slope on the road that made you go faster or the fact you're so overloaded and busy you 'had to' rush. Human nature can struggle to look within during challenges, wanting to defend the ego.

It can feel more comfortable to say things are going wrong because life is unfair, or you may feel angry believing you have experienced a disproportionate amount of challenges. While it might be easier to justify in the short term, blaming others or thinking that you've been dealt a lousy hand can lead to sense of helplessness in the long term. When you clear your mind enough to see your own part in making things better, you free yourself to find solutions and move forward.

Group discussion: My part in problems and solutions

Share a time when you had a part to play in a problem and its solution. For example, perhaps you arrived late to school one day, your class wondered where you were and the principal looked you over with a puzzled expression. Taking responsibility for your part in what happened might mean merely owning up to sleeping in or forgetting to turn your alarm on. Denying responsibility and blaming others might be making up an excuse like your car broke down or your neighbour needed help or your child was sick. Taking control of the situation might involve being honest with the people you work with, and making sure you have a backup alarm so it doesn't happen again.

Together as a group, allow some time for students to 'come clean' about a time they had a conflict or a problem and placed blame or responsibility upon something or someone else. Together, explore how the situations could be resolved through increased self-awareness, self-efficacy and a sense of agency. Talk about how differently things turn out when you don't reflect on your decisions honestly, focusing instead on the unfairness of what you're going through.

Everyone makes mistakes and has areas they can improve upon. Expecting perfection from yourself and others contributes to feelings of inadequacy and defiance. In other words, if you can't see your part in anything or find it hard to own your mistakes, you will waste time and energy on unhelpful actions like blaming others, or wallowing in a funk of self-imposed hopelessness.

Role plays

Divide the group into pairs and ask students to role play the following scenarios. Have them show the resolution when problems are blamed on someone or something else, compared to solutions dependent upon personal accountability, agency and self-efficacy. At the end of each role play, ask students to compare how they would feel according to whether or not the characters held themselves accountable.

- Sisters Jemma and Ari fought several times a day. After a screaming match that ended in Jemma throwing Ari's iPod into the swimming pool, their dad brings them together to talk things through.
- Your team and your best friend's cricket team from another school are playing against each other for the first time. You're confident you can stay friendly towards each other despite the fierce competition. It turns out to be a close match, with both teams intimidating opposing players and generally being mean. After the match, you and your best friend are furious at each other. You both feel upset that each other's team was such a bad sport. Show how you could talk this through in a respectful way.
- You ate the last packet of biscuits in the cupboard. When your brother asks where the biscuits have gone, you reply, 'Maybe you should ask yourself seeing as you ate two packets last week without sharing them!' Show how you could both come clean and sort this out.
- You failed your science project because you left everything to the last minute. You tell your parents that your science teacher has it in for you and that she expects too much. Your parents aren't convinced. Show how you could take responsibility for your actions.
- You think your mum and dad are mean for taking your laptop away. They say you spend too much time on it.
- You snuck your phone into your bedroom, and you were up all night texting. The next morning you sleep in. Your parents are walking out the door, and you've missed your chance to get a lift to school. You're angry and yell at them for not waiting five more minutes. They respond by taking your phone away.

- You're having a great time chasing your sister around the house. You collide with each other, smashing your nose against your sister's head. There's blood everywhere and you're going to need stitches. You're mad at your sister and blame her for not looking where she was going. Show how you might both talk it through once you've come back from the doctor.

Play and games

Arm wrestles, rock paper scissors and thumb wars

Old favourites such as arm wrestling, rock-paper-scissors and thumb wars are a great way to connect in a relaxed and friendly way. Allow some time for everyone to have a go, making sure people play several rounds with different pairs.

Lesson 6.3

Self-efficacy in problem solving and decision making

New confident minds concept: I can influence my life

Linking problems or their outcomes to external factors such as luck, other people's actions or biased circumstances can be tempting when you're feeling overwhelmed. Developing self-efficacy is a critical part of a confident mindset. When you recognise the links between your own efforts and the resulting outcomes in your life, you gain confidence and build resilience.

When things turn out well, you're able to connect it to your efforts, strengths and support systems. When things go wrong, remember to keep things in perspective, maintaining hope you have what it takes to get through. When a person with self-efficacy sees they had a part in what went wrong, they observe it without taking things personally.

Problems are an inevitable part of life. Most of the time, they involve others in some way and need resolving through self-awareness, a sense of agency and self-efficacy to reach the best outcomes. Many conflicts involve more than one person and might need a few attempts to solve the problem in a balanced, mutually agreeable way.

Mind map and brainstorm: Self-efficacy

Revisit everything you've learned so far about developing a sense of agency and self-efficacy. The topics in this chapter can be complicated for young people to grasp, so take it slow and be prepared to go back over the information. Put simply; this chapter is about meeting problems with confidence and hope. Once you have assessed the situation in a balanced way, your strengths and capabilities can be called upon to respond proactively to whatever comes your way.

Ask the following questions or reframe them to suit your group. A mind map for each item to explore this valuable part of thinking and perceiving is ideal. If time is not on your side, then offer the questions as a brainstorm.

What does 'self-efficacy' mean to you?

What do 'helpless and hopelessness' mean to you?

Can you think of a time when something went wrong and you successfully used your self-efficacy?

Can you think of a time when something went wrong and you felt helpless and hopeless and couldn't take part in resolving the problem?

Skills like self-efficacy are game changers, but thinking habits are the hardest of all to turn around. Be patient as everyone strengthens their understanding, offer encouragement, reminders and of course, keep role modelling.

A problem-solving framework for building self-efficacy

Offer the framework that follows to break problems down into manageable chunks that involve self-awareness, self-direction and decision making.

1 Clearly identify the problem. Think about the outcome you would like to work towards. Talk it through with a trusted person or write it in your journal.

2 Consider your strengths. Tap into your existing skills and values to come up with three possible solutions.

3 Decide which solution has the best chance of working and give it a go.

4 Check on the results. What did you learn? What worked well? What didn't? Return to step 2 and try something else if you didn't have success.

5 Be persistent. Don't give up. Problems are rarely solved first try. Keep going until your problem is solved or you feel it's reasonable to move on.

Remember, practice makes perfect. Problem solving is about trying new things, making use of your skills and resources until you find a way to make things better. Try not to give up or blame others when things don't work out straightaway. Life can be complicated, but most of the time, it works out. Stay hopeful and focused while you build your sense of agency and self-efficacy and stay an active participant in what happens throughout your life.

Journaling: Problem solving

Keep the framework displayed and ask your students to think about a problem they are experiencing. Allow 10 minutes or longer to reach possible solutions using the framework. Invite students to share their responses (some will prefer not to.)

Role plays

Prompt your students to work in pairs. Solve the following problems by making decisions using the problem-solving framework explored previously.

- Jazzie was exhausted and ready for bed when her mum came into her room. 'Jazzie,' she said, 'I've just got an email from your teacher and it says you haven't been listening in class and you're two assignments behind. Can you help me understand what's going on?' Show how Jazzie might resolve this problem.

- Aiiye was full of hope for the world. When her parents decided to move to another country for work, Aiiye felt sad but also very excited and hopeful for the future. When Aiiye's sister discovered they were moving, she became angry at her parents for making them leave their family and friends. Show the kind of thinking Aiiye might have compared with her sister. See if you can find a possible solution to the problem.
- Benito said yes to every invitation from his friends. He would not only turn up to things, he'd try really hard to be the life of the party. This worried his parents, who knew Benito found social situations exhausting. Benito loved his friends but found himself doing more than he could cope with. In the end, he was left with little energy to do other things. How might Benito solve his problem?
- Jalina had a good life. She went to the local school, enjoyed learning and had lots of friends. Her parents had just put in a pool, and a new puppy was arriving soon. Jalina's friends often said how lucky she was to have such a wonderful life. Despite all this, Jalina complained a lot and was never happy with what she had. She always wanted more, and if anything didn't go her way, she felt like her world was falling apart. Eventually, Jalina's friends started calling her spoilt and said they were tired of listening to her complain all day. Show how this group of friends might solve the problem together.
- Alex had never passed a science test in his life. No matter how hard he tried or how much tutoring he had, Alex always struggled. Despite his challenges, day after day, week after week, Alex turned up to science with a smile on his face. Consider his mindset and show the problem-solving steps Alex might be using to stay positive and engaged with science, in spite of his learning difficulties.
- Jerome was in trouble a lot at school, and he often complained about how strict the principal was. Show a conversation between the principal (who is trying to help Jerome use his strengths and take responsibility for his actions) and Jerome (who thinks the principal is unfair). How might Jerome and the principal go about problem solving together?

Stories about problem solving and decision making

Being solution-focused helps children and young people influence the direction their lives take. Making decisions based on a strong sense of agency and self-efficacy gives students the best chance of moving forward with confidence and stability.

Help students learn more about what good problem solving and decision making looks like by regularly sharing stories about well-known people who calmly and constructively problem solve their way through hardship. To get you started you can read about people like Malala Yousafzai (human rights activist), Jacinda Ardern (prime minister of New Zealand), Richard Branson (Entrepreneur with learning difficulties) and Albert Einstein (1921 Nobel Prize Winner in Physics, who struggled socially through school). All resolved their unique challenges and could not have done so without a sense of agency, self-efficacy and optimism.

Play and games

Let's blame the world

This activity is designed to help students have fun reflecting on what blaming others and the world looks like.

Seat everyone in a social circle. Students are asked to come up with a typical problem someone their age might experience (or use the prompts that follow). The person beside them replies, employing a way to blame the world or someone else for the problem. For each problem aim for three possible 'blames' stemming from a sense of helplessness and hopelessness. At the end of a 'blame' round, invite students to come up with a constructive response to the problem that stems from a sense of agency and self-efficacy.

- I forgot to do my homework and it's due today.
- I left the gate open and my dog ran away.
- I don't have enough money to go to the movies with my friends.
- I dropped my laptop and now it's broken.
- I lost my part-time job.
- I was really late home from school and forgot to text my dad, who was really worried about me. Now he's angry.
- My teacher got upset when I handed my assignment in late, and she wouldn't listen to my excuses.
- I fell off my bike and broke my wrist. Now I can't go to the swimming carnival.
- I missed the bus to school this morning.
- I failed my maths test.
- I slept in and got to school late.
- I broke my best friend's remote-controlled car.
- I am behind with all my assignments.
- I forgot to bring my sports uniform.
- I was getting a lunch order but forgot my money.
- None of my school uniforms got washed over the weekend and now I have nothing to wear.

Lesson 6.4

Decision making with a sense of agency and self-efficacy

New confident minds concept: Making confident decisions by seeing yourself as capable and in control

Knowing how to problem solve and make decisions raises a young person's sense of agency, self-efficacy and overall self-esteem. Including these skills as part of the curriculum correlates with higher self-esteem in school-age children. Park and Park (2012)

While the problem-solving framework includes decision making within the process, many young people don't draw the connection between the two forms of resolution. This lesson will further refine their decision-making skills.

Case study: Staying hopeful

Bree was a straight-A student. She was full of creativity and curiosity and always a pleasure to be around. She was confident but never showed off about her achievements. What people didn't know was that Bree really struggled with her learning. She had to put hours of intense effort into things other students seemed to find easy. No one believed Bree when she tried to explain the difficulties she was experiencing. Finally, her maths teacher suggested she see someone to assess her learning.

The assessment confirmed that Bree had learning difficulties. The news hit Bree hard. She burst into tears and told everyone there was no hope for her. She was never going to get anywhere and would not be able to keep up with her school work anymore. Bree's response to the assessment surprised and worried everyone; after all, she had always managed her study by working hard, remaining positive and keeping focused on her strengths.

Bree started coming late to class, and she quickly fell behind with her homework and assignments. Her behaviour in class became disruptive and disrespectful. Bree was invited to attend a meeting in a hope to do some problem solving and make a decision about what to do next.

Solution

Bree and I started by brainstorming together. I asked, 'Before your diagnosis, what got you through all the challenges you were experiencing?' Bree had a long think and began describing all the problem-solving methods and adaptations she had put in place to manage her learning. Her explanations showed that she already had a strong sense of agency and self-efficacy. Although Bree didn't take this brainstorm very seriously, I knew we were planting the seeds that would help her once again see herself as worthy and capable. That knowledge was already there, but had been overlooked in the aftermath of being labelled with a learning difficulty.

Over the following weeks, Bree and I talked about her learning difficulties while I empathised with her ongoing grief and frustration. As Bree debriefed about her experiences, I was able to redirect her towards all the problem-solving and learning strategies she was making use of before her diagnosis. Bree had always known something wasn't quite right, and now as a result of her assessment, she was finally developing an understanding of what had been making things tough, and how to get help where and when it was needed.

Together, we spent time problem-solving and making decisions about what to do next. Bree decided to refocus her efforts as if she had never been labelled. She was going to emphasise what she *could* do, rather than dwelling on what she couldn't do *yet*. She was going to talk to her parents about her sense of grief and ask for their support. She made a conscious effort to once again not let her learning difficulties define her or get in the way of her goals.

Over time, Bree reconnected with her preexisting sense of agency and self-efficacy. She felt proud of her efforts again and knew she wasn't the only person experiencing a learning difficulty. She returned to her problem-solving framework and the decisions she had always made to manage her learning challenges. One of the more effective strategies was encouraging Bree to help younger students with similar challenges learn creative problem solving and decision-making skills. Her maths teacher connected her with a high-achieving senior student with similar learning difficulties. This gave Bree a mentor to look up to while caring for others, which tapped into her compassionate nature.

Steps to good decision making

Ask your students to think of as many things they feel are essential for making helpful decisions. For inspiration, offer the following framework. You might notice, it's similar to the problem-solving framework earlier.

1 Identify what the decision is that you need to make.

2 Consider the possible outcomes for each decision (i.e., the likely pros and cons).

3 Choose the decision that seems most reasonable.

4 Review your decision. What did you learn? How did it turn out? If it turned out well, remember your choice for next time. If it didn't, go back to step 2 and try something else.

Don't forget to keep practicing. From small decisions to more significant decisions, this is a skill that develops over time and with practice.

Brainstorm: Remembering decision making and problem solving are possible in times of hardship

In the heat of a challenging moment, it can be hard to remember you can take part in problem solving and decision making instead of feeling helpless and hopeless. When you're upset or taken by surprise, it's often the emotional part of your brain that takes over. It's hard to switch your rational thinking back on and remember you have the mental tools to get you through any challenge.

Begin a brainstorm with your students. Share with your students anything that helps you remember to use your sense of agency and self-efficacy, or take inspiration from the ones below:

- Wear a friendship bracelet as a reminder to 'be friends with your strengths'.
- Tell yourself before you get out of bed each morning, 'I'll have a great day today. Nothing can stop me.'
- Ask for someone to help you remember not to get stuck when you reach a problem, but to look within and problem solve together.
- Create a secret signal with an adult who can show you the sign to remind you to stay calm and problem solve.

Create short role plays where you're in the heat of a problem and you use your favourite reminder to stay out of a hopeless and helpless mindset. The more you practice, the better your brain will be at using those skills when you are truly in need. Ideas from the role plays below will get you started, and remember to use your own ideas too.

Role plays

Divide students into pairs. Use the following problems to help build their sense of agency and self-efficacy 'muscles'. Students show how they use a decision-making reminder to stay out of helpless and hopeless mindsets.

- Your parents have forbidden you from going to a friend's house because of his bad behaviour at your home recently. Your friend asks you to come over and you really want to go.
- You don't understand maths. You don't get along with your maths teacher and you don't want to ask for help. You are close to failing the subject and are thinking you will quit.
- You're always fighting with your older sister over shared clothes and bedroom space.

- You feel lonely at school. Everyone seems to have found their 'group', but you feel lost and alone. You want to try a different school.
- Your teacher is mad at you for mucking around in class. You plan to do the right thing, but get such a good reaction from your class when you misbehave that you kind of like it. Your teacher asks you to focus on your work, or he will need to meet with your parents and the school principal.
- You desperately want to be a student leader but you're known for being a 'troublemaker'. You're impulsive, you talk in class and can be dishonest. You've also been caught saying rude things about teachers behind their backs. Despite this, you believe you would make a good leader. What could you do to give yourself a better chance at being nominated?
- You want a dog, but your parents don't. You're sure you're ready for the responsibility of a pet. Your parents say there's no way you're ready based on the empty vegetable patch you begged them for and the messy state of your bedroom. You want to prove them wrong. How will you do it?
- You just got into heaps of trouble for something that had nothing to do with you.
- You've lost your brand-new and very expensive football. Your parents look super mad.

Play and games

Human pyramid

Human pyramids are a reminder of everyone's strength and creativity. Start by asking the group to decide how to best layer the pyramid according to each other's personalities, height and strength. Allow time to discuss and only step in with suggestions if necessary. Inspire them by showing appropriate YouTube clips that show other classes and groups of young people creating a human pyramid. For the reluctant students, try giving them different roles like supervising, photographing and advising. Human pyramids are not for everyone.

If you're concerned about this activity, you can instead help them practice their confidence by spelling out words or creating shapes using their bodies by laying out on the floor together. If you're working one on one with a student, use this time to get them to teach you one of their talents as a reminder they have many. Be sure to teach them one of yours.

Lesson 6.5

Poise

New confident minds concept: Staying composed during problems and decision making

Poise (your ability to remain peaceful, composed and neutral no matter what is happening around you) is vital for a confident mindset. Poise supports productive problem solving and decision making by helping students sustain a sense of peace during emotional storms. It's about being the point of clarity and calm despite how others behave around you. Adding one emotional storm to another will always make things worse. By teaching students as early as possible to regulate their feelings and not react to provocation, you are contributing to a crucial part of their emotional intelligence.

Group discussion and mind map: Equanimity

While younger students might not fully retain the word 'poise', introduce it and encourage its addition to their vocabulary. In the centre of the board, write 'Poise' or 'Being peaceful in an emotional storm'. Discuss a time you stayed calm in an emotional storm and how it helped you make good decisions and find a solution to a problem. Next, allow plenty of time to hear from students about their unique ways of not reacting while keeping a clear head no matter what's happening around them.

Journaling

Enjoy some time writing calming thoughts and practices that could help you and your students maintain equanimity during an emotional storm.

Poise mentors

Brainstorm people in your community who are calm and composed no matter what's happening around them. Role models are essential for all young people and highlighting those with excellent emotional management skills will help draw their attention towards healthy behaviour patterns.

Some students need a more focused approach to mentoring and will not feel comfortable actively seeking out mentors themselves. It's important students have people to look up to and see as calm, responsible, resilient and capable. Through these connections, students have people in their everyday life to admire and learn from.

Role plays

Split students into pairs. Their task is to show how maintaining poise in a chaotic or challenging situation can lead to better outcomes. Students can demonstrate their ability to remain in a state of poise despite the urgency of the problem, high conflict or emotion around them.

- You're cooking family dinner on the gas cooktop with your younger sister. She has left her drawing next to the cooktop and it catches on fire. The flame grows fast and your sister is screaming hysterically.
- Your new puppy has just wriggled out of her collar and is running towards the main road in peak hour traffic.
- Your best friend is hysterically crying and shouting at you, accusing you of something you didn't do.
- You're late for your grand final football game. Your parents can't find the car keys and everyone is yelling at each other.
- You're looking after your younger brother in the supermarket. In an instant he runs off squealing, begging you to chase after him. As he runs towards the tomato sauce bottle shelf, you know this is not going to end well.
- Your mum loves her brand-new phone. You're desperate to check it out, but she will not let you near it. When she isn't looking, you grab it, sneak it into the bathroom and check it out. You hear her coming and pop it in your pocket ready to walk out calmly and put it back. You drop it and it smashes. Yikes!
- Your expensive drone just smashed into someone else's very expensive drone. It was an accident, but the other person is starting to get very upset.
- You can't find your money box. There's almost $200 in there. Your parents have been reminding you to put it in the bank. They're going to be furious.
- You're at the beach when a freak wave washes over you. Your dog gets swept out to sea.
- Your parents argue and your two brothers are crying. They think your parents are going to break up and you're worried too.

Play and games

Being calm in the eye of a storm

Not everyone will feel comfortable playing the 'eye' so allow students to nominate themselves and use your judgment on how loud and chaotic you let things get.

The idea in this game is for one person to sit in the middle of the social circle, cross-legged and peaceful. They are the 'eye' of the storm. Closing their eyes, they focus on their breathing and try to remain in a state of peace and harmony. Everyone around them creates a little noise and chaos. They might repeatedly cough, sing, shuffle around, drop things or play music louder than usual. The idea is for the 'eye' to remain calm. When they lose their calm, someone else gets a turn. This game takes a lot of emotional regulation, not just for the 'eye' but for the storms as well! If your group is not emotionally mature enough, exchange this game for another and leave it for another time.

References

Bandura, A. 1988 'Perceived Self-Efficacy: Exercise of Control through Self-Belief.' In *Annual Series of European Research in Behavior Therapy*, Vol. 2, edited by J. P. Dauwalder, M. Perrez, and V. Hobi, 27–59. Lisse, NE: Swets and Zeitlanger.

———. 2001. 'Social Cognitive Theory: An Agentic Perspective.' *Annual Review of Psychology* 52, no. 1: 1–26.

Benight, C. C., and A. Bandura. 2003. 'Social Cognitive Theory of Post-Traumatic Recovery: The Role of Perceived Self-Efficacy.' *Behavior Research and Therapy* 42: 1129–1148.

Bortolotti, L. 2018. 'Optimism, Agency, and Success.' *Ethical Theory and Moral Practice* 21, no. 3: 521.

Chemers, M. M., Hu, L. T., and Garcia, B. F. 2001. 'Academic Self-efficacy in First Year College Student Performance and Adjustment.' *Journal of Educational Psychology*, 93, no. 1: 55–64.

Freire, T., I. Lima, A. Teixera, M. R. Araujo, and A. Machado. 2018. 'Challenge: To Be+: A Group Intervention Program to Promote the Positive Development of Adolescents.' *Children and Youth Services Review* 87: 173–185.

Harzer, C. 2016. 'The Eudaimonics of Human Strengths and Well-Being.' In *Handbook of Eudaimonic Well-Being*, edited by J. Vitterso, 307–322. Basel, CH: Springer. doi: 10.1007/978-3-319-42445-3_20.

Lavy, S. 2018. 'A Review of Character Strengths Interventions in Twenty-First-Century Schools: Their Importance and How They Can Be Fostered.' *Applied Research in Quality of Life*. doi: 10.1007/s11482-018-9700-6.

Niemic, R. M. 2014. *Mindfulness and Character Strengths: A Practical Guide to Flourishing*. Boston: Hogrefe.

Park, J., and J. Park. 2012. 'The Study of the Relationship between Young Children's Decision-Making Ability and Self-Esteem.' In *Computer Interaction, Signal and Image Processing and Pattern Recognition, Communications in Computer and Information Science*, Vol. 342, edited by T. Kim, S. Mohammed, C. Ramos, J. Abawajy, B. H. Kang, and D. Slezak. Berlin: Springer.

Peterson, C. 2006. 'The Values in Action (VIA) Classification of Strengths.' In *A Life Worth Living: Contributions to Positive Psychology*, edited by M. Csikszentmihalyi and I. Csikszentmihalyi, 29–48. New York: Oxford University Press.

Wagner, L. 2018. 'Good Character Is What We Look for in a Friend: Character Strengths Are Positively Related to Peer Acceptance and Friendship Quality in Early Adolescents.' *Journal of Early Adolescence*. doi: 10.1177/0272431618791286.

CHAPTER 7

Managing challenging feelings constructively and responsibly

Introduction

Managing challenging feelings can be difficult. They often bring waves of physical and emotional energy, unhelpful thoughts and general helplessness. To gain mastery over emotional regulation takes self-awareness, acknowledgment and acceptance of your feelings. It also requires conscious commitment and practice.

There are many teachable ways to manage challenging feelings constructively and responsibly. Rational thoughts and impulse control tend to switch off in the heat of the moment. For this reason, it is vital to plan ahead, know the early warning signs and familiarise yourself with your emotional triggers. You also need to be taking enough care of your health and well-being to help maximise your resilience in the face of adversity.

Knowing how to manage challenging feelings has many long-term benefits, including improved comfort and security, increased earning potential and greater socioeconomic status. Côté, Gyurnak and Leveson (2014) When you consider how emotions can pass from one person to the next, it's easy to imagine how being able to handle your feelings constructively, might place you at a social advantage. People tend to seek out people who can keep their feelings in perspective most of the time and avoid those who transfer heavy emotional weight onto others or lose control over their emotions at the smallest of frustrations. This does not mean challenging feelings and conversations are abnormal. It's a typical human experience to go through a broad range of feelings and to work through them with the support of others. The key point is that challenging feelings should not be squashed and ignored, nor should they be thrown onto the shoulders of others.

People who have less control over their thoughts and feelings experience overwhelming anger more often, putting their physical and psychological health at risk. Anger has been shown in studies to increase mood disturbance and heart rate while lowering immunity. Upbeat emotions such as compassion and joy have the opposite effect. Rein, Atkinson and McRaty (1995) Heavy emotions need to firstly be acknowledged, accepted and then exit the body in healthy and constructive ways to protect your psychological health. Thaik (2014)

Lesson 7.1

Intend to have positive feelings

New confident minds concept: Plan to adopt a positive outlook

Practicing optimism and consciously planning to have a positive outlook helps build balanced emotions from within without relying on external events to 'make you happy'. Choosing a hopeful outlook and recognising the good in yourself and others can promote emotional stability. Many people do this by starting their day with an intention such as 'I'm going to have a great day,' or 'Today I will notice what's going well.' When emotions get challenging, they repeat their intention. Practicing a positive outlook consistently every day can rewire your brain to feel happier and interpret life in a more positive way. When you're in a state of contentedness, you're more likely to manage your feelings constructively. Achor (2010)

There are many daily practices that bring about positive feelings of happiness and hope. While the goal is not to stamp out difficult emotions, seeking out experiences that bring about happiness improves your mood and overall ability to regulate your feelings.

Happiness practice 1: Daily gratitude

Deliberately bringing your attention back to things during your day that went well floods your brain with a sense of joy, hope and contentment as if you were experiencing these events all over again. Practicing gratitude strengthens your neurological pathways for happiness. A recent study focusing on people with anxiety and depression found the group that added daily gratitude practice to their counselling had significantly higher levels of longer lasting happiness and well-being than the group that had counselling alone. Wong et al. (2018)

Students can adopt a daily gratitude journal to draw or write about three positive things they experienced, or three things that went well. A classroom routine at the end of each day where everyone states their top three experiences is another way to practice gratitude. Another method is scanning the day to identify who in your day helped and supported you. From the farmers and grocers who made your breakfast possible, to the teacher who brought you new information, to the friend who joined you at playtime and the caretakers who loved and nurtured you. Focusing on the people that make your life better is a wonderful way to embrace gratitude.

When gratitude skills grow with practice and support, consider sharing the benefits with your students' families. To take gratitude to a deeper level, students might enjoy spending a couple of minutes each day writing or drawing in detail about one or more things that went well. Others enjoy writing to people thanking them for their kindness and support.

The more often gratitude is practiced, the better it is for everyone's overall health and happiness. Scientists have found that an attitude of gratitude changes the molecular structure of the brain's central nervous system. Grey matter gets a good workout with gratitude practice and there's potential to be significantly calmer and less reactive as a result. Moran (2013)

Happiness practice 2: Be active

Difficult thoughts and emotions can build up quickly, generating excessive energy and feelings of unrest. It is becoming increasingly recognised that commitment to at least 30 minutes of movement a day has a similar outcome to taking antidepressants for a person with mild to moderate depression. Other benefits in the same study showed increased protection against heart disease and diabetes, as well as improved sleep and lower blood pressure. A meta-analysis of 455 patients by the University of Thessaly in Greece found exercising for 20 to 30 minutes each day reduces anxiety and depression. Morres et al. (2018)

Help your students identify ways they can be more active every day. Many young people struggle with motivation to exercise for a range of reasons including poor coordination, low muscle tone and a sense of inadequacy during competitive sports. Consider adding 5 to 20 minutes of high-energy play and exercise into your students' routine to boost their opportunities to be active.

Happiness practice 3: Daily acts of kindness

Chapter 2 explained the benefits of interacting with kindness and compassion. Creating goals for children and young people to engage in one act of kindness each day can improve their sense of happiness, making it easier for them to control their own emotions. In other words, being kind to others helps you feel good. Cutler (2018) Being kind and generous has also been shown to activate a part of the brain called the striatum, which responds to pleasure from rewarding experiences. Moll et al. (2006)

Adolescents focusing on acts of kindness to build a more positive and considerate identity have shown significant improvements in overall well-being. Cotney and Banjerjee (2017) You can help young people see themselves as kind by drawing attention to and acknowledging even their smallest acts of kindness. You can engage the whole class or school in a random act of kindness challenge to bring the whole community together in a similar way.

Happiness practice 4: Spend time in friendly company

Social connection as a primary contributing factor to happiness and good health was explored in chapter 1 on healthy relationships. Remind your students of the importance of making time for friendship.

Another example of relationship quality impacting upon a person's ability to regulate emotions is spending large amounts of time with moody or excessively negative people. While you can't expect to avoid challenging personalities, it's important for children and young people to understand how easily hopeless attitudes can be absorbed, even if you have high levels of hopefulness yourself. Research has shown that the impact of being around consistently moody people negatively affects cardiovascular and mental health. Friedman and Martin (2012)

Help students identify people who are hopeful, kind and uplifting while coming up with a self-protection plan for when they are around people who aren't; for example, managing stress before and after seeing them and using confident self-talk to cope. Trying to see the person through the eyes of compassion can also be helpful; however, this can be harder in the short term if the person is being intentionally hurtful or challenging. Spending time with people is vital for happiness stability and maintaining a healthy emotional state. Helping young people remain in tune with the kind of friendships they foster is important.

Happiness practice 5: Watch what you watch!

With the news at your fingertips through mobile technology and social media, it's hard not to know when something goes wrong in the world. Watching just three minutes of negative news in the morning was found to increase a person's likelihood of reporting an unhappy day six hours later by 27 percent. Achor and Gielan (2015) Watching negative images such as those in violent video games have shown an increase in aggression and a decrease in empathy and prosocial behaviour. Anderson et al. (2010)

Journaling: Self-awareness about watching what I watch

Allow 10 minutes for students to reflect on the programs, games and social media they watch. Remind them about the research from happiness practice number 5. Students can write down their favourite shows, video games and social media.

- Do you think you, your family and friends have healthy habits around what they watch on TV and online?
- Would you like to make any changes for yourself around what you watch?
- Do you notice yourself feeling moody when you've been gaming for a while?
- How do you feel after watching TV for long periods of time?

Students can write about their observations and experiences, and explain their reasons.

Students don't need to share their answers. If they do, it's important not to be judgmental about what they like or tell students what they should be watching or playing. Instead, use your expertise and experience to craft the conversation in a way that helps them make their own mind up. While you can't control what your students watch or the games they choose to play, offering them information, encouraging self-awareness and allowing them time to reflect upon their emotional states is a step in the right direction.

Case study: Practicing happiness

Meaghan was only in year two when I first met her. She rarely smiled, carrying tension around with her wherever she went. She struggled to make friends and didn't seem to enjoy any aspect of school or family life. Meaghan was in the habit of complaining about everything. She saw the world as a glass half empty.

Meaghan's teacher felt I might be able to guide her towards a more positive and resilient mindset, given that she was developing a reputation amongst the other students as someone to avoid. The children in her class not only felt uncomfortable in her presence, they felt frustrated that she never seemed to share in anyone else's joy.

Solution

Meaghan had no previous experience in working on her thinking skills. She was interested in learning how to intentionally choose optimism over pessimism, and how her neural connections strengthen through the skills she practices most often.

The first step was to develop a daily gratitude routine. Although at first she found it hard to think of things that were in fact working well, over time she became more confident in her ability to identify the positives in her life. Staff knew Meaghan would find it hard to practice this at home, so they structured in regular opportunities during the school day.

On as many days as possible, the whole class engaged in gratitude and optimism exercises. After two weeks of consistent practice, the change in Meaghan's behaviour and self-expression was clearly visible. More tools such as kindness goals, supporting younger students, and increasing physical activity were added. Meaghan also learned about mirror neurons and the impact her smiles and positive outlook had upon others.

As Meaghan's self-awareness and confident mindset grew, she appeared visibly happier and approached interactions with her classmates more optimistically. While Meaghan continues to be pessimistic at times, the table has undoubtedly turned and she is seen smiling and reacting to challenges in a positive way most of the time.

Play and games

Catch my smile

Students work in pairs. They take it in turns to be 'Smiler' and 'Serious'. The Smiler looks into their partner's eyes with a genuine smile for 30 seconds. The Serious player on the receiving end has to use all their energy to stay serious and avoid smiling back. Students take turns to play both roles. Loads of laughs usually follow, and many children without prompting will relate this activity to what they have learned about mirror neurons.

Lesson 7.2

Breath awareness and breathing techniques

New confident minds concept: Focus on your breathing

You can have complete, conscious control over your breathing. Deep, steady and diaphragmatic breathing calms your sympathetic nervous system, allowing thoughts to balance, feelings to settle and behaviour to adjust. Breathing is also a technique to draw the mind back when it's rushing ahead too fast. Breathing sounds simple because it is. You can regulate your breathing by paying attention to it. When you're paying attention to your breath, you're more likely to be both present in the moment and increasingly self-aware.

Brainstorm: All about breathing

Begin by gaining information about what your students already know about breathing techniques. Many young people have attempted to use breathing techniques in the past and may have preconceived ideas about them. Often, they have either not practiced enough or have tried them and found them unhelpful. That's okay.

Asking students more about their previous experiences is one way to help them let go of past disappointments and open their minds to trying breathing strategies again. Empathise with and show understanding for students who might feel suspicious about its effectiveness. It's important to remain understanding and connected if you want to make progress.

Brainstorming questions:

- Have you ever tried breathing techniques?
- What have you found helpful about breathing techniques?
- What didn't you find helpful about breathing techniques?
- Do you know about any research showing breathing as an important tool for handling challenging feelings?

Activity: Breathing practice

The first time you teach your students the skill of breathing into their diaphragm, set aside at least 20 minutes to half an hour. Once they know how to do it, you can pause for breathing breaks before each lesson and it should only take a few moments.

Laying comfortably on the floor is one way to get the hang of slow, deep diaphragmatic breathing. Children can place one hand or a teddy, toy or book on their stomach, with their other hand resting gently on their chest. Students can then focus their attention on breathing deeper into their diaphragm, keeping their chest relatively still as their stomach moves up and down.

Many people develop a reliance on shallow or superficial breathing into the upper lungs. Effective diaphragmatic breathing used to enhance self-regulation relies upon deep breaths into the abdomen. Once everyone is focused on the movement of their breathing, turn the lights off and, if you wish, play soothing music. You might even like to introduce a symbol like a gong, a candle or aromatic scents that mark the beginning of a relaxing breathing period.

Breathing meditation

1 Close your eyes and notice the sounds around you.

2 Place one hand/toy/teddy/book on your stomach and the other hand on your chest.

3 Quietly focus on your breath going in and out, making your stomach rise.

4 See if you can slow your breathing down a little.

5 In your own time, breathe in and out, in and out.

6 Keep noticing your breath. Every time you start thinking about something else, refocus on your breathing. In and out … in and out.

7 Enjoy the quiet for a while. You don't need to think about anything but your breathing.

4-7-8 breathing activity

Another tool to build your breathing skills is the 4-7-8 technique. Weil (1998) Give your students this instruction:

Close your eyes and notice your breath. Is it fast or slow? How do you feel?

In a moment, I'll count to 4 as you breathe deep into your diaphragm, making your stomach rise. Next, hold your breath as I count to 7. Finally, breathe out for 8 seconds through tight lips.

Don't worry if you take less time than I count. This skill takes time and practice.

Let's begin.

1 Breathing in (1…2…3…4)

2 Hold (1…2…3…4…5…6…7)

3 Breathing out through tightened lips (1…2…3…4…5…6…7…8)

Offer a few rounds of this breathing. There are many other forms of relaxation breathing you might like to try. Encourage your students to teach the class any that they already know.

Case study: Learning to interrupt unhelpful thoughts with breathing practice

At the ripe old age of eight, Joel was one of the biggest worriers I'd ever met. Frown marks crisscrossed his forehead and the look in his eyes was that of someone profoundly preoccupied with stressful thoughts.

Joel struggled with learning and making friends, and life rarely went according to plan. If he wanted to make a new friend, things would usually start okay but after a few weeks of social clumsiness and awkward communication, Joel would inevitably and unintentionally hurt someone else's feelings. New friends would lose interest because Joel spoke in a monotone voice, talking exclusively about topics that only he was interested in. He was still trying to learn many of the most fundamental social-emotional literacy skills.

Every night Joel went to bed thinking and worrying about all the things that had happened during the day and all the things that might go wrong the next day. He rarely got a good night's sleep and the dark circles under his eyes were very telling.

Joel's teachers and family noticed he was starting to hold his breath and stare out into space during class time. At playtime, Joel wandered around alone in his thoughts and stopped reaching out to make friends. His eyes were always tired, and he would often fall asleep during quiet reading time.

Solution

I began by teaching Joel and his class how to focus on their breathing to keep calm and take their minds off their thoughts. I explained how everyone got 'hijacked' or 'interrupted,' by their thoughts sometimes—especially when something difficult was happening in their life. Breathing can be easier for children to control than their thoughts. With this in mind, I talked them through how to pause and focus consciously on diaphragmatic breathing. Joel's class teacher agreed to try focused one-minute breathing sessions to the start of each lesson. She found it made a noticeable difference in how well students were able to concentrate on their work and manage their feelings when faced with a challenge.

When working with Joel on his own, he would tell me all about his overactive mind. He said that unless he was watching TV or playing video games, he just couldn't switch off all the thoughts and worries that constantly buzzed through his head. I let Joel know that he wasn't alone and that lots of children had similar experiences. I told him that managing his racing thoughts wouldn't always be this hard and things would improve as he learned new skills over time.

Together, we practiced our diaphragmatic breathing in and out, counting 1...2...3 as we slowly inhaled and 1...2...3 as we slowly exhaled. Initially, Joel would get frustrated as the thoughts would return even before starting the exhalation, but I reminded him this would happen for a while. Until he was doing the breathing practice more often than the worrying, things couldn't get better. Brains make connections for whatever gets the most attention. Joel understood.

It was hard work. Joel wore a neat little friendship bracelet his dad made to remind him to breathe when his feelings and thoughts got challenging. His teachers established a secret signal that only Joel knew about, where they would walk past his desk and gently touch his shoulder if they noticed a distracted, faraway look in his eyes. This helped Joel to focus on his breathing rather than becoming preoccupied with his thoughts and feelings.

While breathing was only one part of the support provided to Joel, it helped build a solid foundation for his continued development in emotional regulation. It enhanced his self-awareness and increased control over his own responses. In time, Joel's behaviour improved as he learned new skills in how to get along with others, and he even began sleeping better.

Sleeping better through conscious breathing

Focusing on your breath can help you fall asleep at night, especially if you tend to stay up worrying or thinking things through more than is necessary. When you can't fall asleep, bring your mind back to your breath. Talk through each breath you take (breathing in, breathing out, and continue). Every time a thought enters, go back to thinking about your breath until you fall back asleep.

Role plays

The following role plays pose difficult situations that with a calm response won't end in conflict or challenging behaviour. Prompt students to incorporate being breath aware into the role plays.

- Your sister is confronting you about taking her Bluetooth speaker to school without asking permission.
- Your brother lost your head torch that he borrowed for school camp.
- Your teacher tells you to stay in at lunch, accusing you of something you didn't do.
- Your parents ask you to clean up your bedroom, but you've come home from school feeling tired and stressed and don't want to do it.
- You lost your house keys and no one's going to be home for another hour.
- Someone says something really mean to you in front of everyone.

- You're off to get a new jacket. On the way your mum puts a limit on how much you're allowed to spend. She has no idea about how much a new jacket really costs.
- You did something wrong at school, and you're lying awake in bed worrying about a meeting with your parents and principal in the morning.
- You just got caught cheating on a test.
- You have to give a talk in front of your class. Some of the kids up the back are calling out some mean remarks before you get started.

Play and games

Feather, balloon, ping-pong or bubble blowing

Hand out some bubble mix, or for older students, feathers, balloons or ping-pong balls. Let everyone work in small groups or pairs. The idea is for each student to blow their chosen item in the air or along a flat surface at the same time. Players compete to get ahead of one and other, becoming more aware of what conscious breathing feels like along the way.

Lesson 7.3

Being present and mindful to handle challenging feelings

New confident minds concept: Being present and mindful

Through mindfulness and presence, you can improve your state of mind and strengthen a confident mindset. Mindfulness is the nonjudgmental acceptance of an individual's present state of awareness. Mindfulness reduces stress and rumination, improving emotional regulation. Gu, Strauss, Bond and Cavanaugh (2015)

For most people, only seconds after planning to stay in the present, their minds immediately begin to wander. Thoughts of past regrets or future worries can weigh heavily upon our shoulders. It's generally more convenient to be in the past or future than the present. By nature, our minds unconsciously chatter. If something has gone wrong, it's easy to fall into the pattern of repeatedly going over what happened and what might happen next.

Hopeless thoughts about the past and future are powerful, having a significant influence upon your present experience and state of mind when they are overactive or unregulated. To be present and mindful, you need to acknowledge the thoughts that bombard your mind, then let them go, returning your attention to what is presently in front of you. If you're with another person and you're fully present with them, your connection can expand. Your presence without distraction makes people feel seen, heard and understood. A distracted companion, on the other hand, makes others feel rushed, dismissed and disconnected.

Generally speaking, children are pretty good at existing in the present. For example, when playing, they become easily immersed in play. As children develop, they may become increasingly aware of their social, sporting or academic status (or lack of) in schools, clubs and sports teams. Caught up in their own performance, thinking only of the outcome or what other people may be thinking of them, can make it harder for children to live in the moment and appreciate the present. It's important to acknowledge that children who are naturally more anxious may develop higher than usual levels of mind chatter, becoming caught up in excessive worry sooner and more often than other children of similar age.

The flood of information through devices, email, messenger and social media is a constant reminder that even if you're still for a moment, the rest of the world isn't. Most people are fighting the urge to step out of the present to find out what's happening around them. The impulse to sneak a look at your device can be hard to resist, constantly interrupting the stable focus in your mind. Mindfulness and presence have become more critical than before in the fast-paced, continually changing world. Anxiety, stress and disconnection are made worse by our preoccupation and worry about what's happened in the past and what might happen in the future.

This lesson will help you and your students learn a range of simple ways to start practicing presence and mindfulness. When life is busy, your phone is buzzing or you're going through a tough time, it can be challenging to slow down, pause and enjoy being in the moment. Share your own experiences of trying to stay in the present. Tell your students about how your mind wanders back to past experiences or jumps ahead to future concerns or things that are sitting on your 'to do' list. Let them know that being present and mindful is not easy or natural at first for anyone. This is because humans are thinkers and thoughts come flying into our minds involuntarily all day long.

When you learn to ignore worrying thoughts and focus on what you're doing right now, you can make the most of every interaction and experience by giving it your full, undivided attention.

Activity: Present awareness

Take your students outside. Sit down, with eyes closed. Guide your students to place their hands on their lap and start to focus on their breathing, 1…2…3 over and over. Their task is to put their hand up when their thoughts interrupt their attempt to focus on their breathing. When they return to the present by being mindful of their breath, they place their hand down.

After five minutes of building their awareness around being in the moment, invite everyone to open their eyes and discuss what it felt like to try and stay focused on the present while practicing their breathing.

Activity: Present, mindful, awareness of your surroundings

This activity can follow on from the previous one or be done another day, outside or inside. The idea is to help everyone attune to their senses and surroundings, remaining both mindful and present.

Encourage students to notice the breeze against their skin, the smells in the air, the sounds that surround them and anything else that is happening right now. When thoughts interrupt their focused attention, students can bring their mind back to the present by focusing on what they see, hear, feel and smell.

Daily 'pause for presence' breaks

One short daily break where everyone pauses to be present can help students transition into a calm state of awareness, soothing their minds and recharging their batteries. Through regular practice, neural pathways are strengthened, helping children to instinctively focus on the present when thoughts and feelings threaten to overwhelm them.

When might your class best respond to a daily pause? In the morning? Before lunch or after recess? Before intense learning periods? Could the whole school pause for presence at the same time each day?

- Begin your pause for presence breaks with something to indicate a change in atmosphere, like lighting a candle, playing soothing music or tapping on a gong.
- Everyone closes their eyes. Lead everyone to breathe in and out at their own pace. As they breathe in, they count 1...2...3 and as they breathe out, they count 1...2...3. The counting is done in their mind, not out loud.
- Once everyone is in a solid breathing rhythm, ask, what can you hear? What can you smell? What can you feel? What can you taste?
- Add new presence activities to your 'pause for presence' breaks to extend their skill base.

Mindful eating

Mindful eating is another way of teaching presence. Provide everyone with something small like a raisin or piece of dark chocolate. Lead everyone to look at the piece of food, consciously observing its appearance. Now direct everyone's attention towards smelling it and savouring the scent. Next, students focus on touching it. What does it feel like in your hand or on your fingertips? Pay attention to the details. Finally, students can place it in their mouth, noticing every bite, enjoying the flavour and feeling until it's gone.

Mindful drinking

Mindful drinking activities are similar. You can do this with water, milk or tea. Again, you start by looking, then smelling, then tasting. Another mindful experience might be passing around a flower, lemon or candle (anything fragrant).

You won't have time to extend your 'pause for presence' breaks every day, however, schools I've worked with who have allocated 5 to 10 minutes each day report a shift in their students' sense of well-being, mood and behaviour.

Brainstorm: Pause for presence

As with any new skills or ideas you introduce, it's important children feel they have a part to play in its design and implementation. If they engage in well-being and resilience tools only because they 'have to' or were 'told to' then it's unlikely they will take it on board wholeheartedly and embrace the potential benefits. To explore their thinking, offer the following questions:

- What do you think of 'pause for presence' breaks?
- What might you like about them?
- What don't you like about them?
- What differences might people notice after pausing for presence?
- What would you do differently (if anything)?
- How could we make it better?
- How often should we practice this skill?

Pause for presence poster

To help everyone remember that being present can calm you down, consider making a banner or poster to hang up in the room (for a free downloadable 'Pause for presence' banner, please go to www.positivemindsausatralia.com.au).

Role plays

To stay calm when you're feeling upset takes time. When challenging feelings come your way, your primal brain has a habit of taking over and can dive straight in to a fight, flight or freeze response (explained in more detail later in this chapter).

When you practice pausing and counting to 10, you allow helpful thinking to flourish. You are less likely to say or do something you later regret. What makes this most effective is when you synchronise counting with slow, deep breathing. The following role plays will give you plenty of practice doing this.

- You have a ton of homework tonight and you feel completely overwhelmed. Your thoughts are consumed with worry about how you will get it done in time.
- You've just been suspended and you realise that you won't be able to go on school camp.
- After you've been playing in the rain, your parents tell you off for coming back inside covered in mud.
- Your parents have a flat tyre and you're late for school.
- Your little brother gets you in trouble for doing something you didn't do.
- You fall in the middle of the 100 metre sprint on sports day. You were just about to win and you can feel the tears starting well up.

- The waiter apologises wholeheartedly that they forgot about your meal. The rest of your family are eating theirs. You're upset and want to tell the waiter off.
- You can't find your assignment on your laptop and you didn't back it up. It's due tomorrow and you're sure it got deleted.
- Your brand-new watch breaks. It's under warranty, but you can't find the receipt.

Case study: Slowing down before reacting

Renee was always quick to react. She had a strong sense of social justice and held high standards not only for herself but for everyone else. Renee's moral compass was on overdrive and she couldn't bear comments that seemed uninformed or intentionally cruel. If someone mistreated another person, Renee would jump in and attempt to save them. It was during these moments, her rules about humanity and kindness went out the window—much to her embarrassment afterwards. She would lose any ability to regulate her feelings and she would say and do things she later regretted. These impulsive reactions led to regular conflict with her peers and began to impact on her ability to maintain friendships.

One afternoon, Renee noticed another student say to her sister, 'You're weird.' Understandably, Renee was furious. She leaped up, stood above the little girl and entered into an aggressive monologue, highlighting everything she disliked about her. The child began to cry, and her friends called the teacher over. Despite attempts to smooth things over, the child who had been the target of Renee's withering critique said that she found Renee overwhelming and was going to complain to her parents about what had happened. This was not the first time she had been on the receiving end of one of Renee's sudden outbursts.

Solution

Renee's parents were called in, and it was agreed Renee needed to learn how to handle her conflicts more respectfully and constructively. Renee learned how to pause and count to 10 before saying or doing anything when she found herself getting upset. Renee agreed that when given the cue, 'Give me 10', she would do her best to settle down and focus on her breathing, giving her brain the best chance to switch on and think clearly and responsibly.

Renee was also taught how to repair relationships on the occasions where she hadn't been able to pause and count to 10. Renee and her class practiced asking each other, 'How can I make it better?' This approach to relational repair then became part of everyone's dialogue.

Through time and practice, Renee improved at taking 10 seconds to breathe and pause. It meant she needed less intervention from teachers because she was getting into less trouble each day. Renee also learned to tell herself, 'I am here' and to pay attention to her senses—the breeze on her skin, the smell in the air, the sounds in her ears, and the sights in front of her. This simple strategy went a long way towards helping her stay in the present and regulate her emotions more effectively.

When breathing wasn't enough and her thoughts were relentless, Renee was reminded to move away from the situation and ask for help from an adult. Renee also started using a journal—firstly, to write her thoughts down before she went to bed. Next, to record three things she felt thankful for from her day. After a couple of months, Renee was doing better overall. Through support from home and school, she continues to improve and make new and longer lasting friendships.

Play and games

Pause for presence mindful walking

> **Please note:** You might prefer to choose a mindful eating or drinking activity here.

Take everyone outdoors where there is plenty of space. As everyone begins walking, guide students to pay full attention to the experience of walking. Introduce the Zen saying, 'When walking, walk.' Share how helpful it can be to stay mentally present with what you're doing and to reject the wandering mind from sabotaging the experience.

Lesson 7.4

Developing confident self-talk to manage challenging feelings constructively

New confident minds concept: Confident, encouraging self-talk

When faced with an onslaught of overwhelming emotions, what goes on in children's minds is rarely confident and may lead to feelings of helplessness. Sometimes destructive thoughts are about past regrets or worries about the future, rather than confident, constructive ideas to help navigate the current situation.

Learning to talk to yourself hopefully and proactively, is an essential part of remaining calm in the face of adversity. Telling yourself, 'I am calm. I can do this,' or 'I have what it takes to handle this' is more constructive than 'I'm freaking out,' 'This is too hard,' or 'I'm not good enough.'

Overwhelming feelings like anxiety often follow pessimistic thoughts. When thoughts are confident, or at least neutral, more pleasant feelings will naturally follow. With practice, anyone can choose a different thought.

Brainstorm: Confident self-talk

To develop self-awareness about your style of self-talk, pose the following hypothetical problem:

Imagine you've just heard that you won a family trip of a lifetime. It's somewhere you've always wanted to go. Two days into celebrating your prize, your family receives a phone call. Something is not right. Your dad looks concerned as he strokes your mum's back gently. Then she starts to cry. There was a mistake and you weren't the prize winners after all. You won a basket of goodies but not the three-week luxury overseas holiday you were all looking forward to. You're stunned and your head is spinning.

Begin a brainstorm with the following questions:

- What thoughts might you have if this was you?
- What feelings from the past might come back to bother you?
- What thoughts about the future might you have?
- What hopeful or courageous thoughts could you use in this situation?

Role plays

Students engage in the following role plays on their own, presenting them to the group showing both confident and hopeless self-talk.

- You are at the doctor's waiting to see if you can come out of your 'moon boot' after breaking your foot.
- You have handed in your last assignment. You worked hard and you need to get a B to pass the subject. You won't get the results for three more days.
- You're at the vet with your sick dog. You worry he's not going to make it through the night.
- You are waiting to see if you've been accepted in to the school drama performance but are worried you won't get a role.
- You are due to give a talk to the class. Public speaking is not your strength and you're worried you're going to bomb out.
- Your mum calls to say she's been admitted to hospital after a minor accident. You panic, worrying that she won't be okay, but you can't go and see her until your dad gets home from work.
- Your dad hasn't come to pick you up from school. This has never happened before.
- You left your calculator at home and you have a big maths test after lunch.
- You are excited about going on excursion. When your teacher gathers the group, he notices your parents haven't signed the consent form. When they call your parents, there's no answer. It's likely you can't go with the class.

Play and games

Compliments and encouragement

Allow everyone a moment to sit together in a social circle and encourage everyone to think about each other positively, looking for the best in each other One by one, each person stands up. If they wish, they can state a problem or challenge they have. If they prefer to remain quiet, that's okay. The idea is that group members offer words of encouragement and positive feedback to the person. Remind students to say 'thank you' at the end of each suggestion, even if they don't believe what they are hearing.

Remind everyone that what they have just heard about themselves is also what they can tell themselves when they are experiencing challenging feelings. Many teachers with whom I work have implemented compliment circles at the end of each day to reconnect everyone and finish the day on a positive note.

Lesson 7.5

Talking back to hopeless thoughts when you have challenging feelings

New confident minds concept: Talking back to destructive thoughts

No matter how good you are at being calm, present and mindful, destructive or hopeless thoughts are inevitable. Learning to respond calmly and train yourself back to the present moment through conscious breathing and engagement with what's in front of you is a valuable starting point. Once you can do that, you can interrupt the thoughts by answering back and sending them away. You might recall learning about this in chapter 3 on the inner critic.

Brainstorm: Talking back to your thoughts

Ask your students about the kinds of thoughts they have when they experience difficult or uncomfortable feelings. Thoughts can be destructive and powerful making it difficult to keep calm. Talking back to them is one strategy to regain control and separate yourself from what your mind is telling you. Note: Some hopeless thoughts can alert you to something that is genuinely wrong or be a reminder to talk to someone and ask for help if you're struggling. You don't ignore them immediately, you hear what they have to say. If they are saying something that is untrue, destructive and derailing you from being your best, they are probably created by anxiety and are not helpful.

Examples of how to talk back to destructive and hopeless thoughts:

- You're back again. I'm not listening.
- I don't believe you.
- I'll think about you later. Right now, I'm doing my work.
- I'm more than my thoughts. You're not who I am.
- I'm calm and peaceful.
- I am brave.
- I am willing to give things a go.
- I am not wasting my time thinking about this.
- Things usually turn out fine.
- You're not here to help so I'm thinking about something that will.

Doing this isn't easy; it takes lots of practice. It might even feel strange for a while. In time, everyone can do this. If you're keen, make a poster of these statements as a reminder for your group.

Role plays

In the following role plays, break the group into pairs, with one person sitting behind the other, acting as the destructive or hopeless self-talk. The person listening then responds out loud with confident self-talk. If you're working one on one with a student, you can be the one with the problem and they act as the confident voice.

- You haven't made friends at your new school.
- You weren't invited to a friend's party.
- You've been invited to two places at the same time on the same day and want to do both but that would be impossible.
- Your family just missed out on a beautiful home they put an offer in for. You are tired of looking at houses, and feel like nothing like this will ever come up again.
- Your grandparents have asked if you would make their 50th wedding anniversary cake. It means a lot to them, but you think there's no way you can make something good enough for such a special occasion.
- You've been invited to be ambassador for the environment at your school. You care a lot about the environment, but you've never taken on a role like this in your life.
- You're about to audition for a role in a TV series. This is your dream opportunity. Lots of your friends are also competing for the role.

Play and games

Egg and spoon race

This old favourite will get some energy out and help everyone practice handling their feelings. Feel free to use something less messy on your spoons (or boil the eggs to eat afterward). This game can be played together in one line or as a relay.

Explain that the goal is to run from one point to the other without dropping the egg. If you lose the egg before reaching the end, you need to run back to the start and try again.

Lesson 7.6

Building a toolbox of strategies to manage challenging feelings

New confident minds concept: Feelings need to go somewhere useful

Feelings come with a wave of energy and it's important that energy is directed somewhere constructive. Some people bottle their feelings inside, while others are more demonstrative and show their emotions often. Some people tend to fall into the habit of expressing their emotions by taking their feelings out and dumping them on others. This alleviates the pressure building inside them. It's important to move the energy that can spill out with challenging feelings in constructive ways so you are not hurting yourself or others.

Acknowledge feelings without resistance

Challenging feelings are naturally unpleasant. Resisting them or thinking they should not exist will only create more tension inside, keeping them brewing for longer. The first step in dealing with your feelings constructively is to accept their presence. You might name the feeling in your mind and acknowledge its presence. An example of a thought you might employ is, 'I am feeling jealous.' This is healthier than pretending you're not feeling what you are feeling or resisting the presence of the uncomfortable feeling. Once you have acknowledged its presence, you can do something with the energy it brings.

Cultivate positive emotions

Some of Barbara Fredrickson's (2004) most celebrated research demonstrated that cultivating positive emotions fuels psychological resilience, reduces negative emotional arousal and improves well-being. Remind your students what they have learned about the value of gratitude and savouring positive moments by giving them focused and present attention. Giving to others and engaging in kindness are other ways to cultivate positive emotions not only in yourself but in those around you.

Find something to focus on when feelings get challenging

When you're feeling upset, sometimes it's hard to think about anything else. Paying attention to a focal point nearby is one way to distract yourself from your thoughts and feelings. Focal points might be a tree, a candle or a painting—anything pleasant or neutral to look at.

When you notice your mind wandering or becoming negative and anxious, find your focal point then describe it mentally, in detail. When challenging thoughts and feelings return, revisit to your focal point. Many people find it much easier to maintain focus in this way rather than generating and sustaining positive thoughts.

Ask your students to look around the room to find potential focal points that might help manage challenging feelings. Once they've chosen one, allow some time to pay attention to it and its details for a couple of minutes.

Another way is by using grounding techniques like the 5, 4, 3, 2, and 1 (original source unknown). Focus on: five things you can see, four things you can hear, three things you can touch, two things you can smell and one thing you can taste. This is a great way to interrupt destructive thoughts and replace them with something to do.

The heartbeat, pulse or breath as a focal point

A personal, portable focal point is with you all the time—your pulse, breathing rate or heartbeat. Finding a pulse and concentrating on it, getting moving, then touching your chest to feel your heart beating, or attending to your breathing are all focal points that can help you return to the present and manage difficult feelings.

Find flow

'Flow' is the feeling of being happily immersed in what you're doing, so much so you lose all sense of time. You're engrossed in an activity you love and engage in with ease, for the pure sake of enjoyment. Csikszentmihalyi (1990) Art projects, creative ventures and hobbies are examples of endeavours that can put you in a state of flow. Allow the group time to identify, brainstorm and journal about the kinds of activities that put them in flow. Encourage students to think of ways they can spend time in flow every week.

Savour the moment or savour a pleasant experience from the past

It's easy to leap through life's moments without paying full attention to them. Savouring is about noticing, embracing and enjoying what's in front of you. Making the conscious effort to immerse yourself in what you're doing as well as savouring moments from your past through joyful reflection, allows you to experience a fuller range of joy in everything you do. Fredrickson's (2014) research highlights the value of savouring to create and maintain positive feelings.

Change routines on purpose

Most people have a predictable daily routine, from daily walking and familiar driving routes to visiting certain shopping spots or cafes with friends. If your routine offers little room for variety, you can find yourself zoning out into 'automatic pilot'. Find ways to change routines and help keep things interesting. For many people, adding variety or encouraging change can lift their mood and make them feel more energised.

Encourage students to reflect on their daily routines and journal small ways they can change things around a little. Here are some subtle ways you can make small changes every day to get you started:

- Play music while having a shower.
- Eat breakfast outdoors.
- Take a different route to school.
- Pretend to be a tourist and notice new things in your town or city.
- Buy groceries somewhere out of your neighbourhood.
- Learn a new skill or Google a topic you know nothing about.
- Talk to someone in your class you've never properly connected with.

Identify and prepare for your triggers

When learning to master challenging feelings, planning is crucial. Developing self-awareness by figuring out what bothers us can help us face tricky situations with increased confidence. For example, if you identify that you are agitated by other people's dishonesty, acknowledge the feeling, accept it and plan a response for when it does happen. You can't control other people, but you can learn to manage your own thoughts, feelings and reactions.

Journaling: Planning for your triggers

Allow time for students to write down what triggers their challenging feelings and what helps them to calm down. Support children to develop a handful of confident self-talk statements like 'I am calm,' or 'I can handle this,' as well as thinking up ways to respond, like moving away from the trigger, focusing on breathing or finding a peaceful focal point.

Help them get to know the recurring situations they are often triggered by, before they enter them, so they do so with self-awareness and focus to regulate their feelings responsibly, For example, if a young person has identified she is triggered when losing at sport, before the game begins she prepares herself by saying in her mind, 'I can handle losing by focusing on something else and breathing calmly.' Next time she finds herself triggered by a particular situation, increased self-awareness and careful planning gives her the best chance to stay calm and respond in a thoughtful manner. Emotional regulation takes conscious effort and lots of practice before it becomes routine.

Play and games

Tug of war

Find a long, thick rope for this activity. Divide the group into two. Mark a central line that needs to be crossed by the group in either direction to win. On 'go' each team pulls the rope in opposite directions with all their might. This is another great game for being in the moment, focusing on one thing at a time.

References

Achor, S. 2010. *The Happiness Advantage: The Seven Principles that Fuel Success and Performance at Work*. New York: Currency.

Achor, S., and M. Gielan. 2015. 'Consuming negative news can make you less effective at work'. *Harvard Business Review*, September 14.

Anderson, C., N. Ihori, B. J. Bushman, H. R. Rothstein, A. Shibuya, E. L. Swing, A. Sakamoto, and M. Saleem. 2010. 'Violent Video Game Effects on Aggression, Empathy, and Prosocial Behavior in Eastern and Western Countries: A Meta-Analytic Review.' *Psychology Bulletin* 126, no. 2: 151–173.

Côté, S., A. Gyurak, and R. W. Levenson. 2014. 'The Ability to Regulate Emotion Is Associated with Greater Well-Being, Income, and Socioeconomic Status.' *Emotion* 10, no. 6: 923–933.

Cotney, J. L., and R. Banerjee. 2017. 'Adolescents' Conceptualizations of Kindness and Its Links with Well-Being: A Focus Group Study.' *Journal of Social and Personal Relationships* 36, no. 2: 599–617.

Csikszentmihalyi, M. 1990. *Flow: The Psychology of Optimal Experience*. New York: Harper Perennial.

Cutler, J., and R. Banerjee. 2018. 'Five Reasons Why Being Kind Makes You Feel Good—According to Science.' *The Conversation*, February 27.

Fredrickson, B. L. 2004. 'The Broaden-and-Build Theory of Positive Emotions.' *Philosophical Transactions of the Royal Society B: Biological Sciences* 359, no. 1449: 1367–1378.

Friedman, H. S., and L. R. Martin. 2012. 'The Longevity Project: Surprising Discoveries for Health and Long Life from the Landmark Eight-Decade Study.' New York: Penguin Putnam.

Gu, J., C. Strauss, R. Bond, and K. Cavanaugh. 2015. 'How Do Mindfulness-Based Cognitive Therapy and Mindfulness-Based Stress Reduction Improve Mental Health and Wellbeing? A Systematic Review and Meta-analysis of Mediation Studies.' *Clinical Psychology Review* 37: 1–12. doi: 10.1016/j.cpr.2015.01.006.

Moll, J., F. Krueger, R. Zahn, M. Pardini, R. de Oliveira-Souza, and J. Grafman. 2006. 'Human Fronto-Mesolimbic Networks Guide Decisions about Charitable Donation.' *PNAS* 103, no. 42: 15623–15628.

Moran, J. 2013. 'Pause, Reflect and Give Thanks: The Power of Gratitude During the Holidays.' *Huffington Post*, October 29.

Morres, I. D., A. Hatzigeorgiadis, A. Stathi, N. Comoutos, C. Arpin-Cribbie, C. Krommidas, and Y. Theodorakis. 2018. 'Aerobic Exercise for Adult Patients with Major Depressive Disorder in Mental Health Services: A Systematic Review and Meta-analysis.' *Depression and Anxiety Journal* 36, no. 1.

Rein, G., M. Atkinson, and R. McRaty. 1995. 'The Physiological and Psychological Effects of Compassion and Anger.' *Journal of Advancement in Medicine* 8, no. 2: 87–105.

Thaik, C. 2014. 'Why laughing is good for your health.' *Huffington Post*, March 16.

Weil, A. 1998. *Eight Weeks to Optimum Health*. New York: Random House.

Wong, J., S. McInnis, L. Toth, and P. Gillman. 2018. 'Does Gratitude Writing Improve the Mental Health of Psychotherapy Clients? Evidence from a Randomized Controlled Trial.' *Journal of Psychotherapy Research* 28, no. 2: 192–202.

CHAPTER 8

Well-being to uphold a confident mindset

Introduction

The Oxford Dictionary defines well-being as 'the state of being comfortable, healthy, or happy'. Many young people, particularly those who struggle to learn and make friends, may not identify well-being as a predominant emotional state. Adding well-being to the social-emotional curriculum is still relatively new and often undervalued. A recent study suggested the middle years are in particular need of well-being and social-emotional learning. It points out that, above all, students need to be involved in the process to truly create impact. With so many experts researching what is necessary for a young person's development, at times, children and young people's opinions about what they need to flourish have been missed. Redmond et al. (2016) It is important to keep this in mind when tailoring a well-being approach for your unique setting.

By now, you have planted many valuable seeds for a confident mindset. Students have learned about healthy relationships, constructive problem solving, conflict resolution, compassion, emotional intelligence, optimism and more to uphold a more hopeful way of thinking, feeling and behaving.

Inevitably, there will be many times you forget how to handle challenging situations and your responses might not be consistently constructive. Keeping calm will be more of a struggle on some days and you will naturally find yourself thinking negatively from time to time. This is okay, just don't stay there too long. Social-emotional behaviour is changeable but not without a fight. Old habits tend to die hard.

By adding well-being to *The Confident Minds Curriculum*, you will be better prepared to rise to challenges and responsibly manage difficult feelings. Without well-being, improvements can be short-lived. You will access your best thinking, mood and behaviour when self-care and well-being are prioritised. Well-being is the foundation for better emotional health and resilience.

Mental health and well-being are nourished by self-compassion and self-care as well as involvement in character strength and personality-related endeavours. This final chapter is the scaffolding to uphold a confident mindset. By encouraging healthy well-being, a springboard for a confident mindset is at your fingertips.

A different structure to previous chapters follows. Rather than dividing topics into individual lessons, this chapter offers essential well-being tips that can be added into your own and your students' day as needed.

Case study: The missing link

After three months of working closely with me to build a confident mindset, Tara had everyone confused. She could tell you logically what she needed to do during hardship, what her triggers were, what her inner critic said, and she even knew how to stay present. Two or three days into a calm patch would usually end with Tara falling into an emotional heap. She felt devastated, declaring one day, 'It's not working!'

Solution

I acknowledged how hard Tara had been working on her new skills and what a brilliant job she was doing despite the challenging moments. I reminded Tara how thinking skills were hard to retrieve during times of stress and that despite what she thought, she was calmer than ever before, handling things well most of the time. I mentioned I had noticed she seemed preoccupied when I observed her in the yard. She didn't fully understand what I meant, but she said, 'I always feel yuck.'

I realised we'd left the final phase of *The Confident Minds Curriculum*, 'the well-being check', out of her plan. The reasoning at the time was Tara's school already had a well-being program in place, so I thought it best not to overlap.

What I failed to see was that Tara couldn't generalise new skills unless they were related explicitly to her specific circumstances. Although she was learning about well-being in class, she wasn't applying it independently. She didn't have her own well-being goals and there was no process to monitor her. It's one thing to learn the lessons and be encouraged to use them, it's another to remember when and how to apply them.

When well-being was placed under the spotlight, it didn't take long to see that Tara didn't have the necessary foundation for learning, thinking and behaving well. She wasn't sleeping anywhere near enough; she didn't exercise and a heavy after-school schedule didn't allow time to rest and recuperate. She needed help to map out a tailored approach to her well-being.

I arranged a meeting with Tara's parents to explain how Tara's long-term academic and social emotional achievement relied on healthy well-being. Tara couldn't get on top of this without their help. While they understood Tara might benefit from more down time and an earlier bedtime (without a device in her hand), they worried about reducing after-school tutoring and were frustrated she didn't listen when they asked her to go to bed.

I empathised with their challenges and let them know these concerns were common for most parents. I felt that Tara's challenges couldn't be overcome without these adjustments, so along with Tara, we worked together on a plan for earlier bedtimes and more time outdoors being active. Tara's parents met with her teacher to see if the extra tutoring was giving more stressors than benefits at this stage.

In time, and with a few adjustments, Tara's well-being increased. Her stress levels reduced and she became more capable of applying the skills she had embraced in her heart but couldn't use because she was too sleep deprived and overworked.

Well-being tool 1: Ask students what they need for their well-being

While this chapter offers several ideas for healthy well-being, it's essential to identify what is uniquely relevant and helpful to you and your students. There isn't a one size fits all approach to well-being. A student with many friends compared to one who is more socially isolated will require different well-being measures. Other factors like personality, temperament, strengths, difficulties and interests will also have an impact on what contributes to a person's well-being. What one person finds energising and rejuvenating, another person might find exhausting and emotionally taxing.

Journaling: What I need for my well-being

Read your students the well-being definition from the introduction to this chapter. If you have another definition you prefer, use that.

Once you are sure everyone understands what well-being is, ask the following questions:

- What is important to you?
- When do you feel healthy?
- When do you feel happy and relaxed?
- What energises you?
- What exhausts you?
- What helps your sense of well-being grow?
- What gets in the way of your well-being?
- What support do you need when things get tough?

Allow some time for the group to discuss their answers. Next, pass a piece of paper to each student to record anonymous responses to this question:

- It would help my well-being at school if...

Once you have everyone's answers, use this as 'data' to discuss at your next meeting with colleagues. This child-centred approach will help you support the unique well-being needs of your students.

Well-being tool 2: Grow your emotional intelligence

New confident minds concept: Emotional intelligence matters

Unlike IQ, emotional intelligence (EQ) can be taught and improved. Goleman (2011) Emotional intelligence comprises of self-awareness, being attuned to other people's feelings and knowing how to manage your thoughts and feelings in healthy ways. Mayer and Salovey (1997) Healthy social connections with others are essential for well-being. While how much social interaction between one individual to the next might be on a spectrum, a disconnected and emotionally unbalanced person is likely to report lower well-being and have compromised health. Bar-On (2012) Without strong emotional intelligence 'muscles', your relationships with others are more likely to experience conflict.

The Confident Minds Curriculum has explored emotional intelligence skills in detail in previous chapters. In context of well-being, the following framework will help you and your students reflect again on the necessary groundwork for strong emotional intelligence, crucial for well-being. Seven key aspects to a healthy EQ are the primary focus in the framework that follows based on Goleman's (2006) research and recommendations.

A seven-step emotional intelligence framework

Each step can be complicated, particularly for children who naturally struggle with social-emotional learning. Remember that developing social and emotional skills is a lifelong process that takes conscious effort and practice. One way to reduce the complexity is by setting goals to work on one small aspect of the framework at a time. A class, group or whole school/community/health care setting approach will always bring you the best results. Through encouragement, gentle guidance and opportunities to practice, the skills will become easier for everyone to apply.

1 **Feelings awareness:** Learn to pay attention to your feelings. When feelings arise, practise asking yourself, 'What am I feeling?' Naming your feelings is an integral part of handling emotions constructively.

2 **Feelings acceptance:** Accept your feelings—they visit for a reason. They might be telling you something isn't right and needs your attention. Alternatively, they might be telling you your thinking needs rethinking! Wishing them away or fighting them won't work, no matter how hard you try.

3 **Do something with your feelings:** Do something helpful with uncomfortable feelings so you can think clearly again. You might need to get moving or slow down. Either way, meet your emotions with something useful.

4 **Pay attention to other people's feelings:** Notice what other people feel. Are they frustrated? Jealous? Angry? Sad? Accept their feelings even if you don't agree with them. They are allowed to have their emotions. Doing this shows empathy. Empathy builds healthy relationships.

5 **Welcome other people's thoughts and feelings:** Respectfully welcome (or at the very least, acknowledge and accept) other people's opinions, thoughts and feelings. You don't have to agree to be friendly. If this gets hard, try imagining how you might feel if you were them and saw things their way.

6 **Communicate and behave calmly:** Talk and behave in understanding, nonjudgmental and respectful ways. If you don't know how to do this or find this confusing, let a trusted adult know so they can help you learn this skill.

7 **Be compassionate about other people's feelings:** Be caring and helpful when someone else is upset or going through a tough time. This is known as compassion. If you're too upset yourself, go back to steps 1, 2 and 3 to slow down. If your feelings take over and you do something hurtful, do what you can to make things better with the person. Be kind to them and to yourself.

Role plays

During the following role plays, students practice building emotional intelligence by using the framework and trying to include all seven steps.

- Your friend has sent you a rude and hurtful text message.
- Your friend has invited you over this Friday night. You want to go, but you have already made plans with someone else.
- Your parents read your phone messages and are unhappy about a conversation you had with some friends. You're furious about them reading your messages without asking.
- Your friend argued with your closest friend. They both come to you for advice later that day.
- You asked to borrow your sister's bike to ride to school. She agreed, but when you are about to leave, you see her riding off to school on it. How will you handle this?
- You have a personality clash with someone in your class. You know better than to judge her or expect her to be more like you, but you are struggling to be kind to her. She has just joined you for lunch and is particularly chatty, talking about rabbits—her favourite animals.
- You desperately want your friends over this weekend. There are a lot of exciting things happening in your social life and never enough time to talk it through during the week. You ask your parents if you can have everyone

over on Saturday night. They immediately say no because you haven't been keeping up with your chores or homework. You're upset.

- You find a note that your brother wrote about you after you teased him about his pimple. He writes about how you're never nice to him and that he hates you. You decide to bring it up with him.
- Your friends pop by on the weekend. They ask you to come to the café for a milkshake. You have a different group of friends on their way right now to pick you up for a milkshake.
- A boy in your class gets teased. You often step up and tell people to leave him alone. You go to the bathroom and see the door shut and cries coming from inside. You know the boy sobbing is the one that gets teased. You call out and ask if it's him. He tells you, 'Go away—what would you care?'

Journaling: Keeping emotional intelligence strong and healthy through conscious practice

Just as one visit to the gym won't mean you walk out with instant muscles, building emotional intelligence takes time and practice. Allow some time to reflect on situations where people might practise their emotional intelligence. Set some individual or group goals to practise emotional intelligence often, to carve new neurological pathways that build this critical part of your thinking.

When you notice students using any part of their emotional intelligence, compliment the specific behaviour and the good feelings it brought about. Identify situations that trigger emotional reactions and remind students before those moments to call upon their emotional intelligence to handle whatever lies ahead. Before competitive sport is an example of when tempers might flair for some young people. Reminding them just before that everyone playing wants to win and see the game played fairly.

For younger students, a poster such as 'Our class is emotionally intelligent' serves as a nonthreatening reminder that emotional intelligence is valued within the group.

Feelings awareness check-in

To build emotional self-awareness, consider adding a 'feelings check-in' throughout the day. This might be as simple as asking your students to briefly close their eyes and bring their attention to their feelings by asking themselves, 'What am I feeling right now?' Many schools use laminated emojis, providing a 'How am I feeling?' record sheet for each student. When students come in and out of activities, they can post the emoji that best represents what they are feeling at the time. Not only does this help build their emotional self-awareness, it provides you with insight into how individual students are feeling throughout the day. This can be a helpful predictor for behaviour.

Play and games

Pass the frown

Seat everyone in a circle. Ask for a volunteer to practice a 'fake' frown. The leader starts by frowning at the person next to them who then replicates the frown, passing it on until everyone in the group has received a frown. This is a fun way to explore emotions, their contagion and how hard it can be to control them—get ready for lots of laughs.

Well-being tool 3: Find a well-being 'shake off'

New confident minds concept: Shake off and reset after a problem

Have you ever noticed a duck shake off its feelings after a squabble with another duck? Dogs engage in a similar 'shake off' after interacting with another dog or feeling stressed. Animals are present beings and have in-built mechanisms to move on after a problem.

Animals in conflict tend to move towards each other to 'have it out'. They move about rambunctiously for a while. Soon after, they resolve things—or agree to disagree, heading off in opposite directions. When they are far away enough from each other, they 'shake off' what just happened and calmly move on to the next thing, like nothing ever happened.

Humans, on the other hand, tend to get agitated and stay upset for hours, days and in some cases, years. Without some kind of emotional 'shake off', painful feelings can linger, becoming harmful and lowering well-being.

Journaling: Shake off and reset

Allocate time to ask students what they've observed in pets and animals around them in terms of moving on from conflict. Once you're certain they understand the concept of a 'shake off', it's time to figure out their own version to help leave conflict and problems behind.

Here are some ideas to get you inspired:

- Confident self-talk. Tell yourself, 'I'm done with this, no more.'
- Take a short, brisk walk.
- Mindful breathing.
- Think about your happy place.
- Create a mantra like 'I am calm' or 'I am peaceful' in your head.
- Drink some water.
- Laugh.

- Stretch, tense and relax your body.
- Enjoy a cup of tea or warm drink.
- Do star jumps.
- Write in a journal.

Well-being tip 4: Find meaning and purpose in everyday things

Meaning and purpose is a crucial aspect of healthy well-being, lowering stress and anxiety and benefiting psychological health. Hadden and Smith (2019) When people think of finding meaning, they often overcomplicate things, searching for a 'why' for their entire life. Finding meaning doesn't have to be complicated. Meaning can be found in almost anything when you're focused and present with what's in front of you. Paying full attention to what happens in your day and around you (instead of thinking about what you need to get done or worrying about the past) is one way to add more meaning to your life.

Journaling: Finding meaning and purpose

Draw your students' attention to what they already have in their lives that brings meaning and purpose. Ask, 'What is going well in your life?' This is more optimistic and constructive than beginning from a state of inadequacy, where you search for meaning from scratch.

Heading towards finding meaning and purpose can be as simple as asking your students questions like 'What are the things you most love doing?' Allow plenty of time for journaling and discussion.

Finding meaning and purpose is ultimately up to the person. If your mind focuses on what you don't have instead of gratitude for what you do have, you may find yourself constantly searching for something new to give you meaning. The trouble is, once you find that, your focus will change again to the next thing that you don't have. Meaning is best sourced by noticing and celebrating what you already have and spending time enjoying it.

Well-being tool 5: Music

There are many known scientific benefits to listening to music, including its contribution to pain relief and improving your mood. Onevia-Zafra (2013) Listening to uplifting music shows changes in your brain's pleasure centres, as well as releasing the feel-good hormone dopamine. Increases in dopamine have even been noted in people who are just thinking about music. Instrumental music shown to make you feel happy are referred to by researchers at the Montreal Neurological Institute as 'chills' songs. They are songs that gave the listeners 'chills', causing the brain to release dopamine. They include 'Claire de Lune' by Debussy; 'First Breath After

Coma' by Explosions in the Sky; and 'Adagio for Strings' (Parade of the Athletes version) by Tiësto. Salimpoor, Beovoy and Zatorre (2011)

Playing uplifting background music in your home, classroom and therapy setting supports a positive mood, contributing to emotional well-being. From upper primary through to middle and high school, music is often part of a young person's identity. Making a class playlist with everyone's favourite songs is one way to build group well-being.

A study using the Australian Unity Wellbeing Index identified six areas of music consumption that improved well-being. They were listening to music, dancing, singing, playing an instrument, attending concerts and composing music. People engaged in high levels of music consumption rated higher on levels of happiness and well-being. Within this group, the leading scores were from those regularly attending concerts and going out dancing. This result was linked to the social connection both activities tended to bring with them. Weinberg and Joseph (2017) Finding ways to increase music consumption can help improve your own and your students' well-being.

Mind map: Music

Share with your students the six areas of music researched to contribute to healthy well-being. Allow them a moment to reflect, then write 'Music and well-being' in the centre of the board. Students can explore the benefits of music through their mind map, as well as explore ways to incorporate its benefits into every day.

Play and games

Old favourites like musical chairs and musical statues will be fun for younger students. Older students might just enjoy the opportunity to listen to a favourite radio station or playlist for 10 minutes while journaling gratitude or personal reflections.

Well-being tool 5: Move

Research has demonstrated the value of daily exercise to improve happiness and well-being. Zhang and Chen (2018) You don't have to join a gym, jog for miles or climb to the top of your closest mountain. Just try to add some form of movement into each day. The human body is designed to move and serves you best when it gets enough movement. It's often the last thing anyone wants to do after a long day working, learning or engaging in difficult things; yet movement can be your daily reset button that makes all these challenges easier to live with.

Journaling: Movement

Explain to your students there is plenty of scientific evidence to show the benefits of daily exercise for their physical and mental health. Not everyone feels motivated to move and some young people might feel embarrassed if the discussion about movement exposes this to their peers. Talk briefly about how daily movement is not only important to your cardiovascular health but also to your well-being and happiness. Show empathy for how hard moving can sometimes be, allowing some time for students to engage in private journaling. Then ask the following questions:

- What can get in the way of being active?
- What can help get people out the door to be more active?
- How do you feel after you have been active?
- How do you feel when you haven't been active?
- If you were to add some time for movement in your day, what might be the best time?

As a group, you might also like to consider adding movement into your day.

Well-being tool 6: Take time to check your well-being

Gather your students and ask, 'Do you take time to relax and do things you love?' Give examples of the kinds of things you love to do and share whether or not you make the time to do them. Explain you're going to take a well-being check together to tune into what they love and find a way to include those things more often. Encourage them to choose things that don't cost money or require travel to experience (otherwise their list may end up being impossible to enable, as much as a trip to Paris would nourish everyone's well-being!).

Write 'Ways to well-being' on the board. Encourage students to brainstorm what contributes to their daily well-being. Exercise, sport, friends, family, music, nourishing food, sleep, love and hobbies will hopefully find their way onto the list.

Finally, take out journals so students can record what is most meaningful to their personal well-being. Help them set a goal to engage in one a day. Touch base with them often so they are more likely to remember to do it. Young people tend to need lots of reminders, especially when it comes to behaviour change.

Well-being tool 7: Do something for fun, without a goal or purpose

How many of you engage in activities just for the fun of it? Even pleasurable activities like hobbies and pastimes are often done with a purpose in mind. Take for example a hike. You might love hiking and engage in it often. It's likely you see the hike as a form of exercise too and this becomes a core reason you keep doing it. Without a purpose or reason, people often think what they are doing is indulgent or unnecessary. Fun for the sake of fun is valuable to your well-being.

It's important to remember you don't have to be 'good' at something to delve in and enjoy it. Many people avoid creative endeavours that could bring about a lot of fun, because they don't see themselves as good enough. Creative pursuits like painting, sewing, crafting and gardening allow you to be present, mindful and enter a state of flow. Try avoiding the expectation that you'll be an expert immediately. Go in for the fun of it and see what happens. Mastery takes time.

Journaling: Fun for the sake of fun

Students write a list of fun activities that interest them. Set a challenge for everyone to have a go at something new and creative, asking for help from supportive adults where necessary.

Well-being tool 8: Healthy nutrition

While most children have heard about healthy nutrition, it's not an easy one to implement—even for adults. In the case of children, they often rely on what's available in their environment, as they're too young to organise their diet independently. Older children might know the principles of healthy nutrition but prefer eating fast foods and aren't emotionally mature enough to make consistently healthy decisions.

A lecture on healthy eating doesn't usually go far, yet the value of healthy nutrition and its impact on learning and behaviour is an integral part of the well-being curriculum. Tread carefully, as it can be a particularly sensitive topic for some. Don't take it personally if students don't take it on board—there are lots of variables at play that affect their understanding and choices related to food and nutrition.

Case study: Jack needs a nutrition reset

Jack grew up in a busy home with little parental supervision around food. Jack and his siblings could choose what they ate. The choices were limited—high in sugar and fat and all prepackaged or frozen. Jack was often sluggish and always felt hungry. He often felt embarrassed when other children would ask, 'Why don't you eat real food?'

Despite their challenges around providing nutritious food, Jack's parents gave plenty of love and care. They showed affection freely, listened to and spent time with Jack and his younger siblings as much as possible. They did their best. In a busy house with many children and a low income, nutrition wasn't a priority. Nutritious food was not only more expensive, but it took longer to prepare.

Jack went to a warm and supportive school. Staff knew the parents well and kept an eye out for the family. They understood Jack's parents weren't able yet to change their own or their children's healthy eating. They weren't going to make Jack feel bad because the food he brought in was always prepackaged and high in all the energy-sapping ingredients.

Solution

Jack's school mind mapped with the whole class to help them tune into their own understanding of nutrition. They added the 'nonjudgment' role plays to remind the students not to make judgments about other people's choices. They hoped the nonjudgment role plays would reduce the commentary about Jack's weight and the contents of his lunch box.

Jack had a mentor in the school who took him under his wing. With his parents' permission, Jack came by his mentor's office each morning to grab some fruit and vegetables from his basket. Jack's parents appreciated this. The school understood to treat their involvement in what went into Jack's lunch box sensitively, to avoid the risk of making his parents feel small or inadequate.

Finally, Jack was supported to build ways to contribute to the family shopping list, which we shared with his parents. He took on the responsibility of packing everyone's school lunches and loved cutting fruit up into interesting shapes, which got his brother and sisters excited about fruit too. He used the pocket money he was given for making the lunches to ride his bike to the local shops and buy fruit, cheese and crackers.

Note: Although this case study was executed beautifully to plan, there are many times when food is such a sensitive topic your impact will be limited. You're the best judge for working out what you can and can't do for a constructive resolution.

Tuning into how different foods make you think, feel and behave

Self-awareness is vital for any change, but this is by no means about making children feel self-conscious. It's about building awareness of the impact what you eat can have.

Nutrition is essential for well-being, but it can be a complicated process. Proper nutrition for children is not something they have much control over in the early years, and when they're teenagers, it's not necessarily something they value. Think back to when you were a teenager—it was fun to socialise at the local deli with food that had zero nutritional value!

One way to develop awareness about how food makes you feel is by considering this question before eating: 'How might eating this make me feel, think and behave?'

Of course, no one will or should ask themselves this question every time they're about to eat. It's important not to get self-conscious about what you eat. This is just one way to increase mindfulness and self-awareness around food. Many people eat without conscious awareness and later feel sluggish or hyperactive and experience regret. Learning to be more mindful through questions like this can be a positive step forward.

For more information about healthy eating, check out www.eatforhealth.gov.au.

Well-being tool 9: Accept others without judgment

Being socially disconnected and experiencing difficulties in your relationships will impact on your mental health and well-being. Hartneck (2015) The conflict that grows from unreasonably judging other people, expecting they should think and feel more like you, can disconnect you from potential friends. An important part of a confident mindset and healthy well-being is seeing others with compassion and understanding. Limiting judgmental, superior thinking early on can help people feel less angry about their differences with others and contribute to better harmony overall.

Journaling: Accepting others for who they are without judgment

Understanding you're not 'better than' or 'less than' others is a helpful way to reduce the natural tendency to judge people who aren't exactly like you.

Encourage your students to put the following statement into their own words:

> *'I am not above anyone. I am not below anyone.'*

Allow some time to discuss your students' answers and practice further with the role plays that follow.

Role plays

Divide your students into groups of three or four people. One person plays the part of the person struggling, while the remainder of the group are the observers. After the situation is role played, observers discuss what might be going on for the person, looking at the situation with curiosity and compassion instead of judgment and close-mindedness. If you're doing this one on one with a young person, just use the role plays as a discussion point.

- Bea arrives late to class—again. She's never on time.
- Sia's mum turns up to school drop-off every morning in her pyjamas.
- Jasper runs angrily into class and throws his backpack across the floor. He never arrives at school in a good mood.
- Your teacher doesn't seem enthusiastic about what he's teaching. He often yawns and seems to be thinking about other things. He teaches you what you need to know, but his delivery is a little short of inspiring.
- A girl in the yard often looks sad, wandering around alone. Whenever you invite her to join you, she never wants to.

- Elijah has a lunchbox full of lollies and chips almost every day.
- A teenage boy in the supermarket has a massive meltdown and starts throwing food all over the floor and hitting himself in the head.
- A mother in a playground shouts at her wailing child and says, 'You're ruining everyone's day, I'm sick of you!'
- Your school has a strict uniform policy. Alexa always turns up with at least one part of her uniform worn incorrectly.
- Mia brings her dog along to your class picnic. She does nothing while you watch in horror as the dog runs through the picnic rugs and eats all the food off the picnic tables.

Well-being tool 10: Create time for 'flow'

'Flow' has featured already in chapter 7 on handling challenging feelings. In context of your well-being, finding flow is a valuable source of rest and rejuvenation. Doing what you enjoy engages your whole attention and enters you into a state of flow. Examples include being artistic and creative, dancing, bike riding, socialising and listening to music. There are many other examples of flow that vary between people. Csikszentmihalyi (2008)

Well-being tool 11: Know, enjoy and share your talents

Engaging in your talents is an essential part of nurturing your self-esteem and well-being. Du, King and Chi (2017) Talents are skills and strengths that come naturally to you and help you feel good. Engaging in them often is not only fun but a reminder of your strengths.

Share your talents and strengths

Giving to others by using your strengths and talents improves your well-being significantly. It even promotes physiological changes in your brain associated with happiness. It also enhances your connection to others, bringing meaning and purpose while strengthening your sense of self. Mental Health Foundation (2012)

The statement below from Dr Maya Angelou is one I share with many young people. As a generation today, children are often more naturally driven to make a difference and contribute positively. Maya Angelou's statement can offer a lovely framework for one way to do this.

'When you learn, teach. When you get, give.' Angelou (1969)

Journaling: Learning and teaching, getting and giving

Allow time for students to discuss Dr Maya Angelou's words, then identify what they can teach and give to others. They can record these ideas in their journals.

Continue encouraging students to share their time, talents and skills, keeping them connected in positive ways with those around them. Turning too far inwards and engaging with life solely for your own benefit reduces opportunities for compassionate interactions that can improve well-being. Being kind and helpful is particularly important for students struggling to hold an identity other than that of the class clown or troublemaker. Providing them with opportunities to lead and share their strengths and talents will build their self-esteem and confidence in many ways.

Well-being tool 12: Know your values

People are born with their unique character, personality and temperament. Values develop over the years according to how these interact with a person's environment, family, community and experiences.

In a decade where images about the ideals of 'success' and 'happiness' frequently flow via advertising and social media, it can get confusing (especially for young people) to remember what they truly value. Having a value system you genuinely believe in and feel motivated to uphold strengthens your well-being. Sagiv, Roccas and Oppenheim-Weller (2015)

Values are like a moral compass to uphold your sense of character and integrity. Start by sharing your most treasured value and demonstrate how it plays out in your life. Let them know they don't have to agree with your value, but they do need to be respectful.

Next, ask students to break into pairs or small groups to discuss the following questions (or brainstorm together as a group).

- What do you think the world needs more of?
- What do you think the world needs less of?
- If you had a million dollars to make one thing different, what would you choose?
- When you're in a difficult situation or about to do the wrong thing, what values come into your head so you end up doing the right thing?
- What are your top five values? Write them down.

Allow anyone comfortable with the idea to share their answers with the broader group. Continue to encourage students to keep tuning in with their values, especially at times of conflict or challenge.

Role plays

Divide the group into pairs and remind them the focus is to identify a value system to resolve the problem. They can also solve it negatively, showing what might happen when ethical values get neglected.

- You have plans to sleep over at a friend's place. You can't wait—that ism until you get another invitation to go somewhere even better.
- Your little brother wants to walk to school with you. It means a lot to you, but you feel so embarrassed and don't want to do it
- No one likes your best friend who has just joined your school. Your classmates are feeling very unsettled about her and you want everyone to get along. You're feeling the pressure not to let her sit with you and your group.
- Your sister just found a box of chocolates in the cupboard, and you both decide to cover up for each other and scoff the lot. Your mum is horrified when she finds the empty box and asks you both what happened.
- You desperately want to buy something from the Tuck Shop at school. Your parents never let you buy anything from there because healthy eating is a high priority for them. You're walking out the door to head to school and see $2 on the kitchen bench top. It would be so easy to take it and sneak a treat in at school.
- You're tired and haven't showered in three days. Your parents ask, 'Have you showered recently?' You don't want to get into trouble, but you don't want to be forced to take a shower either.
- The dentist finds three holes in your teeth. You know it's because you've been sneaking lollies into your bedroom and eating them at night. The dentist asks you if you are brushing regularly (which you're not) and if you have been eating lollies or drinking sugary soft drinks. Your dad is looking right into your eyes and you feel like you're going to explode.
- You drop your teacher's iPad and crack the screen. Your teacher has no idea you did it and is sighing and groaning when he discovers it.
- You know your neighbours are mistreating their animals. They are always yelling at them, and the animals often wander over to your house hungry. They are friendly to people—just not to animals.

Remind your students that everyone makes poor value judgments from time to time. It's crucial they forgive themselves and others when this happens and look instead at how to make things better.

Well-being tool 13: Choose who you spend time with

Throughout this book, there's been plenty of reference to the importance of investing in healthy, supportive and reciprocal relationships. Everyone needs a supportive family and friendship circle who genuinely accept you, treat you well and want the best for you.

In many of the chapters, we explored the contagion of emotion. Trying not to absorb other people's negativity can be challenging. Young people can struggle to navigate tricky friendships and establish and maintain healthy boundaries with people who don't treat them well. Your expertise, guidance and support are essential. Too much time around negative and hurtful people can be damaging for well-being, resilience and maintaining a confident mindset.

Spend time together discussing their choice of friendships with the following ideas:

- Showing you understand how hard it can sometimes be to make friends in the first place and how that can mean any association is better than no friendship at all.
- Reminding them of their supporters with whom they can discuss their friendship troubles.
- When they're not sure if a friendship is harmful, the give-away is usually taking note of how you feel after being around them. Good friends tend to energise you. Questionable ones tend to undermine and exhaust you.
- Build confident self-talk and coping mechanisms for when they are around people who aren't good companions but can't be avoided. Many of these are found throughout the chapters in this book.

Case study: Jak puts himself first

Jak had a complicated family life. One of six children, he would do anything for any of them. They expected nothing less. His parents and siblings weren't in the habit of thanking him, and he intuitively knew if he didn't help or do what they asked, they would disengage emotionally and even bully him.

Jak did the grocery shopping for his parents, made the school lunches for his siblings, kept the house clean and helped with his little sister's homework. He didn't start his homework or relaxation time until he finished his obligations. When he dedicated time to his own needs, someone would usually arc up and ask for something or call him 'selfish' for doing his own thing.

Jak had served his family like this for years and was exhausted. When I saw him for a well-being check to look at what energised and what drained him, he couldn't answer. Instead, he burst into tears. The years of effort and dedication had taken their toll. While he loved being kind and helpful, it felt like no one in his home was being kind and helpful in return. Jak's 12-year-old heart felt sad and alone.

Together, we role played ways he could say no and found strategies that worked for him to 'shake off' those tough feelings when his family rejected him for saying no. We also engaged Jak in enriching experiences at school to balance out his struggles at home.

It took months of practice, encouragement and guidance before Jak started laying healthy boundaries with his family. The consequences of this decision made life difficult for him; it was tough being harshly judged when he wasn't doing anything wrong.

Jak needed lots of support from other trusted adults in his school and sporting community. We drew his attention to 'Kids Helpline' where he could call confidentially to talk any time he wasn't coping at home. He received empathy from his supporters and regular reminders that things wouldn't always be this hard and that he had a good life ahead of him.

In time, Jak got more comfortable with his family's reaction and was able to keep calm and not personalise it. Jak started looking within and finding things he loved to do, developing new interests, using his strengths and placing his own needs back on the priority list. While he has a long way to go and nothing has changed within his family unit, with extra care and support, Jak is doing much better within himself than ever before.

Well-being tool 14: Fire and wire well-being thoughts

The most frequently used thoughts will build the most robust neurological pathways in your brain. These pathways become our thinking habits, and our thinking habits affect our feelings. Hanson (2016)

Together with your students, create some reminders to pin around the room to cultivate optimism and a confident mindset. You can come up with your own or use the ones here for inspiration:

- I have plenty of great people who care about me.
- There are always people to help me.
- I am active.
- I'm going to have a brilliant day.
- I take care of myself.
- I'm as kind to myself as I am to others.
- I take time every day to do what I love.

- I am strong.
- I am healthy.
- I am capable.
- I work hard.

Continue to encourage your students to choose healthy, helpful and optimistic thoughts as much as possible. When they are in a rut and having a tough time, help them choose another thought.

Well-being tool 15: Make time for laughter

Laughter releases endorphins and can quickly change even the worst of moods. Researchers around the world studying the value of laughter have shown it makes a positive impact on your mental health and well-being. Manninen et al. (2017)

The joke monitor

For your primary age students, designate a different joke monitor every week who has the responsibility of choosing two appropriate jokes a day to make sure your group laughs together. The ideal times to get them to share the jokes are at the start and end of the school day.

Watch funny clips together

Brainstorm what your group tends to find funny and make a commitment to watch a funny YouTube clip each day. Laughter is a great way to reset and reconnect the group, especially after a stressful lesson or experience.

Fake laughter

If there aren't any good reasons at the time to laugh, why not give 'fake laughter' a go? Be brave in front of your students and show them what a fake laugh is. Think of something that makes you laugh and start laughing, loud and clear. Your students might laugh at you—be prepared for this. If they do, be understanding; what you're doing and asking them to do would make most people feel awkward.

Once you have demonstrated and told them how you felt, it's their turn. Remind them that their mirror neurons and the contagion of emotion will help them do this. Why not make it a daily practice to spend a couple of minutes at the start or end of the day laughing without any reason other than the fun and joy of it. For inspiration, check out Annie Harvey's TED talk, 'Silence to LOL' at www.ted.com/talks/annie_harvey_silence_to_lol.

Well-being tool 16: Get enough rest and sleep

Getting enough sleep each night is crucial for your mental health and well-being. Bartel, Richardson and Gradiscar (2018) Some people naturally struggle to sleep. Worrying too much, not being sufficiently active, poor nutrition, social isolation and spending too much time on devices are examples of factors that can affect the quality of your sleep.

Brainstorm: Sleep

Divide your board into two columns. The first column can identify, 'What makes it hard to sleep?' The other column, 'What makes it easy to sleep?' Take some time to explore the questions and help each other out with ideas.

The previous chapter on managing challenging feelings will also help you find strategies for sleeping better. If your students are not sleeping enough, it might be valuable to meet their parents to build strategies to support better sleep at home.

References

Angelou, M. 1969. *I Know Why the Caged Bird Sings*. New York: Random House.

Bar-On, R. 2012. 'The Impact of Emotional Intelligence on Health and Wellbeing, Emotional Intelligence New Perceptions and Applications.' *InTech Europe*. doi: 10.5772/32468.

Bartel, K., C. Richardson, and M. Gradiscar. 2018. 'Sleep and Mental Wellbeing: Exploring the Links.' Melbourne: Victorian Health Promotion Foundation.

Csikszentmihalyi, M. 1990. *Flow: The Psychology of Optimal Experience*. New York: Harper Perennial.

Du, H., R. B. King, and P. Chi. 2017. 'Self-Esteem and Subjective Well-Being Revisited: The Roles of Personal, Relational, and Collective Self-Esteem.' *PLOS One* 12, no. 8.

Goleman, D. 2011. *The Brain and Emotional Intelligence: New Insights*. More than Sound, audiobook.

———. 2006. *Emotional Intelligence: Why It Can Matter More Than IQ*. New York: Bantam.

Hadden, B. W., and V. Smith. 2019. 'I Gotta Say, Today Was a Good (and Meaningful) Day: Daily Meaning in Life as a Basic Psychological Need.' *Journal of Happiness Studies* 20, no. 1: 185–202.

Hanson, R. 2016. *Hardwiring Happiness: The New Brain Science of Contentment, Calm, and Confidence*. New York: Harmony.

Hartneck, P. 2015. '9 Ways You Can Improve Your Mental Health Today.' *Psychology Today*, October.

Manninen, S., L. Tuominen, R. Dunbar, T. Karjalainen, J. Hirvonen, E. Arponen, R. Hari, I. P. Jaaskelainen, M. Sams, and L. Nummenmaa. 2017. 'Social Laughter Triggers Endogenous Opioid Release in Humans.' *Journal of Neuroscience* 37, no. 25: 6125–6135.

Mayer, J. D., and P. Salovey. 1997. 'What Is Emotional Intelligence?' In *Emotional Development and Emotional Intelligence: Educational Implications*, edited by P. Salovey and D. J. Sluyter, 3–31. New York: Basic Books.

Mental Health Foundation. 2012. *Doing Good Does You Good: A Pocket Guide to Helping Others*. London: Mental Health Foundation. Available at: https://www.mentalhealth.org.uk/publications/doing-good-does-you-good

Onevia-Zafra, M. D., Catro-Sanchez, A. M., Mataran-Pennarorocha, G. A., and Moreno-Lorenzo C. 2013. 'Effect of Music as Nursing Intervention for People Diagnosed with Fibromyalgia.' *Pain Management Nursing* 14, no. 2.

Redmond, G., et al. 2016. *Are the Kids Alright? Young Australians in Their Middle Years: Final Report of the Australian Child Wellbeing Project*. Flinders University, University of New South Wales and Australian Council for Educational Research.

Sagiv, L., S. Roccas, and S. Oppenheim-Weller. 2015. 'Values and Well-Being.' In *Positive Psychology in Practice: Promoting Human Flourishing in Work, Health, Education and Everyday Life*, edited by S. Joseph. Hoboken, NJ: Wiley.

V. N. Salimpoor, M. Beovoy, and R. Zatorre. 2011. 'Anatomically Distinct Dopamine Release During Anticipation and Experience of Peak Emotion Music.' *Nature Neuroscience Journal* 14: 257–262.

Weinberg, M. K., and D. Joseph. 2017. 'If You're Happy and You Know It: Music Engagement and Subjective Wellbeing.' *Psychology of Music* 45, no. 2.

Zhang, Z., and W. Chen. 2019. 'A Systematic Review of the Relationship between Physical Activity and Happiness.' *Journal of Happiness Studies* 20, no. 4: 1305–1322.

Index

Made in the USA
Monee, IL
07 August 2021